AF593791

THE 1982 DALLAS COWBOYS BLUEBOOK III

THE OFFICIAL 1982 DALLAS COWBOYS BLUEBOOK

VOLUME III

TAYLOR PUBLISHING COMPANY
Dallas, Texas

Editor: Olivia Lane

Photographs by: Bukki Erwin, Steve Harris, Russ Russell, Ron Scribner, ©Dallas Morning News/David Woo
Cheerleaders' action photographs by: Shelly Katz, Suzanne Mitchell, Russ Russell, Dan Sellers

Book design: Steve Harris

Published in cooperation with The Dallas Cowboys.

1550 West Mockingbird Lane, Dallas, Texas 75221

Library of Congress Catalog Card Number 82-060349

ISBN: 0-87833-324-X

Printed in the United States of America

The Dallas Cowboys Bluebook, the third in a continuing series of reference books, serves as a guide to the fine points of both the team and the season. Grateful acknowledgement is given to the Dallas Cowboys organization for its cooperation and perception in providing the kind of information that is helpful, if not essential to the serious sports reader.

CONTENTS

Introduction with Roger Staubach

The Dallas Cowboys Bluebook, in its dedication to present things of the (immediate) past, present and future, prevailed upon a distinguished and expert panel to discuss the 1982 team and its prospects. Roger Staubach was designated Chairman of the Board for his role in the only two Dallas Super Bowl championships. "I go along with that," said Staubach, "because the Bluebook keeps track of how it all goes on, but there were a lot of other people out there who might ought to sit in this chair."

Never mind, Roger. You have some illustrious board members:

Larry Cole, the highest scoring defensive tackle in the history of the National Football League.

Lee Roy Jordan, middle linebacker and possibly the hardest nose that ever protruded beneath the Cowboys star.

Bob Lilly, a pussycat until the ball was snapped.

Rayfield Wright, an All-Pro from an Itty-Bitty State.

STAUBACH: Fellas, I'm sure you know why we're all gathered here today—to lend our expertise to the Old Firm and get a fix on the current situation . . .

JORDAN: All right, let's get on with it!

STAUBACH: Sure, Lee Roy. Calm yourself. Now, before we get to the nitty-gritty, let's address ourselves to the psychological factor—that the Cowboys have come up short two years in a row in the game that could have put them in the Super Bowl.

COLE: I'd rather we started off talking about coming back with the tackle-eligible play. Tackles should be allowed to score, too.

STAUBACH: There is no rule that can benefit *defensive* tackles in scoring. What are you, on some kind of ego trip? Now let's go back to the original question.

JORDAN: Psychology is not a factor. This team is too damn young to know about psychology. The last two years they should have been delighted to get as far as they did—the first year with a new quarterback like Danny White taking over for you, Roger, and then last year starting out with what seemed to be a bunch of nothing in the defensive backfield.

STAUBACH: I want to interrupt here, just to agree with Lee Roy. That third-year thing is going to come up when Dallas gets into the National Conference championship game again, which I think they'll do. But that will be a con job, and I don't think that's going to affect Danny White or any other people on the team.

JORDAN: All right, let's get on with it!

COLE: The first thing they've got to do is get last year behind them. Forget about San Francisco. They can't be psyched out if they get in the same situation. They have to listen to their guru, Tom Landry, who sayeth, "If you're better prepared, if you give it a little more sacrifice, it won't come down to the last game."

STAUBACH: Robert, you've been quiet through all this.

LILLY: You know I was never much for psychology. You either did it or you didn't. But I'd like to say that this year and the next year are the best opportunities I've ever seen for the Cowboys to go to the Super Bowl. The defensive line and the offensive line are at their peaks. The defensive line is the best it's ever been. After two more years they might all start going downhill—that's the way it works, unfortunately, as I can testify. But right now that's where they've got it going pretty good.

JORDAN: All right, let's get on with it!

STAUBACH: There are a lot of teams in the NFL who would dearly love to get into the conference championship game, but, of course, that is not enough for Dallas. What do you guys think it will take for the Old Firm to get over the hump? I might add, I have my own ideas.

WRIGHT: They just need some more of what they had last year. The attitude of the team as a whole was what brought them through—the veterans lifting the spirits of the young players. You tell them, "You can *do* it, even though you're a rookie." You've got to give the next person support.

COLE: It seems more and more important to have the home field advantage in the playoffs. Dallas has lost its last two NFC championship games on the road, and yet we have an 18-game streak at Texas Stadium. That tells you something right there. It might be a good "goal" for this team to come up with the best record in football.

JORDAN: They need more consistency on defense. The Cowboys seem to have evolved into a big-play defense. They set a record in interceptions and turnovers last year, but they didn't shut down a lot of people. In the championship games, they were so close, but a little bit away.

STAUBACH: It seems to me, Lee Roy, you have been through that "little bit away" experience yourself.

JORDAN: Yeah, back in 1966 through 1969, when we couldn't win *the* game. The only difference between now and then is that now we know damn well we can win it: we've been there (to the Super Bowl) five times.

COLE: These last two years, we lost in the NFC game. We've got to stop thinking about "next year's champions." If you start thinking "jinx" then you are sure to be jinxed.

WRIGHT: Forget about any talk of being jinxed. I think the Cowboys have an excellent shot at going all the way. The offensive line has the potential to be the best. (Pat) Donovan and (Herb) Scott are the anchors, just like Blaine Nye and Rayfield Wright were on the other side. You build an attack that way.

LILLY: If we are going to talk about strength—other than the two lines—I'd like to point out that there are enough good defensive backs to make up a pretty good secondary. Of course, the linebackers may need a little shoring up.

JORDAN: Hey, look back a year ago. They didn't know what they had back there in the secondary. That was the weakness of the team. I know I didn't give the Cowboys defensive backfield much chance to become something. Just about all they had was Charlie Waters on bad wheels. Now they are going into the season with a helluva boost: being confident in their defensive backfield. Last year, Michael Downs and Everson Walls came in new, and Dennis Thurman did a great job at cornerback. That secondary is a big plus going into '82.

COLE: Yeah, but the front four has to have some backup help. It takes about five years to develop a defensive lineman, and I don't see that happening. You must have some people on the bench who can come in and make sparks. We haven't had them, and that's what worries me. I see that as trouble down the road.

STAUBACH: We're looking just at Dallas' problems. Now let's put them into perspective with other teams' problems. Dallas looks pretty good there. The 49ers were on a roll; they couldn't do anything wrong in 15 games. Barring unforeseen circumstances like that—which I don't think is likely to happen again—and injuries to one or two key Cowboys players, I think Dallas will be stronger than last year and should go all the way.

LILLY: I'd agree with that, for another reason—the schedule. Dallas doesn't have any breathers. And the Cowboys have always had their best years when the schedule was the roughest.

JORDAN: All right, let's get on with it!

STAUBACH: I take it then, Lee Roy, you are not as bullish about the Cowboys chances?

JORDAN: You've got me wrong. I didn't give 'em much of a chance to be anything at this time a year ago. I hope that Anthony Dickerson can come in and give them some solidity at linebacker in place of D.D. Lewis. It may be, that in this new form of "special" players, you ought to have linebackers in there on first down—like Randy Hughes, when healthy, and Cornell Green—big enough to stop the run and quick enough to cover the fast guys out of the backfield.

COLE: If Dickerson can step in, they'll be better off. He's more mobile and he's faster.

STAUBACH: Hey, let's not go overboard on this deal. The Cowboys intercepted an incredible number of passes (37) last season. If that doesn't happen again, then they'll have to take up the slack in some other way.

LILLY: The defensive line creates the turnovers, and the defensive line will be better than ever.

WRIGHT: You guys have been overlooking a main point about Dallas. It's all right to talk about this and that, but let's get to the thing that's made the Cowboys great. You have to work with each other, and you must put in that additional time. I was brought up in the generation of Frank Clarke and Pettis Norman. Then when I was an All-Pro, I stayed out after practice to work with Harvey Martin. He was a left end at the time and I was the right tackle, and, hey, it wasn't out of the goodness of my heart entirely. I may have made him a better end, but he was at the same time making me a better tackle. So that's what has to go on with the team today. If it does, they'll get there.

JORDAN: All right, let's get on with it!

STAUBACH: Are there any areas we haven't touched that you gentlemen think are important?

COLE: Yeah. The club lost its "quarterback" in the secondary in Charlie Waters. Who's going to take his place in that role? I've got to believe it's Dennis Thurman, because from what I've seen of him, he's an instinctive player. I mean, things happen so quickly back there that you don't always have time to think, you just have to *know* where everyone else is. Of course, he must be able to read the defensive signals sent in by Ernie Stautner, which is an arcane art in itself.

STAUBACH: I have another question to put before the board: Has the game passed us by?

WRIGHT: With the new rules helping the passing game, it's more like the Canadian Football League; where they have only three downs to get a first. That produces excitement, and that's what the fans want. The Cowboys were the first to put in trick plays and now everybody is doing it.

JORDAN: I could cut it.

LILLY: Me, too, Lee Roy.

COLE: I never could cut it, under the old rules.

STAUBACH: I am amazed that none of you have brought up the single most important person in the Cowboys' 1982 season, namely, the quarterback.

COLE: The guy that always gets the car after the Super Bowl?

STAUBACH: Well, sometimes he takes a station wagon.

LILLY: So lead off.

STAUBACH: Danny White is at the top of the game right now. I wouldn't take any other quarterback in the league over him, and I'm sure the Cowboys wouldn't trade him for any other quarterback in the league. I knew he was that good a long time, and that's what made it easy for me to retire.

JORDAN: Last year he proved he could run an offense, and didn't throw interceptions like he did his first year as a starter. Whether he didn't throw some passes he should have thrown—passes that make a great quarterback—I don't know, because it's been some years since I have looked at the game films.

STAUBACH: Is there anything else we haven't covered?

COLE: Yeah, what about reviving the tackle-eligible play?

PART I

1982 Preview: Shooting for Something Super

It was the set-scene of the 1981 season. And it came at the zenith of Cowboys fortunes, the 38-0 playoff win over Tampa Bay.

It happened at the end of the third quarter . . . But let someone else tell the story. Out-of-town writers, sentimental as they sometimes are, seized on the moment and made much of it.

Wrote John Jeansonne in (Long Island's) *Newsday:* "The picture can be drawn out to a thousand words. At least. The picture is of Ed (Too Tall) Jones lying on his left side, down near the 20-yard line. The third period has just ended, and above Jones toward one end zone is the scoreboard, seeming to lean to one side: Dallas 31, Tampa Bay 0. All of the Tampa Bay players and the rest of the Dallas players have just turned to jog their 'elephant jog' down toward the other end zone, to begin the final period.

"Except that Harvey Martin has noticed that Jones is down. And Randy White has noticed. And John Dutton. So the three of them, these padded monsters protected against all harm, suddenly do an about-face. And they quickly assume this tender pose, *kneeling* around Jones. Seeing to his apparent pain."

"When Too Tall was hurt," Martin said later, "and I was down there, I looked around me and found we were all there. All the defensive linemen. We're a very good group and we play well as a group. When one of us makes a play, we feel *all* of us makes the play."

That scene is now particularly pointed as the Cowboys head into yet another quest for the Holy Grail—the Super Bowl game at Pasadena.

According to Tom Landry, defense is the vital ingredient to winning the supreme championship. Circa 1965, he was asked, "Suppose you had the best offense in the league, and you had only an average defense?" He answered succinctly: "You would get beat."

Supposing that this dictum is still operative (and no one should doubt that it is), the Dallas defense had better hustle if the Cowboys are to go to Pasadena. And who do you think will be leading this defensive charge? None other than that commiserating bunch we left a moment ago: the Dallas front four, known as "Harvey, Randy, Dutton and Jones, a fearsome foursome to rattle your bones."

"The defensive line is the strength of our defense," says Landry. He acknowledges that the other factions are none-too-shabby, either. Yet it was the front four who wreaked most of the havoc of the season: trapping quarterbacks 42 times and creating most of the 53 turnovers, including a league-leading 37 interceptions (a team record, by far). "We have a chance," says Harvey Martin, "to establish ourselves this year as the best front four of all time. I think we're dedicated to that. Well, heck, most games last year we *lived* in their backfield."

The bottom line for Martin in the '82 season: "We've got to win the Super Bowl for our egos."

Indeed, co-captain Bob Breunig, the middle linebacker, starts his pre-

(Top) Benny Barnes, Waters' successor at strong safety, races 72 yards for a touchdown with a fumble recovery last October at San Francisco, one of the few bright spots in a lopsided defeat. *(Bottom)* Charlie Waters (41) played on one good leg and one big heart the final two seasons of his fine career. Charlie retired after the 1981 season as the Cowboys' second all-time leading pass interceptor.

season discussion with the stated "team" goal: Winning the National Conference. "We do that," said Breunig, "we're in the Super Bowl, right?" (The Cowboys' goal for '81 was winning the NFC East, because Philadelphia had usurped that title in 1980; the Dallas team invariably achieves its stated goal.)

But Breunig must be almost forcibly drawn into a discussion of Dallas achieving a Super Bowl victory, because he believes other things come first. "We have to think about the first game," he says. "Then after that one has gone, you think about the second. Before that, in camp, you work on your shortcomings of the year before, usually fundamental stuff. You keep putting it together, and you're on your way to the playoffs."

Breunig, a cerebral player, spells it out further: "We need to limit the big play—passes or runs for more than 20 yards. One team goal for '82 is to reduce the average yards-per-attempt rushing. That was 4.3 last season and it's too much in some categories."

The chief worry among the linebacking corps is that a weakside linebacker must emerge. "The obvious first choice to replace (retired) D. D. Lewis," says Tom Landry, "is Guy Brown, who's started games for us and has the experience. But the position is wide open with the competition coming from Anthony Dickerson, Angelo King and Bill Roe." Nevertheless, the light and speedy Dickerson, a big play fellow all his life, is the railbirds' favorite to take over this job. He has earned it by captaining the Cowboys kicking teams with notable valor.

The defensive backfield, a devastated and suspect area at this time a year ago, has now become a team strength. As ex-Cowboy Lee Roy Jordan so charmingly (but also possibly unanimously) put it: "Last summer they had a Charlie Waters on bad wheels and three suspects." What a difference a year makes! The Cowboys now have a solid and set (if they want it) back four, with a wealth of supportive strength:

Cornerback Everson (Unconscious) Walls led the league with 11 interceptions, breaking Ring of Honor honoree Mel Renfro's team record. Free safety Dennis Thurman was thrust into the breach at right cornerback and thrived. He recorded nine interceptions and a removal of Philadelphia Eagle, Chief Ron Jaworski. Mike Downs, a rookie as was Walls, stood out at free safety, with 110 tackles, second only to MLB Breunig.

Gone, however, is Charlie Waters, the charismatic fellow who was so much a leader and defensive signal-caller that the last two defensive backfields had been dubbed "Charlie's Angels."

(Top) Pat Donovan (67) has reached the taken-for-granted stage of his career. He's a Pro Bowl offensive tackle as a matter of routine. *(Bottom)* White and Jones make passing a risky business for NFL quarterbacks.

Who can replace this paragon? The effervescent Dennis Thurman? "It's going to have to be spread around," says Thurman. "I'm a cornerback now. The strong safety—probably Benny Barnes, who has been playing in the Cowboys secondary so long—is one we should look to. But I'll try to do my part."

Landry is almost paternal when he considers his '82 defensive backfield: "Without the play of the guys back there, I don't think we would have accomplished what we did. Everson Walls was our biggest surprise as a free agent rookie and he can only get better. Other than Walls, the biggest surprise was Thurman. Nobody expected him to play as well as he did after moving over from free safety. So, for the first time, we'll go to camp pretty secure at the corner position." (Landry was not exaggerating. Since 1960, the Cowboys have never been secure entering the season at *both* corner positions.)

Behind Barnes at strong safety, there is Dextor Clinkscale, who missed the '81 season with an Achilles' heel injury. But, in a long talk with Thurman, another star candidate emerges. "You know who the best athlete in the defensive backfield is?" asked Thurman. A wise answer was: Thurman? "No. Ron Fellows. As far as agility and quickness and speed, he is the best." Fellows may be Thurman's candidate to take over his right cornerback job thus returning him to his natural (All-American, USC) position at free safety. This would result in Mike Downs moving to strong safety and a standard secondary for the Cowboys for the next six or seven years: Fellows and Walls at corners, Thurman and Downs at safeties.

Aside from that, Thurman eyes the coming season with an immediate goal: "We have to play a lot better defensively at the start of the season, so we don't lose that crazy game that eventually costs us the home field advantage. (In 1980, Dallas lost 38-35 in New York and had to play Philadelphia in the title game at Veterans Stadium; in 1981, Dallas lost at St. Louis and wound up playing San Francisco in Candlestick Park.)

For his own department's role, Thurman said: "If we can cut down the other side's big plays, then we won't have to make so many big plays ourselves." He perhaps got this line from one of Landry's stated goals for the '82 team.

Of course, the bell cow of the defense—line, linebackers or defensive backs—is the incomparable Randy White, the fellow that made Landry bite his tongue when he said, "I never expect to see another player like Bob Lilly." "Last season," says White, "left one feeling like if he had just done a little more—like if I hadn't gotten the cramps in my leg on the last San Francisco drive. So now we know we have the capability to be as good as we want, because it's up to us."

But Randy White is baffled when you ask him about Dallas' chances for a Super Bowl championship. He's looking to Super Bowl XVII, of course, but that's putting a lot of cart before the horse in his mind. "I'm going to training camp to get sharp," he says, "then I'm just going to take 'em one game at a time. When you get to the end of the season and you're in the playoffs, you hope you've played well enough all year to get the home field advantage. Then you start thinking about beating your opponent in the playoffs, and then you're in the Super Bowl. The Super Bowl—that's something we know something about."

In between the defense and the offense is an important department that could mean the difference between ending the season in Texas Stadium instead of Pasadena—the kicking game. Last season that segment of the game was Orphan Annie. Various kicking teams were sorted out to members of the coaching staff (whereas the year before Mike Ditka had been the K.T. coach). The results were not good. The

(Top) "Beneath that gentle exterior lies a heart of ice," says Pat Donovan of teammate and All-Pro guard Herbert Scott (68). Scott has been voted to three straight Pro Bowls and been chosen All-Pro the past two seasons. *(Bottom)* On the right side of the offensive line, tackle Jim Cooper (61) and guard Kurt Petersen (65), are the young, developing stars of their unit. It shouldn't be long before they're going to Pro Bowls a la Donovan and Scott.

Cowboys ran punts back 5.2 yards a crack, but opponents had 6.1. On kickoffs the Cowboys logged 18.2 per kick (poor) and foes got 21.2. In some games, this is dangerous yardage to yield. Now Dallas will have another fulltime kicking team coach, Alan Lowry, a tiger from the University of Texas (both as player and assistant coach). Presumably, because of his familiarity with Texas A&M's "12th Man" tradition, he will also be aware of the Cowboys 12th-man tradition of the last few years that have cost them a few ball games.

But he will have something more positive going for him, too, in first-round draft choice Rod Hill of Kentucky State. Hill has been a college standout in both punt and kickoff returns—including an astounding 30-yard average on punt runbacks as a junior. The Dallas return job seems in good hands.

For many years now the onus has been on the defense, because it has been recognized that Landry's offense is one of the most—if not *the* most—productive in the league. The expectations are no less this season. Roger Staubach rates Danny White as the top quarterback in the league, and Landry is staunch in his agreement: "He's an excellent quarterback. His knowledge of the game is unsurpassed by any quarterback we've had."

But can he get Dallas to a Super Bowl championship?

"That," says White, "is the question people will be asking me the rest of my life—not what your winning percentage was during the season, but how many Super Bowls did you win? Remember Fran Tarkenton? One of the great quarterbacks of all time. But he'll always be remembered by being 0-3 in the Super Bowl."

White is not at all bitter about that qualification. Instead, he welcomes it, because he believes he and the Cowboys are going to get there. One reason is that Landry has decreed this year's target the winning of the National Conference championship game. "Coach Landry," says White, "is absolutely phenomenal at picking out weaknesses and setting goals. Last summer he told the defense it had to have more turnovers, more interceptions. Well, we led the league.

"This year our objective is to be more effective in 'plus territory' (inside the opponents' 20-yard line), which we didn't do too well last season. He has the pulse. We were 4-2 last season and coming up against a four-game streak against championship contenders. He told us, 'Now we got to bear down. This is make or break, the next four games. If we can win three out of the four, we'll be in great shape.' Well, it turned out we won four-of-four, but it was mainly because he had laid it out for us."

Roger Staubach noted in the introduction that White is at the "top of his game." And White responds, "He just means I have played enough to have settled into the position. Yes, I think I have established myself as one of the leading quarterbacks in the NFL, but I also realize you never stop learning as a quarterback. You should learn something every play you execute. You're in the middle of an ocean of knowledge, and you try to become a sponge in absorbing as much of that knowledge as you can. Now, I feel it's time to set my sights a little higher, time to assume more leadership. And, of course, if you're a Super Bowl championship quarterback, everything else falls into place."

White's right hand that throws the ball is not his real right hand—that is personified by halfback Tony Dorsett. He makes White so much more dangerous, because he can break for a 75-yard touchdown on a run at New England, or he can take a short pass for a 73-yard TD against Buffalo.

Many Cowboys fans were skeptical about the kind of person Dorsett was when he first came to Dallas. He was a flashy, highly publicized

(Top) Rafael Septien kicked his way to the top of the Cowboys' record book in 1981. He set club records for field goals (27) and points (121) and became the team's all-time leading field goal kicker (73). *(Bottom)* The offensive fireworks are about to be lit.

phenomenon at the University of Pittsburgh. Apparently, those Cowboys fans did not pay attention to the first scouting report on Dorsett, before he was drafted by the Cowboys: "A great practice player, runs out 25 yards every carry, great team player since high school."

Finally, last season, after his marriage, after a full off-season of sweating the weights and three-mile runs, after being "canonized" by Landry as one of the offensive captains (with Pat Donovan), Dallas fans kept giving Dorsett standing ovations at Texas Stadium. He responded as he had planned all along by gaining 1,646 yards—second in the NFL.

Dorsett is now one of the established, veteran leaders of the ball club, so his remarks must be attended: "The last two years we came up a game short of the Super Bowl and this past year by just one point. That should be enough to make everyone participate harder in the off-season program. That's where you get started. It might all boil down to the off-season program.

"I think it might even be tougher to get to the Super Bowl this year, though, because our schedule looks tougher. But they say the third time is a charm, so hopefully we'll be able to make it. I miss the Super Bowl. I think I got spoiled my first two years, and I miss it. Individually, I've just got to keep on keepin' on. In any business you always want to improve, and those 1,600 yards (in 1981) aren't going to remain the highlight of my career. It's going to take a lot of work by a lot of people (blockers) because what an individual accomplishes in this game depends on the group. All I know is I want to do better."

And Dorsett knows he has the people up front to help him do better. Last season when he had accumulated five MVP awards and the gift certificates for boots that accompanies them, he gave the certificates to the five starters in the offensive line.

With the All-NFL pair of Pat Donovan at left tackle and Herb Scott at left guard, the Dallas line going into the '82 campaign is a blend of youth and experience that figures to bolster the offense for many years to come. Right tackle Jim Cooper has been singled out by Landry as "underrated . . . he had a lot better season than many people recognized."

At center and right guard there's a dramatic battle shaping up, titled, "three into two won't go." Guard Tom Rafferty moved to center last season when center Robert Shaw had a knee injury. Into Rafferty's job strode Kurt Petersen, perhaps the strongest player, physically, on the squad. Now Shaw's knee is healed and it is expected to take all summer to sort out who starts where.

Notably, the Dallas receiving corps is the admiration of the league with wide receivers Tony Hill and Drew Pearson and Butch Johnson, plus tight ends Billy Joe DuPree, Doug Cosbie and Jay Saldi. Pressing the illustrious trio at wide receiver this season will be second-year Cowboy Doug Donley, the blond whiz out of Ohio State, who caught only three passes last season but is expected to play a large role this year in the team's formation which features four wide men spotted here and there. Only Dorsett is faster than Donley in the 40-yard dash.

Rafael Septien became a Pro Bowl kicking star last year, despite lingering injuries. He was 27-for-35 in field goals and a perfect 40-40 on extra points. Quarterback White figures again as team punter and therefore that job is in talented hands.

But, as the Cowboys stand—poised to bust out of the starting gate—they should pause to reflect on how the road to the Super Bowl all began, especially with most everyone in the country expecting Dallas to reach the ultimate game and win it. It was both a glorious and torturous road.

DALLAS
24
PART II

1981 Review: Just 58 Seconds Short

In retrospect, Everson Walls was the perfect metaphor of the Cowboys in 1981. After he had intercepted three passes early in the regular season, he was asked, "What are you trying to do—steal 11 like you did last year at Grambling?" And Walls replied, "NO-O-O. I'm just trying to make All-NFL."

All Cowboys personnel with the exception of the players—especially the players—have a great affection for Thousand Oaks, California. In the beginning, 1963, it was the balmy daytime weather and the crisp, sweater-clad evenings and the comfortable, cozy dormitory quarters. Later, when the first two losing seasons of that era were behind them, the Cowboys' six weeks of training camp began to take on the heady atmosphere of hope and even expectation.

Now, all these many years later, the California Lutheran facilities breathe a life of their own—first part renewal, second part confidence.

Oh, there have been a lot of detail changes on the fringes of camp. Everyone has been split into five condominium-style dorms. Los Robles, a nightclub-restaurant on top of a country club, long ago under new management, is not *the* place to go at night. Some 40 miles north of Los Angeles on the Ventura Freeway, Thousand Oaks in the '60s was a "bedroom community." Now, though it still has no real center, it is a sprawling mini-metropolis. And, the natives are still friendly.

But none of the aforementioned are prevailing factors as the Cowboys come to camp in the early '80s. What matters is that in the ensuing years the team has gone to the playoffs 15 times, traveled five times to the Super Bowl and fought on twice to the only goal that matters—the championship.

It is almost the only thing the veteran players talk about in July. Charlie Waters and D.D. Lewis could have called it quits after the '80 season, and not many would have lifted an eyebrow. "I want to get Philadelphia," Waters kept saying. "I want to go out as champion." And Lewis, typically understating: "Yeah, I'd like to go out on top. That'd be a great way to end it, wouldn't it?"

Waters and Lewis, along with all the other '80 Cowboys, were chafing about getting to the lip of the cup in the Super Bowl tournament, then tripping over their shoddy offensive play in the NFC title game at Philadelphia. That they had already beaten Oakland, on Oakland's home field, put the irritation specifically on their posteriors. The Eagles had told "funny stories" after their victory over Dallas, and now the Cowboys were growling, "Deal the cards."

Because the club had been dethroned as rulers of the NFC East, Gil Brandt and his scouting department were galvanized into the club's greatest manhunt since the early '60s. Brandt brought in 93 free agents to go with the 12 draftees. Some other NFL teams only had 40 or so from the overlooked pool of collegians.

Tom Landry was growling, too, unimpressed by the 105 rookies in

The much-heralded and much-honored defensive line was the key to the Cowboys' defense. Led by All-Pros Ed Jones and Randy White, the front four specialized in harassing offenses.

camp. But he had an eye open: "Right now you find yourself paying more attention to the draft choices, especially the high-round guys. The free agents and the lower-round guys are the ones you hope to get a little sign from. D.D. Lewis is a good example of what you look for. He was pretty lousy when he was a rookie. Then one afternoon he fought off the end and got to the running back. What it boiled down to is that he made the team in one day, which is not that easy to do."

The practices at Thousand Oaks are open to the public and a few grandstand seats are provided, well away from the action. Inside the red-composition track that circles the field gather the "inside" camp followers, the scouts, the doctors, visiting college coaches and the media people, the latter strolling the sideline and denying information to each other concerning their inevitable hangovers from the night before.

These interested parties, during the early parts of each practice, may select from a smorgasbord of action—Ernie Stautner working his defensive linemen against Jim Myers' opposite numbers, Jerry Tubbs slinging not-so-easy spirals for his linebackers to intercept. But the greatest throng this summer was positioned to watch the pass-skeleton drills.

A pass-skeleton drill involves only a quarterback (taking a phantom snap from an absent center), wide receivers and tight ends, cornerbacks and safeties. Of particular interest, of course, were the cornerbacks.

That focus had been assured for months, since Landry's April assessment of incumbent cornermen Steve Wilson and Aaron Mitchell: "If Wilson and Mitchell improve in training camp, we'll be okay. If they don't, we've got a problem." Somebody looked it up and discovered there had not been a rookie starter in the defensive backfield since Cliff Harris (at free safety) in 1970. Landry agreed: "You can't anticipate having rookie help." This would later prove, of course, an ironic remark.

(Top Left) Despite the firm grip of the folks who blocked him, Harvey Martin led the Cowboys in quarterback traps for the ninth consecutive year, every one he's been with the club. *(Top Right)* Ron "Bird" Fellows hauls down Tampa Bay's Theo Bell in Cowboys' playoff victory last season. Fellows, one of the team's quickest players, was a surprise seventh-round draft choice in 1981 who played his way onto the regular third-down pass defense by season's end.

So, the favorite pastime in the early weeks of training was to sidle up to a knowledgeable party and ask, "Who do you see that you like?"

"You mean besides Donley?" said John Wooten, one of Brandt's top aides. Wooten should know a player when he sees one, because he himself was an All-NFL blocker for the great Jim Brown at Cleveland. "I know all about Donley," the writer would say, referring to the club's second-round draft choice. "He hasn't dropped a pass in eight days."

"Well, then you are probably interested in defensive backs. I like Ken Miller, the kid out of Eastern Michigan, seventh round. He's quick. And I like Ron Fellows and Everson Walls and I'm beginning to like Mike Downs." Fellows was selected right before Miller, but the other two were signed as free agents.

Ermal Allen, the special assistant upon whom Landry relied to grade every single player in the National Football League, was another dependable source. A salty fellow, Allen wouldn't give a twin brother a blue chip rating if he didn't merit it. "Oh, I think so-and-so can play," Allen would answer. "And so-and-so is better than we thought he'd be." The point was, when he had completed a rundown, he had also singled out Miller, Fellows, Walls and Downs.

By now they were heading them up and shipping them out by the carload, to make room for the veterans coming in. The names chalked every other day on the slate in the press room read like a casualty list from the front. "But I'm not ready to quit football," a rookie would protest to administrative aide Dan Werner, as he handed him a plane ticket and arranged a ride to the L.A. airport. Another would promise, "I'll be back here next summer and *make* this team." Some, like receiver Mike Wilson of Washington State, never said a word. Wilson merely went up the coast to San Francisco and wound up catching a crucial pass in the Super Bowl.

D. D. Lewis set an NFL record with his 27th playoff game appearance. Unfortunately, it was D.D.'s last game with the Cowboys after 13 seasons.

Full-speed scrimmages offered exciting yet fearful occasions for weeding out the prospects, even if it was, for example, a quasi-game against rookies from the San Diego Chargers. That affair ended 0-0, but it was notable in Landry's assessment of the action. He singled out Miller, Fellows and Walls for praise. Now even "The Man" was joining in. He also noted that Mike Downs had intercepted a pass in the end zone to stop one San Diego threat and made a goal-line solo tackle to halt another.

But when Landry took stock of the men he would rely on in the defensive backfield, no newcomer was on the list. "We'll go with Barnes and Wilson at left corner," he said, "Mitchell and Manning at right corner, Waters and Clinkscale at strong safety and Hughes and Thurman at free safety."

The injury factor loomed over this group like a dark cloud. Charlie Waters had endured the second of two knee operations, Randy Hughes the second of two shoulder operations, and Benny Barnes had been nursing a bad foot for several years. Barnes no longer wanted to play cornerback, where quick cuts and starts and stops invariably had him limping. One day back in April a writer saw him emerging from Landry's wing of the Cowboys offices and said, "He must have told you you were moving to strong safety, judging by that smile on your face."

"That's what he said," Barnes replied, the smile getting broader. "This turns out to be a happy day in my life."

As time drew nearer to the pre-season games, Landry was asked if he meant to ease Hughes and his shoulder back into action. "No," he said. "There's no reason for him to play less in these games. He's either going to hold up or he isn't."

Hughes, an All-American at Oklahoma in 1974, had seen his way blocked for years by the tandem of Waters and Harris, and once Harris got out of the way the shoulder kept dislocating. He was now a fatalist: "Maybe I'm going to have some luck. You've got to have the opinion that it's finally going to be your turn. I haven't had any luck since I got here."

Through the years, the Cowboys had been notoriously inept when they came east from training camp to play the first pre-season game in Dallas. After the barracks life of Thousand Oaks, the pleasures of homecoming have taken priority over football. So the Green Bay Packers, a team going nowhere, beat them 21-17 for an 11th defeat in 22 summertime openers. "We were so glad to be home," Drew Pearson said, "we just forgot about the game." Landry was only partly surprised: "I knew we would have trouble playing well, from the way they were working last week, but I didn't think we would be down 21-0 in the first half."

The defeat itself was not important, but the way it happened was worrisome. Green Bay's Lynn Dickey completed 13 of 18 passes and three of his misses were dropped. Rookie Ken Miller seemed lost on a TD pass. Cornerback Steve Wilson had a 49-yard completion taken out of his hands by James Lofton at the four. The other cornerman, Mitchell, gave up his share of the 259 yards passing. The bright spot of the game for Dallas was that Mike Downs blocked a punt and Everson Walls picked it up and ran for a touchdown.

That next week back in Thousand Oaks, Charlie Waters tried to rally his troops: "We have to make the plays, be able to cover one on one, but it's an overall team problem, not just a secondary problem. We need pressure on the passer and we need those drops by the linebackers."

The second summer game, at Anaheim, Calif., made the first one seem like a lark. Not only did the Los Angeles Rams wipe out the Cowboys,

(Top Left) Everson Walls got burned occasionally, but more than made up for it with a record-setting 11 interceptions. *(Top Right)* They call this man "Stoneface"? The key is to watch Landry during plays. That's when he's emotional.

33-21, they also marked finis to the career of Randy Hughes. As L.A. ran out the clock late in the fourth quarter, Hughes reached out with his left arm to hook a Rams rookie on a sweep . . . and his shoulder went again. As Hughes knelt there on the field, his left arm limp, a Cowboys player on the sidelines yelled, "Oh, my God, look at Randy!" The troubled shoulder had suffered its third and final dislocation. Earlier in the week, Hughes had told the press, "If I'm hurt again, I've had it," and so went his last play for the Cowboys.

Pat Haden, the little Rams quarterback from Oxford, hit 17 of 25 passes, again building a 21-0 lead before Dallas could get out of the starting blocks. Twice the Cowboys were called for pass interference in the end zone.

Harvey Martin came up with a brutal bottom line: "We can't cut it," he said, "with the cornerbacks we got."

The back-to-back losses did not do much for Landry's disposition. When he suggested that the Cowboys problems were simply having to use too many people, a writer asked if that wasn't true for the other side as well, and Landry, untypically, barked back: "I don't care what *their* problems are. I'm telling you what *our* problems are."

Therefore, it was a grim Dallas team that left Thousand Oaks to return for the last two pre-season games, both at Texas Stadium, versus Pittsburgh and Houston.

Fate had begun to reshape the Dallas secondary.

Hughes was gone. And now cornerback Aaron Mitchell was out with an ankle sprain. At the insistence of secondary coach Gene Stallings, free safety Dennis Thurman was moved to right corner: "He's a football player." And at the insistence of everyone, rookie Mike Downs was installed at free safety.

(Top Left) Harvey Martin (79) has led the Cowboys in quarterback sacks for nine straight years. He gets lots of help from teammates like blitzing linebacker Mike Hegman (58), a player with a knack for making the right move. *(Top Right)* "Tony Dorsett had a super year in 1981, says Tom Landry. "Now, you ask, can he repeat it? Well, he can if he wants to. It's also possible for him to be even better because he's maturing to a point where there's not much limit anymore in what he can do."

Everything that had been all wrong in the first two summer games suddenly became everything *all-right* in the last two. Danny White threw for 382 yards to rout the Steelers, 24-14, and Thurman was a stickout with several vicious hits at cornerback. Houston was dispatched just as neatly the following week, 28-20, as Tony Dorsett rolled up 129 yards rushing and looked flashier than anytime since his rookie year four seasons before.

Rookie Everson Walls intercepted his third pass of the pre-season against Houston. On being congratulated on his three-for-four, Walls said, "And I ran in that blocked punt in the other game. I'm just a lucky guy."

Preparing for the league opener at Washington, Landry looked back and judged: "We have so many weapons on offense. We're in good shape there. On defense our front people (linemen and linebackers) are playing well. If we can get the secondary together, we'll be a contender. If we can't, we won't."

In the final cutdown to the 45-man roster, Landry made his decision to give up on cornerback Aaron Mitchell, trading him to Tampa Bay and keeping rookies Fellows, Downs and Walls. Thurman and Steve Wilson would start at the corners against the Redskins, with Waters and Downs at the safety positions.

A year before, with an unproven Danny White taking over for the retired Roger Staubach, Dallas was not rated highly as a contender. Some people picked the Cowboys to finish third in their division. Not so now. Las Vegas had Dallas the short-priced favorite to win the Super Bowl. "I like that," said Harvey Martin. "Let 'em all know how *bad* we are."

(Top Left) Versatile Tom Rafferty's (64) ability to switch from right guard to center to replace injured Robert Shaw was a key to the success of the 1981 season. *(Top Right)* "The California Quake" got another rousing ovation, meaning Butch Johnson (86) scored another touchdown, this one against the Eagles at Texas Stadium.

One of Landry's "so many weapons" exploded in the Washington faces as Dallas won its 17th straight opening game, 26-10. That weapon was Tony Dorsett—"in late season form," according to Landry—with 132 yards in 21 carries.

There were other complements to the solid Cowboy win: Dallas coaches knew that the Redskin secondary concentrated on stopping intermediate-range passes, confident it could do this and also defend the long ball. Dallas decided to test the waters, and the result was a 33-yard TD to Billy Joe DuPree and a 42-yard bomb to Drew Pearson, both down the middle. Pearson's score put Dallas ahead, 14-7, and the Cowboys never trailed thereafter, adding the final 12 points on four Rafael Septien field goals.

But it was Dorsett's 132 yards that announced a new surge to the Dallas offense. The "most misunderstood" Cowboy had always been a team-player, as it said on his initial Dallas scouting report. But a change in lifestyle and a new dedication early in 1981 finally made his role apparent to all.

On April 7, Dorsett had wed a Thousand Oaks sweetheart, Julie Simon. In contrast to his former off-season wanderings, Dorsett now stayed at home, and at the Cowboys practice field, pumping iron and running miles. "I'm probably in the best shape, mentally and physically, that I've been in since my rookie year," he said before the opening game. "I'm ready to roll. Ever since losing that Philadelphia championship game last season, I've been wanting to play football. I figured I had something to prove to myself. All I'm trying to do is just be productive and work hard and play with consistency week in and week out. If I do that, everything else is going to fall into place. Our guys have the 'Super Bowl Itch.' "

Landry had watched it all go on, and the week of the Washington opener he did something about it—he named Tony Dorsett one of the Cowboys captains. (The others: Pat Donovan, Bob Breunig, Randy White and Anthony Dickerson.) "He's got a great attitude," Landry said, "and he's always doing that little extra something in practice to help us become a better team."

There was one other significant element in the Washington game—the rebuilt and "suspect" defensive backfield intercepted four of Joe Theisman's passes. Netting one apiece were Mike Downs, Steve Wilson, Everson Walls and Dennis Thurman, the latter for a 96-yard return (no TD) that sealed the victory. Said Walls: "We want to get out of the Rodney Dangerfield mold. The defensive backs on this team are no weak link."

Tony Hill caught 13 passes for 216 yards and a touchdown in the two victories over defending division champion Philadelphia.

The win over Washington in the opening game of 1980 had pumped Dallas up to a 5-1 start. This victory worked the same, and the Cowboys rolled to a 4-0 record with wins over St. Louis, New England and the New York Giants. They dispatched the Cardinals, 30-17, with three short TD plunges by fullback Ron Springs and 129 yards from Tony Dorsett, as Septien kicked three more field goals.

A fateful quote about the New England game came from Patriot safety Tim Fox: "We've had trouble with the San Franciscos but our team has a history of playing well against the good teams and Dallas is one of the best."

Nobody knew it then, but New England was on its way to the worst record in the NFL. Dorsett helped them along with a 75-yard touchdown and 162 yards for the Monday night game. On the other side of the ball, rookie Walls stole two more passes. "I'm just trying to make All-NFL," he said. Dallas won comfortably, 35-21.

Dorsett's teammates signaled his new worth. "Everybody knows Tony is running a lot better," said Drew Pearson. "He's cutting upfield and getting more yardage. In cases last year, he would just string it out to the sideline."

A 41-yard fingertip catch by Butch Johnson powered Dallas to an 18-10 win over the Giants, a game in which the Cowboys never trailed. Suddenly, there were only three undefeated teams in the NFL after four weeks—Miami, Philadelphia and Dallas.

The unbeaten record had been built on 13 interceptions, five fumble recoveries and 13 quarterback traps. Everson Walls now replaced Steve Wilson at left cornerback. The one cloud on the Dallas horizon was an inability to score touchdowns inside the opponents' 20-yard line. In the four wins there had been 19 such opportunities, but the Cowboys could only get the TD five times. They had to settle for Rafael Septien field goals.

"I don't think it's real critical yet. But if we lose one it will be. If we lost a game because we had to kick three field goals that will be a different matter," said Landry.

As it happened, that week in St. Louis, the flaw did cost Dallas a defeat. But not before some quirky happenings kept the lowly Cardinals in the ball game. James Jones fumbled the opening kickoff away at the nine and St. Louis scored on one play. A 48-yard pass from Danny White to Butch Johnson set up a seven-yard TD sweep by Dorsett, but St. Louis went back ahead on a field goal.

When Ed Jones recovered a St. Louis fumble, Dallas soon had a first down at the Cardinal 13-yard line, but had to settle for a Septien field goal. That difference, getting three instead of a probable seven, would haunt the Cowboys at game's end. A muffed punt gave St. Louis the ball at Dallas' 30-yard line and quarterback Jim Hart threw for a TD on the first play, to two-way hero Roy Green, making a highlight-film fingertip catch diving into the end zone.

But the "in close" jinx plagued Dallas again, at the St. Louis eight yard line, when Danny White threw an interception. An interception by Downs quickly gave Dallas another shot, at the St. Louis 21. From the 11, White found Dorsett with a screen pass behind Herb Scott's convoy and the game was 17-17 entering the fourth quarter. "It all came down to who could drive to get a field goal and who couldn't," said Landry.

With less than five minutes remaining, that looked like a Dallas formula. But at midfield, with third down and less than a yard, Danny White fumbled the center snap from Tom Rafferty and had to run the ball himself, for no gain.

After the punt, and a personal foul penalty on Timmy Newsome on the

(Top Left) "Randy White's performances range anywhere from spectacular to spectacular," says Tom Landry, who's not known for exaggeration. *(Top Right)* Tony Dorsett did it all in 1981, e.g., here against the New York Giants.

play, the veteran Hart milked all but 23 seconds off the clock before Neil O'Donoghue kicked a 37-yard field goal.

The Cowboys were in shock. "I don't know what happened," said Dorsett, who had 99 yards rushing. "In my opinion this team doesn't belong on the same field with us." Then the after-shock set in. "Losing in your own division," said quarterback White, "always comes back to haunt you at the end of the season."

On the plane ride back to Dallas, Tex Schramm put it in specifics: "This is the kind of defeat that costs you the home field advantage in the playoffs."

The following Sunday in San Francisco pounded the idea of playoffs right out of the Cowboys' heads. "We can't be thinking about Philadelphia and our division now," said Danny White, after the shattering 45-14 loss to the 49ers. "We've just got to focus on the next game."

Two solid drives had gotten San Francisco away to a 14-0 lead, when a Cowboys play occurred that symbolized the whole day. From his own end zone, White threw in the flat to Drew Pearson. As the ball got there, cornerback Ronnie Lott spun Pearson by his jersey. The ball popped loose near the sideline, hit an official's leg and stayed in bounds. The ruling: Complete pass, fumble, recovery by Lott and "tough luck about the leg, fellas." San Francisco punched it in for a 21-0 lead.

"When you get into a game like this," said Landry, "all you can do is stand there and watch it."

Dallas still had hopes in the third quarter, trailing by 24-7, but one play wiped the hopes away. Quarterback Joe Montana threw a sideline pass to Dwight Clark and rookie Walls over-ran him as he moved for the tackle. Clark slid past him and down the sideline for a 78-yard touchdown. "I felt good about things," said D.D. Lewis, "until they hit that little pass and broke it open."

The 49ers, who were 6-10 in 1980, now were 4-2, identical to the Cowboys.

It appeared that Dallas had cratered at exactly the wrong time. In the next four games the Cowboys would have to face title contenders Los Angeles, Miami, Philadelphia and Buffalo. "We've got to streak sometime if we're going to make the playoffs," Landry said. "That'll be hard to do against the schedule we've got. We'll find out pretty soon where we stand."

The travesty gave the players a new perspective on the season. "Maybe this team is flawed more than people thought," said tackle Pat Donovan. "I think we're a pretty mediocre group right now." Said another Dallas captain, Bob Breunig: "I just hope we're all scared to death and we'll respond to it."

Landry said it looked like the Eagles, 6-0, were a shoo-in for the NFC East title. He said he would take a 2-2 tradeoff in the next four games.

Perhaps part of Landry's dimming view was due to the situation at center. Third-year man Robert Shaw, a onetime first-round draft pick, had beaten out veteran John Fitzgerald in training camp, and then Fitzgerald's tender knee collapsed again. Shaw's emergence as a top flight NFL center was a result of the Dallas weight program, in which he built himself from a 235-pound suspect to a 255-pound Pro Bowl candidate. Then Shaw hurt his knee. Finally, when he tried to return to action in San Francisco, he hurt it again, badly enough to require an operation.

October 25, 1981, the day the Cowboys beat Miami, Mel Renfro was inducted into the Ring of Honor.

So guard Tom Rafferty moved over to become fulltime center, and second-year man Kurt Petersen was installed at right guard. Petersen had played defense in college.

It was mindful of the French general who was told that his army was flanked right and left and that the center could not hold, so he said, "Well, *mes amis,* it is time to attack!"

In other words, the Cowboys had everybody just where they wanted them.

In the next four weeks, in national telecasts, America was re-introduced to the Dallas Cowboys. The Rams went down in a Sunday night game at Texas Stadium, 29-17. The Miami Dolphins were the next victim at the Irving site, which NFL Films has labeled "the Bermuda Triangle," 28-27. A trip to Philadelphia brought a 17-14 Dallas win. Finally, on a tough Monday night back at the Triangle, Buffalo fell, 27-14.

Landry was asked then if he would still settle for 2-2 over the four games, and he returned a sheepish smile. The coach doesn't answer sarcastic questions.

The Rams were done in by their ofttimes nemesis, Tony Dorsett. Runs of 18, 15 and 14 yards set up the first Dallas touchdown. A 44-yard lightning burst right up the middle brought the second. In between, there was a Septien field goal and a safety-sack of Pat Haden by Harvey Martin.

And when L.A. got it back to 10-19, big-play man Tony Hill, returning to a starter's role after his summertime muscle pulls, broke open the ball game with a 63-yard touchdown pass play. He caught a medium pass against the sidelines between two Ram defenders, who then knocked each other out of the play.

In the aftermath, somebody looked it up. The last eight times Dallas had lost by 21 points or more, it came back to win the next game.

Philadelphia had lost its first game of the year, to Minnesota, and Dallas now trailed the Eagles by one game.

The following Sunday belonged to Everson Walls, who contributed almost equally to the Miami offense and to the Dallas salvation. On a day when Cowboys great Mel Renfro was inducted into the club's Ring

Despite Washington's acquisition of Joe Washington (25), the Cowboys beat the Redskins twice last year to run their winning streak over their longtime rival to five games.

of Honor, Walls intercepted his seventh and eighth passes of the year to break Renfro's rookie (1964) record. Walls also yielded eight receptions for 253 yards. "I had an up-and-down day," was his calm response.

The way the Dolphin game tallied, it was one of the outstanding comebacks in Cowboys history, which is saying a lot. The Cowboys' 14-6 first half lead had become a 27-14 deficit with 5:16 remaining. Thousands of faint-hearted fans left the stadium to catch the windup on their car radios. ("I'm sure a few people missed the last quarter," Landry said, slapping his thigh.) What they missed was a 38-yard completion to Tony Hill at the Miami five, followed by a TD toss to tight end Doug Cosbie. Now there was 3:48 left in the game.

Dennis Thurman came up with the interception, his second of the day, to give Dallas possession at the Miami 32. Landry then sent in a call to throw to fullback Ron Springs on an "out and go." Springs beat a Dolphin linebacker to grab a 28-27 lead. But there was 3:17 left in the game, and young David Woodley was working on a 400-yard passing day, only the third opposing quarterback (Billy Wade, Sonny Jurgensen) to rack up such a number.

Surely enough, Woodley passed Miami to the Dallas 26, where a field goal was an easy option. But Don Shula called for just one more pass (perhaps remembering that his kicker, Uwe Von Schamman, had missed an extra point earlier). And Everson Walls got his second interception, at the four-yard line, returning it 18.

"Everson," said Randy White, "usually breaks even—the passes he catches and the passes he lets them catch." Oh, frivolity reigned around Walls. When a Dallas writer said, "Did it surprise you that they came out throwing at you?" Walls replied, "You ask me that every week."

Too Tall's sack of Ron Jaworski provided the field position needed for the winning touchdown at Philadelphia.

Now it was showdown time in Philadelphia. "I don't know of any game better guaranteed to get our attention," said Landry.

Drew Pearson picked up on that. Early in the week, he told a media luncheon audience: "I've been lifting weights since last season getting ready for (Eagles cornerback) Roynell Young. If I don't get thrown out of the game, it should be a good matchup. It'll be like the Ali-Frazier fight, the Thrilla in Manila. This one is the Thrilla in Phila."

Eagles linebacker Frank LeMaster took another tack: "I respect (Dallas), but I don't like them one bit. They're America's Team. We're the Working Man's Team."

Finally, they teed it up, and all the talk meant nothing. The Eagles led 7-3 at the half, though Dallas had moved the ball up the field and down the field, pell mell. A Dorsett fumble at the Eagle four kept the margin intact. Dorsett later tipped up a pass in the third quarter for an interception by linebacker Jerry Robinson in the end zone.

Ron Jaworski then completed an 85-yard TD pass to Harold Carmichael over Everson Walls and the sellout crowd came unglued in celebration of a 14-3 lead. There was still no panic on the Dallas sideline. Ed Jones remembered the defensive platoon's discussion: "We decided all we had to do was get the ball back, because our offense was moving it every time they got it. We knew sooner or later we were going to cash in."

The cash-in came sooner than later. Dallas drove 75 yards with the ensuing kickoff and scored on a peculiar pass play where Danny White threw for Tony Hill in the back of the end zone and had it "intercepted" by Doug Cosbie in the front of the end zone. White smiled as he recounted the play saying, "I knew one of them would get it."

Landry thought the Cosbie reception was worth a lot psychologically. "They had to remember the touchdown Cosbie caught against Miami," he said. "That's got to get them thinking, and when you're thinking and

(Top) Dennis Thurman, a marked man in the rematch against Philadelphia, intercepted three passes to seal the Eagles' fate in the victory that clinched the NFC East title for Dallas. *(Bottom)* Ed Jones was one reason Detroit needed an "extra" man to beat the Cowboys. "Too Tall" applied lots of pressure to Eric Hipple, who cried "We beat America's Team!!" when it was over.

worrying you're off balance." Ed Jones sacked Jaworski at the Eagles' three-yard line and Dallas had the field position for Dorsett to wreak havoc. He gained the first 15 yards of the drive, and the last nine, when he took safety Brenard Wilson into the end zone with him. "I'm little," Dorsett said, "but I'm tough." The Cowboys had seized control of the game, 17-14.

Then Dennis Thurman speared Jaworski on a blitz, drawing a penalty that gave the Eagles a last life. Joe Pisarcik replaced Jaworski and brought Philadelphia to the Dallas 16. Everson Walls then broke up "sure" TD passes to Harold Carmichael and Rodney Parker and kicker Tony Franklin hooked a tying field goal attempt to the left. The Eagles had finally been caught, at 7-2, but Dallas had a 1-0 lead in the first tie-breaker.

Now came Buffalo, a contender out of the AFC East, led by quarterback Joe Ferguson, who had an awed view of the occasion: "It's like going into Yankee Stadium or the Boston Gardens, and it's on Monday Night Football." As it happened, the Monday Night Show turned on a poor decision by Ferguson at the end of the first half and a spectacular play by Dorsett at the outset of the third quarter.

Ferguson racked the Dallas secondary for 259 yards in the first half and had only a 14-7 lead to show for it. Then just before the second quarter ended he had the Bills knocking on the door at the Cowboys' nine-yard line, 33 seconds left. Even a 17-7 halftime margin would have been devastating to Dallas, but Ferguson got rushed by Ed Jones, fell to his knees untouched and *still* tried to complete a TD pass that when deflected, fluttered like a wounded duck into the awaiting hands of safety Michael Downs.

On the second play of the second half, Danny White threw 20 yards down the middle to Dorsett, a linebacker bounced him away from two other Bills defenders and Dorsett took the play 73 yards for the tying score.

That play killed the Bills. Another Walls interception set up a flea-flicker play in which Dorsett going into the line, lateraled back to White, who threw a 37-yard pass to Tony Hill wide open at the goal line. Two Septien field goals completed the scoring.

By now everyone had forgotten the disastrous trips to St. Louis and San Francisco, but Landry was present with a typical warning: "We have Detroit, Washington and Chicago coming up. They are teams who are coming back, better than their records show. There is only three points or so that separates you. Of course, sometimes it's difficult to explain this to your team." No one in the jubilant Cowboys entourage could hear his warning.

Everson Walls stole two passes to tie Renfro's best-season record. Dorsett went over 1,000 yards for his *11th* straight year (dating back to high school). But a cloud no larger than a man's hand loomed over the Dallas fortunes. Conrad Dobler, the self-certified Dirty Uno of the NFL, had leg-whipped John Dutton twice in the Buffalo game and incurred a third 15-yard personal foul penalty on another occasion. Dutton had a bruised thigh and was listed as doubtful for the Detroit game.

The Lions were 4-6 when the Cowboys visited their Silverdome—as Dallas eyed the new place for a January 26 Super Bowl return. And when the Cowboys zipped to a 17-0 lead in the first half, it seemed there was no room for surprises. But Landry didn't think that way. "We were sacking their guy and getting good field position," he said, "and they fumbled at our two-yard line going in." It was the Lions' remarkable Billy Sims who coughed up that ball, but later he was to redeem himself greatly.

Tony Dorsett got loose against the Lions. Tony was hoping this would be his warm-up act at the Silverdome, but they played the Super Bowl there a few months later without him.

A three-yard TD run by Sims narrowed it to 17-7 at the half. And in the third quarter Detroit added 10 points to tie the score. Reviving some of its previous spirit of four-weeks duration, Dallas mounted an 80-yard drive climaxed by a 14-yard White-to-Jay Saldi touchdown. It came with only 2:28 remaining and looked like the game-winner. But on the first play after the kickoff, young Eric Hipple found Sims racing down the sideline with only linebacker D.D. Lewis in pursuit. It was an 81-yard TD and a 24-24 tie.

What happened next was the *cause celebre* of the season. With no timeouts and only 25 seconds left to play, the Lions called field goal kicker Ed Murray onto the field and he used 23 of those seconds to kick a 47-yard game winner. The Cowboys took exception in that Detroit had 12 men on the field, *and that none of the officials counted.*

NFL Commissioner Pete Rozelle happened to be in Detroit for the game, and the next day at a luncheon he said, "I'd like to congratulate all 12 or 13 who participated in the winning field goal." As you'd imagine, Tex Schramm did not think that was funny.

The Cowboys, even in defeat, did chalk a certain milestone at the end. When holder Hipple saw the Murray kick go through the uprights, he tackled the kicker and yelled, "We did it, Eddie! We did it! We beat America's Team!" No sarcasm there, just pure emotion, and the Cowboys' oft-ridiculed designation was certified.

But Dallas was now again one game back of Philadelphia. Losing to "bad teams" was a flaw in the program. Except that looking across the NFC divisions, one of the bad teams, San Francisco, had the same record as Dallas at this stage, 8-3. The Cowboys rebounded to put away Washington at Texas Stadium, 24-10, on a Sunday, and Chicago with greater difficulty the following Thursday, 10-9. Danny White was knocked out of that game, with Glenn Carano presiding over a victory by grace of a last-minute Bears' field goal miss. Carano also had to play the whole game 10 days later at Baltimore, for a 37-13 laugher.

While all this was transpiring, the Philadelphia Eagles were going down the tubes, losers to the Giants, Miami and Washington. The climactic game foreseen in October was now an anti-climax. Dallas owned a two-game lead over the Eagles with two games left to play. Mathematically, Philadelphia still had a chance. A win over Dallas, a mop-up of St. Louis on the final weekend, while the Cowboys were losing to the New York Giants in the Meadowlands—and, presto, the Eagles would be NFC East champions again. It was a scenario that would not work.

First of all, Danny White's bruised ribs were no longer sore from the Thanksgiving Day hit. He would go against the Eagles. Secondly, nothing was happening right for Philadelphia down the stretch, and it happened wrong again just before halftime when the Eagles were enjoying a 10-0 lead. Punt returner John Sciarra muffed Danny White's short kick at the Philly 20-yard line, and in three plays White had a TD pass to Tony Hill. On the first Dallas possession in the third quarter, White hit Butch Johnson for a 36-yard bomb and the Eagles could forget about the NFC East. Final: Dallas 21, Philadelphia still at 10.

(Top Left) This was the day the Cowboys put it all together and, as Danny White said they would be when it happened, they were awesome. *(Top Right)* No, Too Tall didn't play offense, too, against the poor Bucs. He did intercept a pass deflected by John Dutton as Dallas pounded the NFC Central champs to advance to the NFC title game.

It was the 12th division title for the Cowboys, and the finale at New York was rendered meaningless. Besides, Walls got his 11th interception of the year to lead the league and set a new club record.

But the game in New York was not meaningless to the Giants, who could make it into the playoffs as a wild card by beating Dallas. And so they did, in overtime, 13-10, after two Dorsett fumbles and an interception thrown by Danny White. What hurt more was that Danny White blew his chance to lead the NFL in the pass standings and Tony Dorsett lost his NFL rushing lead to George Rogers of New Orleans.

But Dallas had a wild-card week off and just two games between it and the Super Bowl.

"One of these games we're going to put it all together," Danny White had said way back in October, "and when that happens we're going to be awesome."

Well, "one of those games" happened to arrive simultaneously with the Tampa Bay Buccaneers for the first playoff round. Harvey, Randy, Dutton and Jones "hounded and pounded" quarterback Doug Williams into the Texas Stadium turf, sacking him four times, creating four interceptions, forcing him into two grounding-the-ball violations, all of which created a shutout. Meanwhile, the Cowboys offense was scoring 38.

On one occasion, Dutton batted a Williams pass attempt high into the air and Jones intercepted it when it came down. The quarterback was later asked, "But when you did have time to pass, were your receivers covered?"

Williams stared back at his interrogator. "When I had time to pass? When was that? When *did* I have time to pass?"

Still, amidst all the mayhem, Dallas led only 10-0 at halftime. An 80-yard drive at the beginning of the third quarter, most of it courtesy of Tony Dorsett and Ron Springs, produced a 17-0 lead that began to turn the game into a rout.

So there was offense and defense—and there was also the kicking game. No little part of Tampa Bay's problems was due to Danny White's talents as a punter. Twice he kicked out of bounds at the Buccaneers' eight and twice the Cowboys got the ball back to go in for scores.

"Punting is part of our offense," White said. "We were keeping them

(Top) Dorsett gained 86 yards on only 16 carries in the whitewash of the Bucs at Texas Stadium. *(Bottom)* This was the moment when Tampa Bay quarterback Doug Williams asked himself if maybe he should have gone to law school. After the play, Ed Jones, said, "Excuse me."

(Top and Bottom) Tony Hill opened the scoring barrage against Tampa Bay by catching a nine-yard bullet from Danny White. Hill's "Wings of Victory" provided an extra flourish.

down in-tight and not letting them out. The kicking game becomes more and more important. When you kick them down to their five-yard line, you can feel the intensity of the defense pick up. They're a bunch of animals down there. Then we get the ball back on our 50, and it's amazing the attitude you carry back onto the field. It's a big morale booster, an offensive and defensive weapon. The key was to keep them off balance and not give them field position." (The Tampa Bay offense had averaged 27 points in its previous five games, winning the NFC Central championship.)

Washington Post columnist Dave Kindred filed these words back to Redskin fans: "This Dallas team is the next Super Bowl champion."

The Cowboys had waited-out an off week while the wild card games were settled and had plenty of time to reflect on their dismal ending at New York. "We were on pins and needles," said D.D. Lewis. "We just couldn't wait to hit somebody."

But the Cowboys were not ready to count themselves into the Pontiac, Michigan, Silverdome Super Bowl. Their triumph over Tampa Bay happened on a Saturday. On Sunday the New York Giants, surprise victors over the Philadelphia Eagles, were defeated at San Francisco. "The Eagles started making errors over the last four weeks of the season," Landry said. "And after reaching the Super Bowl last year, they had something to lose. New York had nothing to lose. After you reach the Super Bowl, it has a mental effect on you."

The bottom line was this: for the second straight year, because its regular season record was inferior to the other survivor, Dallas would have to travel to an opponent's field to vie for the NFC championship, the ticket to the Super Bowl. And for the second straight year, it was a field where the Cowboys had lost their regular season game.

The field at Candlestick Park had been soggy in sunny weather when the Cowboys fell, 45-14. Now torrential rains in Northern California had forced the 49ers to flee to Anaheim, the Rams' camp, for their title game preparations. Would Dallas' hopes sink in the soggy turf—a speed-defeating factor for a team built on speed—as they had years before on the ice floes at Green Bay?

On Wednesday morning of championship week, that factor was paled by another. During the night a blood vessel burst in the right thigh of John Dutton. Marc Antony once said, "The evil that men do lives after them," and so it was with Buffalo guard Conrad Dobler. The illegal leg-whipping Dutton had received from Dobler, way back on November 9, had caused him trouble off and on. Now the rupture periled Dutton's appearance against San Francisco.

The "matched pairs" of the Cowboys' front four had been broken. Backup tackle Larry Bethea would start in Dutton's place. "Larry knows the defenses," said Ernie Stautner, "but you hate to see a winning combination fouled up."

In a careful review of the regular season, a case was made that the Cowboys had created this Frankenstein monster on the city by the bay. The 49ers had been only a 3-2 team when Dallas fell flat on its collective face. Then they proceeded to win nine out of their last 10 games, and another in the playoffs.

And yet, not many neutral people in the press box, or the millions in front of TV sets around the country expected that Dallas would lose this showdown. But, lose the Cowboys did—four touchdowns and four extra points to three touchdowns, three extra points and two field goals, 28-27—denied again in the penultimate game.

The drama, however, was to exceed anything that happened on Super Sunday.

Bob Breunig (53) grimaces at an official's questionable call in the Championship game.

On its first possession of the game, San Francisco went 63 quick yards to take a 7-0 lead. The key play was a 24-yard pass to running back Linville Elliott, isolated on a first down against middle linebacker Bob Breunig, which reached the Dallas eight. Quarterback Joe Montana then passed to wideman Freddie Solomon on the right side and when Dennis Thurman's body-block attempt didn't stop him, he bounced into the end zone. A 44-yard field goal by Septien narrowed the gap, and Mike Hegman soon claimed a 49er fumble to set up Dallas at the 49er 29-yard line. On second down, Danny White hit a beautifully lofted pass down the left sideline to Tony Hill for a 26-yard touchdown and a 10-7 Dallas lead.

For some magical reason, Tom Landry had decided this was the day he would unleash rookie Doug Donley, mostly absent all season, on the 49ers. A third-and-13 situation had Donley in the lineup just before the end of the first quarter. He caught a pass for four yards. This kind of employment would be fateful for Dallas when the game was on the line.

The one "great" questionable call in the game then happened. Everson Walls, the leading NFL interceptor, stole another one, but this time he did it at the Dallas one-yard line and fell into the end zone. The officials ruled that it was the Cowboys' ball on the one, instead of a touchback with possession on the 20. The 49er defense was the equivalent of Danny White's earlier description of a down-in-the-hole proposition—animals. And White punted out of the end zone to the Dallas 47.

Four plays later, Montana was falling to his knees under a Dallas blitz and still got away a 20-yard TD pass to Dwight Clark, who had turned Dennis Thurman completely the wrong way on an All-NFL fake. San Francisco 14, Dallas 10. A 17-yard completion to Hill, and a 35-yard pass interference penalty against Ronnie Lott on Drew Pearson, led to a five-yard TD sweep by Dorsett and Dallas had regained the lead for the halftime.

Midway in the third quarter, a classic case of what-might-have-been reared its unfortunate head. Randy White alertly intercepted a tipped-up pass at the Dallas 13, and the Cowboys had seemed to dodge a dangerous bullet. But two downs later a Danny White pass went off Ron Springs' hands to an interception by linebacker Bobby Leopold. From the Dallas 13, San Francisco quickly punched in a go-ahead touchdown, 21-17.

Another pass interference call against Lott, the Rookie Of The Year on defense, gave Dallas a first down at the 49ers' 12, but it resulted only in a three-point boot by Septien.

The 49ers had led the NFL in turnover ratio—turnovers claimed versus turnovers yielded—and this statistic was heralded by both coaches as a pre-game gauge. The 49ers were plus-21, but Dallas was second in the NFL at plus-18. And this day the Cowboys would claim six turnovers—so much for statistics.

The turnover, a fumble, claimed by Everson Walls (usually an interceptor turnover-person) was caused by Breunig's hit on Walt Easley and gave Dallas the ball at midfield. Dorsett got 11 and 6 yards and a 12-yard pass to Springs set up the 21-yard TD to tight end Doug Cosbie down the middle.

There was 10:41 left to play in the game, and Dallas led, 27-21.

Walls intercepted yet another pass to halt the 49ers' comeback drive, this one at the Dallas 27. And now the marbles were on the line. The Pontiac Silverdome was clearly gleaming in the distance.

From the 27, Dallas worked its way to the 49ers' 47, where third down came up, with only five yards for a first. Just a few more yards would put Septien in position for a field goal and put the 49ers out of their misery. But White had to pass to the wrong side of rookie Donley and he could

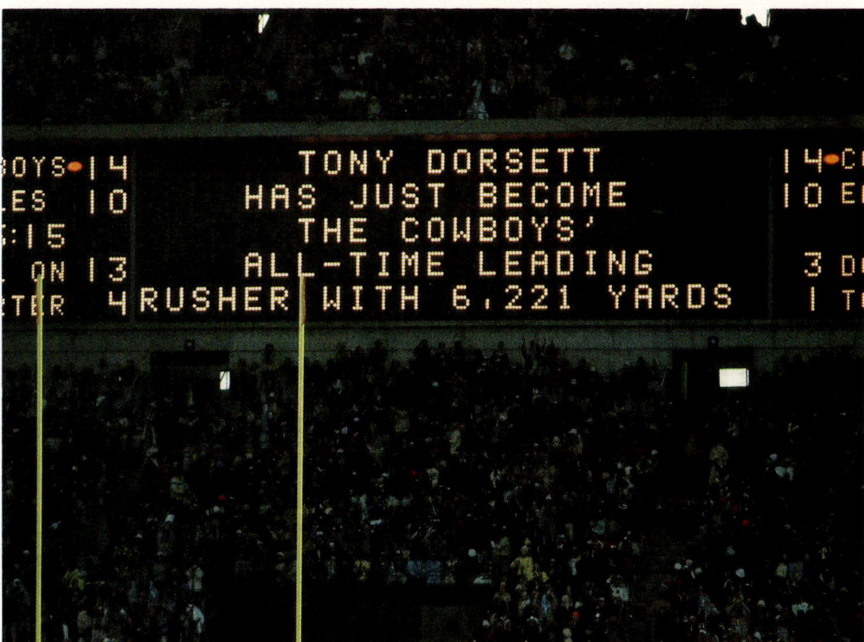

The postscript to a championship afternoon: Dorsett continues his assault on the Cowboys' record book.

not get a handle on the ball. It would have been a great catch, but that's what Super Bowl teams are made of.

White soft-footed a punt to the 49ers at their 11, and now it was all on the line. With 4:54 to play, San Francisco had to move from its own 11 for a touchdown, or else it would never get to Pontiac. Dallas, the only team that had ever been to five Super Bowls, would only have to deny a first down to make it to the sixth.

What happened from there to the end of the game will go down in Dallas history alongside the Cowboys failure at the two-yard line in 1966, the "Ice Bowl" drive by the Packers in 1967, the tipped up passes (and other things) that cost the Cowboys Super Bowl V. The 49ers took it 89 yards for a Super Bowl touchdown, and there is a lingering feeling that the drive was more a failure of Dallas strategy than a failure of Dallas players.

On first down from the 11, a Joe Montana pass was incomplete, so Dallas pulled its linebackers and put in its "4-0" defense, in which there is no middle linebacker. And Dallas kept this defense in the game for the next 12 succeeding downs.

The result was that Elliott gained six, then 11, then seven, then four, then swift Freddie Solomon ran a reverse for 14 and the Cowboys were not only on defense—they were back on their heels. When Montana, passing from the Dallas 35, hit Dwight Clark for 10 yards at the Dallas 25, Cowboys partisans began to fear that this was somehow not their day. Walls had Clark covered like a barracuda, flailing his arm in front of the ball, and still Clark caught a tippy-toe boundary-line catch for the completion.

Unaccountably, after Elliott had racked up another seven-yard gain, Dallas inserted its linebackers for a run defense at the Cowboys six-yard line. There were 58 seconds left to play.

"I don't know why we put in our run defense on that down," Landry was to say on the plane ride home, somewhat uncomfortably. The next play, a Montana pass to Clark in the back of the end zone—the TD that sent the 49ers on to supremacy—will remain in Dallas' memory as "the pass that Montana was trying to throw away, but Clark got up and caught it."

Randy White, as usual, gave it everything he had. He suffered severe muscle cramps late in the game.

Despite the Cowboys failing in their bid to reach a sixth Super Bowl, losing 28-27 at San Francisco, Tony Dorsett gained 91 yards, bringing his 12-game career playoff total to 1,000.

However, by the genius of NFL Films, which had a camera in the end zone area, with a zoom lens focused on Montana's eyes, you know that the Notre Dame gamer knew what he was doing. Montana's eyes were on Clark all the way, as Ed Jones and D.D. Lewis forced him out of the pocket and made him scramble right. Perhaps Too Tall mis-timed his jump, the one that had devastated Tampa Bay's Doug Williams. In any case, Clark was leaping high in the air like a basketball player doing an alley-oop dunk, to get San Francisco into the Super Bowl.

"Michael Downs and I had Clark double-covered on the play," said the ever-honest Everson Walls. "Mike had him inside and I had him outside, but when Montana broke out of the pocket I lost Clark."

The rabid 49er fans—who had pulled some of the most unconscionable acts of the season against Dallas fans—went berserk at Clark's touchdown. But a number of NFL writers in the press box (some of whom had bet on Dallas) looked at the clock and saw 51 seconds remaining. "It ain't over yet, babe," one of them said.

And surely enough, Danny White quickly hit Drew Pearson over the middle for a 31-yard gain to the San Francisco 44—on *first down.* "The guy grabbed my jersey," said Pearson, "or I would have gone all the way."

It was not to be. Defensive end Lawrence Pillers, who was once cut by another team because he was not a good pass rusher, leaped a Dallas offensive lineman and stripped Danny White of the football before he could pass to a wide-open Tony Hill 15 yards downfield. The 49ers slumped out the last 30 seconds on the clock, but Dallas knew it had a whole number of months to evaluate its anguish.

There was the Dutton absence. There was the crucial loss of Randy White during the last 89-yard 49er drive due to leg cramps. There was Tony Dorsett's slashed eye (by an accidental 49er cleat in the second quarter) that limited his playing time. He still gained 91 yards, and only once had Dallas lost (28-1) when he had reached 100.

The Cowboys had claimed six turnovers but got only three points out of them.

The Dallas players in the postgame locker room were unbelieving that this could happen to them again. Most of this squad had known nothing but victory, and quite a few were veterans of the Super Bowl XII victory. "You're supposed to say," said the retiring D.D. Lewis, "hey, we'll get 'em next year, but I can't say that. This club will be good again, though. The machine just keeps rolling."

PART III

Landry: The Constant Star

He has become one of the country's icons. The stoic face—in victory or defeat. The erect posture, the impeccable clothes. The hat.

Of course, the people who know Tom Landry best, know he doesn't have to concern himself with keeping his hat on straight.

It may not have occurred to many observers yet, but perhaps the saddest thing that has ever happened to Tom Landry is that he has been defined completely as *the* coach of the Dallas Cowboys—or, in Pat Summerall's fateful words, "The only coach that Dallas has ever had."

Actually, it is an image he can take pride in, given the accumulative success of the Dallas franchise. It is doubtful Landry pays much heed when his persona is ridiculed publicly, such as the time announcers on national television poked fun at him for wearing a trench coat with a fur collar while his team was coming back in the fourth quarter to beat Atlanta in the playoffs.

At first, and for quite some time, the subject of Tom Landry's personality weighed lightly upon the public consciousness. At least that was the case in Dallas when he arrived in 1960 to coach the expansion Cowboys.

His first team finished 0-11-1. That record stirred few Texans, and fewer still elsewhere, into wishing to know more about him. Even though he was one of their own, born in Mission, down in the Rio Grande Valley, Landry kept his distance from everyone and kept his own counsel. He seemed to be walking to a drumbeat only he could hear, especially on the sideline.

Except there was a Dallas writer in the middle '60s who knew more about Landry than most. He knew him as the University of Texas fullback who would get you three yards when you needed one on third down, and also knew something hazy about his experience as a bomber pilot in World War II who flew 30 bomber missions over Europe and came back once, by virtue of the French underground.

So when this writer chatted with Landry, the subject (games) was both serious and light-hearted. He may turn away good stories, but he never prevaricates, unless it is to prevent criticism of one of his players. Glen Davis, now the director of the L.A. Times charities and once the Mr. Outside of Army, regaled a group at Thousand Oaks training camp one night with his nomination of cornerback Landry as one of the meanest players he'd ever faced. "I ran a stop-and-go and completely faked Tom out of his jock," Davis said, recalling a Giants-Rams exhibition game in the L.A. Coliseum, "and he not only chased me to the end zone, but through the end zone and into the area behind, where the peristyle is, to tackle me. I was so mad I shoved the football in his face. Then he chased me all the way back to the bench."

Landry, confronted with this tale the next day, smiled a small smile before saying, "That makes an interesting story, doesn't it?" Question mark and period.

Landry's assurance—though we cannot be sure of this—may have stemmed from an unusual dialogue between general manager Tex Schramm and owner Clint Murchison following the 1963 season, the fourth disastrous (win-loss) season of the franchise. "I'm getting a lot of heat about Tom," said Schramm, "and that kind of thing might hurt our program."

Murchison, forever a bottom-line man, replied, "Well, then, why don't we extend his contract for 10 years?" So it was done, for the first time in the history of American sports (barring Cornelius McGillicuddy who was both owner *and* manager of the Philadelphia Athletics). The move got the immediate attention of the players, and somehow the program got on track. "When Clint did that," Bob Lilly said recently, "we realized all of us had to get on board or the ship would leave without us."

Time—and some remarkable deeds—have altered the state of curiosity about Landry. Now 58, and having finished his twenty-third season with the Cowboys, he's the dean of National Football League coaches. Many are familiar with Landry's and the Cowboys' record. But the man behind the numbers? To begin with, one myth must be dispelled here and now. Landry *does* have a sense of humor. He laughs. He smiles. His wit is dry, deft, and usually a counterpunch. It is forever a surprise, because he makes spare use of the comic touch.

When pressed by flattery about his longtime tenure at the Cowboy helm, Landry said, "Yes, but look at it this way—I've been at the same job all these years and have never gotten a promotion." Once, when he learned of a bomb threat to the New York press box, Landry was asked how he would have reacted if the thing had exploded. "I suppose we would have observed thirty seconds of silent prayer," he said. "Then we would have continued playing, with enthusiasm."

A few years ago, there was a banquet scene where photographers wanted a shot of Landry and the only middle linebackers he'd ever coached. They were Sam Huff of the Giants and Jerry Tubbs and Lee Roy Jordan of the Cowboys. Tubbs, Huff and Landry stood together as Jordan approached. Said Landry: "Here comes the one with speed."

On the overall scale, Landry does not claim that he is aloof from normal matters or emotions. If he appears as such to others, particularly players, it's through a combination of his nature and necessity. "I've always been quiet and conservative in my approach to everything," Landry says. "I don't think it's aloofness. I enjoy friends and fellowship. But in the position of head coach, you have to create a certain aloofness, although I don't know if that's the right word.

"There just has to be some distance between yourself and the players. No one was closer to the players than I was in New York (as defensive coach of the Giants). Some of my best friends through the years have been those players—Sam Huff, Jim Katcavage, Andy Robustelli, Harland Svare, Dick Nolan. I feel a great warmth and closeness to them." (Huff, who has been voted into the NFL Hall of Fame, asked Landry to be his "presenter" at the Canton ceremonies this summer; Dick Nolan has rejoined the Dallas staff.)

"I'd love to have the same relationship with players now as I did in New York. It's what I miss more than anything. But I can't afford that luxury. I can't afford to be that close and sensitive to players as I was then because I have the full responsibility of this team. When you have that, you have to make hard decisions."

Landry means personnel decisions. His defense mechanism here is obvious: Don't form emotional attachments to players. Judge them solely on athletic merit. That approach eliminates personal bias leading to mistakes in judgment. It also unfortunately eliminates, in large measure, contact on a personal level.

There are other reasons why Landry maintains distance from players. As the authority figure, he must demand they train and play to their physical limits. In periods of exhaustion, pain and frustration, it is human nature to seek a short cut. Part of Landry's job, as he sees it, is to put a roadblock in every passageway leading to lesser performance.

D

"When you're in an especially challenging field like pro football, where you get physically beat, it demands much more of a player," Landry says. "There's a lot of difference in being mentally beat. Therefore, there can't be too much softness from authority. From coaches or anywhere.

"What you're trying to do in football is get guys to do what they don't want to do in an effort to achieve their goals. That's the whole purpose of athletics. If you want to demand that kind of dedication from players, then you can't be too close to them to achieve it. Nobody wants to lift iron for four months. I mean, who *wants* to do that? But at least they respect you if you make them do it, and you can't if you're close to people. They're going to take advantage of you because it's natural to take advantage in that situation.

"So my responsibility is to gain their respect, not for them to like me particularly. But they respect me because they achieve their goals. That's all a coach can ask. If he gets any more that's a plus. If he had a guy or two who cares for him personally, that's a plus in this business."

Leadership is the key ingredient, and has always been, to Landry's role as head coach. "What they see in me, hopefully, is that I'm always in control of the situation. And they're confident it will work out the way it should. That's leadership in a strong way. Players have certain keys they look for in a game. They look at the coach first. If he doesn't appear confident, or looks defeated, then all of a sudden they are defeated. They are limited in overall knowledge as to what's really taking place. So the key for them is to look at me or the quarterback on the field to see how he's reacting.

"That's the one thing I hope they see—that I am in control and I am confident things will work out."

What of other times, when wheels are coming off and spinning in all directions?

"We all have doubts," Landry says. "But it's really the ability to overcome doubt that makes the difference. I don't think you can teach it. I believe the greatest thing in football or any other sport is concentration. Look at Jack Nicklaus or Bjorn Borg. There's something about a winner. They have control of themselves under the toughest situations. Borg knew he was in trouble at Wimbledon against John McEnroe. But you couldn't tell it by looking—even when he left the court. The way he walked off—there was nothing but a winner's attitude about him."

Win or lose, Landry walks off a football field the same way. He is immersed in the game to the exclusion of all else. He doesn't hear crowd noise. He seemingly is unaware of elements and will work a game in 95-degree temperature without removing his coat or even loosening his tie. The last thing he does is change expression. His face is grim. His lips move only when sending in plays. Again, there's a reason.

"Emotion is something you can express if you don't have the

responsibility of making important decisions immediately," Landry says. "If you call plays, you don't have time for emotion. Any time you show emotion, your concentration or train of thought is broken. Any time you look at the scoreboard and start thinking whether you're ahead or behind, whether you're going to win or lose, there's a blank spot in your concentration. You won't do anything positive at that point. I believe anyone who's outstanding in sports must have the ability to concentrate completely. Any time there's a break in concentration, your chances of winning may slip past at just that moment. That's why I've trained myself. I believe the key to success is concentration during the battle.

"I very seldom see or hear what's going on (other than the play on the field), and that's where my whole reputation comes from. A fan can get excited over a play. He looks down at me, and I don't do anything. I don't show any excitement. Well, to him, that's no emotion. More than likely I didn't see it to start with. I was looking at the blocking on the play.

"I can watch a game that I'm not involved in but have an interest in and get just as upset or excited as anyone. My stomach churns when I want someone to win but have no control over the game. I'm sitting there like a fan, and I have the same emotions. I don't have those emotions on the field because I'm too involved in what I'm doing."

Win or lose, there is something else about Landry. He doesn't change. He's not one to agonize over what might have been, in either case. Losing means you work harder to win. Winning means you work harder to keep from losing. Victories and defeats don't clutter his mind long, because there's always the next day, the next game, or the next season. Landry forever marches forward, leaving the past for others to contemplate.

And for the present, Landry remains in command of it all—offense and defense. He rarely mentions his working hours, but his normal schedule includes Monday through Friday nights at home with film and game-plan detail. On the average, says his wife Alicia, those sessions last from two to three hours. If the Landrys manage an evening out during the week, it's on Friday. They share Saturday night dinner on the road because Alicia is a constant companion.

One question about Landry remains: What skills make him a great coach? The subject is broad and worthy of technical study, but shorter answers are necessary. Perhaps the following cross-section touches most of the key bases.

From defensive coach Ernie Stautner: "I almost fainted when I saw Tom's playbook. It was all there, the things that it had taken me 16 years to figure out. It made me mad."

From Danny Reeves, now coach of the Denver Broncos, and a onetime Cowboys player and assistant coach on Landry's staff: "He's such a competitor for one thing. Lose and his jaw gets square. He doesn't say much the next week, just works harder. He *hates* to lose. His football knowledge is extraordinary. Plus, he's been there and has the experience. Very few occasions arise that he doesn't have the experience to know what to do. Another thing is foresight. He can say, 'If we do this now, the situation will be better in three weeks.' It may not be better today but, sure enough, in three weeks the guy he's put in is playing good."

"He's extremely cool under fire," Reeves continues. "You can be getting the hell kicked out of you—he doesn't like it, he bows up a little and the hair raises on the back of his neck—yet he's the same. You can count on him being the same, day in and day out."

Now this "Constant Star" in the Cowboys' firmament takes Dallas into the league campaign for the 23rd straight year, once again as the favorite. What does Landry expect the 1982 Cowboys to accomplish? He expects them to win their third Super Bowl title.

PART IV

Coaches: High Expectations

Up to this point the 1981 team has been reviewed somewhat in terms of being the best since the Cowboys' Super Bowl appearance in 1978. "One of the key developments was the individual performances we received from such players as Tony Dorsett, Rafael Septien, and the emergence of Walls, Downs and Thurman," says Coach Tom Landry. The Dallas Cowboys have had several months since that day in San Francisco to reflect and plan for the 1982 season.

Here are the coaches' expectations for the upcoming season and the 1982 Cowboys team.

Jim Myers: Offensive Line

The questions which Offensive Line Coach Jim Myers poses are not the result of worry. They are, in fact, asked with a smile. Myers has the kind of problems, if they can be labeled as such, coaches everywhere would like to face.

It boils down, as the 1982 season approaches, to the fact that he's got too many starting caliber players and too few positions for them to fill. As a result of last year's position juggle—which saw guard Tom Rafferty move to center to replace injured Robert Shaw and Kurt Petersen taking over at the vacancy Rafferty's move created—Myers is now facing a three-won't-go-into-two situation in the middle of a Cowboys line which could be one of the club's best in years. And, he is wondering, where does last year's No. 1 draft pick Howard Richards, an athlete of great promise, play this year?

"A great deal depends on whether Shaw's knee is okay," Myers says. "He was our starting center last year and showed signs of being an outstanding one until the injury. Then Rafferty moved into the job with no real preparation and came along very well. And while he was proving himself as a center, Petersen surprised a lot of people at the right guard spot. He has great potential because of his size and speed and willingness to work."

The fate of Rafferty and Petersen, at present, depends on the health of Shaw. If well, and able to continue with the progress he showed last year, the center job will be his, thus pitting Rafferty and Petersen in a "battle royal" for the right guard job. If Shaw has problems, Rafferty will retain the center job, thus leaving the guard spot to Petersen.

"Until we're sure Shaw is okay," Myers says, "I think we'll have to count on Rafferty at center. But even if he is the starter he can expect a run for his money because Shaw is a great competitor who has a lot of athletic ability. And he's made it clear he wants the job badly. If Shaw wins out, then it becomes Rafferty's job to try to take Petersen's spot at guard. It's an interesting situation."

The left guard spot is solid with All-Pro Herb Scott returning and the tackle situation is good with veterans Pat Donovan and Jim Cooper back. "Donovan and Scott are proven players who have been to Pro Bowls," says Myers, "and Cooper, who has progressed rapidly the past couple of seasons, is probably the most underrated lineman we have."

Which is to say, regardless of who triumphs in the Shaw-Rafferty-Petersen battle, the prospects for a championship caliber offensive line are good.

Then there's the matter of depth. "Howard Richards has all the qualities to be an outstanding lineman," says Myers, "so we've got to find a place for him to get in some playing time. Because of the depth we currently have at guard, I anticipate his working more at tackle early in the season. But, if he develops the way we think he can, he's going to be challenging the person in front of him, whether it is a guard or tackle."

Two other candidates for reserve work at tackle are five-year veteran Andy Frederick and Steve Wright, a rookie free agent whose potential caught the coaches' eyes last year. Glen Titensor, the No. 3 draft selection in '81, is a Rafferty-type who could have a promising future. "Glen could be an excellent center and will also work at guard," says Myers. "He has a great deal of quickness and good strength. It will be interesting to see which position he matures at this year. There's no question that he has the potential to become a factor at either spot."

If he can work in some playing time. Such are the problems Myers and his offensive line will be faced with this year.

John Mackovic: Quarterbacks

In his two seasons as a starter, Danny White has clearly proved himself a more-than-worthy heir to the job of quarterbacking the Dallas Cowboys.

"I know there was a great deal of talk about the transition he would have to go through after becoming the starter," says quarterback coach John Mackovic, "but I haven't noticed him struggling much. He's an excellent quarterback in every respect and what's really amazing is the fact that he's still far from reaching his potential. He's going to be even better this year." That in itself lends a positive statement about the prospects of the high-geared Cowboys offense. And when one considers the caliber of those waiting in the wings for an opportunity to displace White, it is obvious that quarterback is one of the club's strongest positions.

Barring any late trade that would send five-year veteran Glenn Carano off to some other club to pursue his goal of becoming a starter, the battle for the No. 2 spot on the depth chart will be one of the most interesting of '82. Gary Hogeboom, entering his third season, has reached a point where he is ready to emerge as a challenger. Now well versed in the Cowboys' offensive scheme, he is eager to prove his worth. And Mackovic predicts he'll get that chance.

"He's at the stage of his career when it is important for him and us to find out just what kind of quarterback he is. Gary has all the physical requirements—good size, a quick release, and delivers the ball well—and is an intelligent football player. This year the plan is to get him on the field more during pre-season and allow him to compete equally with Carano."

Which in no way suggests that Carano has fallen from favor. "There's no one in our organization who isn't convinced that Glenn is a talented quarterback. He's performed well in the opportunities he's had. It's just that he's now at a point in his career where something's got to happen to him."

Carano, then, will find himself in a situation of battling White for the starting job while holding off Hogeboom for the No. 2 spot.

"What you want to emerge from a situation like we have," Mackovic says, "is the confidence that should Danny be injured you have someone who can step into his job and get it done. Glenn has proven he's capable of doing that and now Hogeboom will be given an opportunity to prove he can do it as well. Thus far Gary hasn't had the chance to prove that he's ready to move in should something happen to make it necessary."

If, then, having two promising back-up quarterbacks is a problem, it is one John Mackovic enjoys. "Obviously, we've got a great deal of talent at the position," he says.

Dick Nolan: Receivers

The coach is new, but the make-up of the Cowboys' receiving corps, one of the most talent-rich collections in the NFL, isn't likely to undergo much change in 1982. If anything, it could be strengthened with the additional contribution of second-year wide receiver Doug Donley, who could challenge for more playing time this season.

"Even when you sit down and watch film on these guys," says Dick Nolan, who joined the Cowboys staff in the off-season, "it is still hard to believe the level of talent and depth among the receivers. And what makes the group—wide receivers and tight ends—even more unique is the fact each player has a particular talent that sets him apart from the others. You've got a guy like Tony Hill who is the big play kind of player, the one who really threatens the defense just by being on the field. Then, there's Drew Pearson, a pro's pro, who can get open when no one else seems to be able to and also has a long history of making the clutch catch.

"Butch Johnson is an excellent route runner who can make the tough catch look almost routine. It's not hard to understand his frustration at not being listed as one of the starters, despite the fact his role is as vital as that of anyone else in our style attack. And the quick burst of speed Donley has, along with his ability to make the catch inside or out, makes him a bright prospect. I expect him to be in a more challenging position this year, right in there with Butch."

Johnson, however, would be the most likely to unseat one of the starters after a superlative season in '81, when he did log some time in the starting role early, before Hill recovered from a training camp leg injury. "Butch has made it clear that he feels he is as good as our starters," says Nolan, "and that's the way you want people to think. I want Donley thinking the same way."

There could be times, he hints, when situations call for all four to be on the field at the same time this season.

The major battle among the receivers, however, could be between tight ends Billy Joe DuPree, a ten-year man, and Doug Cosbie, who will be entering his fourth season. "Doug is young and talented," observes Nolan, "and there's no question that he's challenging there. He proved himself last year, making the big plays and showing improvement in his blocking. On the other hand, what can you say about DuPree? He's been a great team player—probably one of the most unselfish players in the league—for years and can still perform exceptionally well. It will be an interesting battle."

The third man in the rotation is veteran Jay Saldi, a key figure in special situations. "He's not as big as most tight ends," Nolan says, "but he's very valuable to us because of the many things he can do. He can even line up in the backfield and catch the ball over the middle the way the Preston Pearsons and Calvin Hills did. And he blocks well."

Nolan will also get a look at former cornerback Steve Wilson who came to the Cowboys three years ago as a free agent wide receiver from Howard University.

"With the receivers we have on hand and the caliber of quarterback we have, there's no limit to what this team can do with the passing game," Nolan says. It is obvious he's looking forward to his new job.

Ernie Stautner: Defensive Line

During the course of the 1981 season, assistant coach Ernie Stautner saw two important things as he watched his defensive linemen gain recognition as the best front four in the NFL: (1) there was, as the season progressed, great overall improvement, and (2) there was a marked downfall when left tackle John Dutton was sidelined with a badly bruised thigh during the playoffs.

With Dutton healthy, there is good reason to believe the starting unit will take up where it left off last year. Finding reliable backup help from players who can one day move into starting roles themselves, then, is high on Stautner's priority list this season.

"I'm expecting improvement from our regulars, too," he says. "As a unit there is still room to improve. Dutton, for instance, made great strides in our system last year, gaining confidence in the second half of the season. And he and (defensive left end) Ed Jones had begun to work well together. I anticipate even greater things from that combination this year.

"Jones has improved dramatically since he came back to football after a year off to try boxing. His intensity level has improved but can still be better. If he can maintain the level he reaches for some games over the course of an entire season he can develop into one of this league's most dominant players."

Right tackle Randy White has obviously already reached that level. "He's the most intense player I've ever coached," says Stautner. "The truth is, you seldom see a player of his caliber. He's one of those who plays every play to the fullest: never concerned with the score or the time remaining. He's got such great pride in what he's doing that he doesn't want the guy across from him to beat him a single time."

While there is no concern over the performance of White as he prepares for his eighth season, Stautner admits that former All-Pro right end Harvey Martin, ten-year veteran, has to re-challenge himself. "There was a time last year," he explains, "when I was concerned that Harvey, who has been a great player for us, might be on the downgrade. But, in the last couple of games of the year (play-offs) he really came on strong. I was extremely encouraged. He did some outstanding things. I'm going to expect that of him again this season."

For a couple of backup players, former No. 1 draft pick Larry Bethea and Bruce Thornton, '82 could be critical—for them individually and the Cowboys collectively. "Both are at a point now where they've got to make a serious effort to become a starter," Stautner says. "Bethea now has the necessary experience in our system and is capable of playing well at either end or tackle. I'm confident he'll do a good job for us this year but it is time for him to show signs that he's ready to replace someone in the starting unit. Thornton got a new lease on life last year when we picked him up off the inactive list after cutting him. He worked hard and showed some improvement but he's had a history of inconsistency which he's got to put behind him."

Don Smerek, who made the team last year as a rookie before suffering a knee injury early in the season, and Ron Spears, a rookie free agent hurt in training camp last summer, are other candidates for backup spots. "Smerek, frankly, is a mystery to me. Twice now he's just about made the team and then was hurt. He's got the physical ability necessary to play and is one of the hardest off-season workers. Spears, who has gained 30 pounds since last year, showed great natural talent in a couple of pre-season games last year and could be a factor this season if he's able to stay healthy."

Gene Stallings: Defensive Backs

For the first time in several years, defensive backfield coach Gene Stallings is not looking ahead to a season while wondering who will play where in his secondary. "This is the first time we've spent an off-season with a pretty good idea of what we have to work with," he points out. "It's not a bad feeling."

Indeed, the surprising success of the secondary last year proved to be one of the team's major plus-factors as the NFC East title was reclaimed. A pair of free agent rookies, Everson Walls and Mike Downs, performed above and beyond expectations at cornerback and free safety respectively while Dennis Thurman, looking ahead to his fifth season, made the switch from safety to corner in a style which many felt should have earned him Pro Bowl recognition.

Even with the retirement of All-Pro strong safety Charlie Waters, things appear solid as ten-year veteran Benny Barnes stands ready to step into Waters' vacated spot.

"The main thing we hope to accomplish this season — and I strongly feel we have the people to do it — is to reduce the number of big plays (gains of 20 yards or more) that people managed against us last year. I think a year's experience will help a great deal," Stallings says. "I think we've got a solid starting group and some backup people who want to challenge. I expect the secondary to play well as a unit in addition to individual performances this season."

Barnes, used as a third down specialist last year, will join a youthful group which accounted for 27 interceptions last year (Walls led the league with a club-record 11, followed by Thurman's nine and Downs' seven). "Benny's been around for a long time and he is probably more familiar with our system than those who are returning starters. He'll be our strong safety when we open camp, but he will be challenged."

The player doing that challenging will be young Dextor Clinkscale who received high marks last year until he developed an Achilles tendon problem in training camp and was forced to spend the year on injured reserve. "Dextor has a great deal to learn," Stallings says, "but he's a fine athlete and a good competitor. There's always going to be some question about how well Benny's foot (which has been operated on three times during his career) will hold up, so Clinkscale's development is important to us."

Stallings predicts giant strides for cornerbacks Walls and Thurman in '82. "Both were new to their jobs last year," he says, "and had to learn as they went. Everson is one of those people with the knack for being in the right place at the right time, and that helped him through the early stages of the season. Then, as he got a grasp of what we were trying to do, he was able to add a steady brand of play to that big-play ability. Dennis made the switch from safety to the corner quite well and also came up with the big plays. He also showed some leadership ability which we'll need to have from him even more this season."

Ron Fellows, preparing for his second NFL season, will provide backup strength for both Walls and Thurman as Steve Wilson, once a starter on the right side, returns to the offense for a try as a wide receiver. "Fellows has a chance to be a player," Stallings says. "He moves well, goes to the ball, and has excellent range. If he comes through like we think he can, he will be a big help.

"And, we're not ruling out the possibility that there will be a rookie or two who will step into the picture," he says.

No doubt after the success last year of Downs and Walls, Stallings will be looking at the newcomers even closer than usual.

Jerry Tubbs: Linebackers

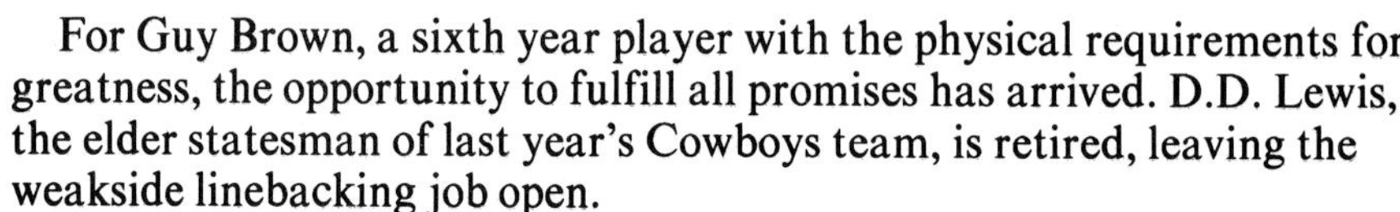

For Guy Brown, a sixth year player with the physical requirements for greatness, the opportunity to fulfill all promises has arrived. D.D. Lewis, the elder statesman of last year's Cowboys team, is retired, leaving the weakside linebacking job open.

"With the experience he has gained since he's been here and the fact he has seen some starting duty in place of injured players," says linebacker coach Jerry Tubbs, "Guy has some pluses in his favor."

Which is not to say the job is automatically his. In fact, Tubbs rates the battle for Lewis' job pretty even with no less than four candidates in the running: Brown, Anthony Dickerson, Bill Roe, and Angelo King.

"Actually, we have two major objectives this season," Tubbs says. "Obviously, we've got to determine as quickly as possible who is going to take Lewis' place. And, once we've settled that matter, we've got to work to control the run better than we did last year. To do so we're going to have to be a group which plays a more aggressive style of football. I want to see us playing with a much higher level of intensity in '82."

With Pro Bowl selection Bob Breunig set to return for his eighth season at middle linebacker and Mike Hegman showing steady improvement at strongside linebacker, a solid performance on the weakside is essential if Tubbs' masterplan is to take shape.

"The reason the competition is so wide open," he says, "is that we have four people who are capable of getting the job done well. When you have a situation like that, you just let them battle for it and hope one player distinguishes himself above the others."

While Brown has shown signs of developing into a starter for several seasons, nagging injuries have interrupted his progress. "But, when Hegman was injured (dislocated elbow) in the playoffs a couple of years ago," Tubbs recalls, "Guy stepped into a difficult situation and came through with flying colors, proving he's capable of getting the job done. In addition to staying healthy, he needs to develop the confidence he must have to earn the starting job. If he's able to win it, I would think his confidence would take a big jump."

A player not lacking in confidence is last year's specialty teams captain Dickerson who will enter his third season with the Cowboys. "He's one of those with big play potential," Tubbs says. "He's the quickest of the people we have and has great explosion. What he has to develop is the level of concentration that will allow him to avoid mistakes and become a steady player."

Bill Roe, a third round selection in 1980, is considered by Tubbs "a competitor" who brings enthusiasm and size to the battle but has some missed time to make up. An ankle problem forced him onto the injured reserve list last year after seeing only specialty team work as a rookie. "He lacks experience right now," observes Tubbs, "but he'll fight for the job." Then, there's Angelo King, a second year free agent, who may best fit the pattern Lewis established at the position. "He's one of those who just seems to perform well when you put him on the field," Tubbs notes. "He doesn't make the spectacular play but he gets the necessary results. He could develop into a solid performer."

Middle linebacker Breunig, the team's leading tackler and a veteran performer, will be called on for more coordination of the linebacking corps this fall. "With a new man on the right side," he says, "it is essential that Bob be in control of what's going on and direct the traffic. He's at a point in his career now where he can handle that responsibility and not have it affect the quality of his own play."

Backing up Breunig this fall will be promising Danny Spradlin who made the squad last year as a rookie. "He showed a real knack for playing middle linebacker last year," Tubbs says, "and is a good hitter who reads and reacts well. All he needs is more experience to become a top flight player."

Al Lavan: Running Backs

Soon after the 1981 season ended, offensive backfield coach Al Lavan summoned his fullbacks to his office and there explained to them the need for someone who can perform at a high level as a blocker, receiver and ball carrier to emerge in '82.

In other words, the job held by Ron Springs a year ago is now open to a field of challengers which also includes third-year man Timmy Newsome, former starter Robert Newhouse and possibly even James Jones, who played well in a backup role to All-Pro halfback Tony Dorsett last season.

"We must have a solid, all-round performance from the fullback position," Lavan says, "and we didn't feel we had it on a consistent basis last year. I've talked with Ron about it, telling him the areas I feel he needs to improve on if he is to keep his job. And at the same time I've made it clear to him and the others that the job is up for grabs."

Unless the decision is reached to switch Jones, a gifted athlete with the qualities Lavan is seeking, but lacking the size of a true fullback, the battle will likely center around Springs and Newsome. "In both cases it is going to be a matter of them making up their minds that they want to be a starter. Springs has to prepare himself mentally to defend his spot and Newsome has to convince himself that he's not ready to settle for being a back-up and make the necessary challenge.

"Jones could figure in as well since he's one of our best blockers and receivers as well as being a fine ball carrier. And Newhouse has indicated he wants to return so he could be in the picture, too."

While the prospect of a Dorsett-Jones tandem in the backfield is interesting, Lavan admits, it would be necessary to do some re-shuffling to fill the backup role at running back. Springs, who served as Dorsett's backup before moving to fullback, could make the switch back but Lavan has reservations. "Once you've been a starter at one position it is sometimes difficult to move to another as a back-up. Generally, what you find an athlete wanting to do is stay at the spot he's been in and challenge to regain his job if he loses it."

Lavan's primary concern, then, is to establish a fullback, then worry about the reserve strength. "When you've got a back like Dorsett, someone who is a real game-breaker, you have to have a fullback who can block well and also take some of the pressure off him as a rusher and receiver.

"Tony's performance last year spoke for itself and he's aware that the pre-season preparation was one of the keys to his reaching some goals he'd not reached before. He's worked hard again during the off-season and I'm convinced it is possible for him to be even better next season. Which, I realize, is saying a lot."

And, while obviously concerned, Lavan is optimistic that a reliable fullback will emerge. "We've got talented people at the position and there's enough experience. All we're waiting for is to see which of them wants the job the most."

Neill Armstrong, Research and Development

Neill Armstrong brings 27 years of coaching experience, including 10 years as a head coach, to the Cowboys' Research and Development Department, where he will work with Ermal Allen in scouting all teams and players in the NFL.

Armstrong joined the Cowboys this year after four seasons as head coach of the Chicago Bears, where he compiled a 30-34 record. Neill directed the Bears to the playoffs in 1979 following a 10-6 finish.

Ermal Allen, Special Assistant

Ermal Allen is recognized as one of the foremost authorities on the NFL. He is in his 21st season with the Cowboys, and is in charge of studying and evaluating all players and teams in the league. His reports provide the basis for the formulation of the Cowboys' weekly game plans.

Allen coached the Cowboys' offensive backfield from 1962-69 following 14 years as an assistant coach at his alma mater, the University of Kentucky.

Alan Lowry, Special Teams

The newest member of Tom Landry's staff is Alan Lowry, who was named special teams coach this year after five seasons as defensive backfield coach at his alma mater, the University of Texas.

Lowry is one of the few players in Southwest Conference history to earn All-Conference honors both as an offensive and defensive star. He was a defensive back at Texas in 1970 and '71 when the Longhorns won a national and two conference championships. Lowry was All-SWC in 1971.

The Conditioners

Bob Ward, Conditioning

Dr. Bob Ward has Cowboys players enthusiastically participating in his innovative conditioning programs, which include running, weightlifting, flexibility training and diet.

Ward directs the Cowboys' voluntary offseason conditioning program, working with computer printouts to devise individual programs for each player. He also supplies each player with an individual weightlifting program during the season. Ward was track coach for 11 years at Fullerton College in California before joining the Cowboys in 1975.

A graduate of Whitworth College in Spokane, Washington, Ward received his master's degree in physical education from the University of Washington and his doctorate from Indiana University. He also has been trained extensively in the martial arts and has taught Cowboys players various martial arts techniques that can be used in football.

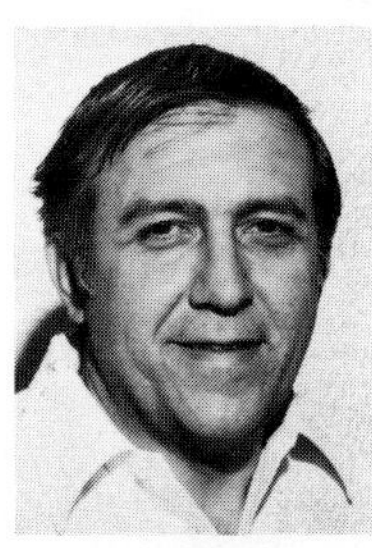

Don Cochren, Trainer

Don Cochren came to the Cowboys in 1965 after experience in college, military and Canadian Football League training.

A graduate of Purdue, Cochren earned his physical therapy certificate at Pennsylvania. He was trainer at Case Institute, now Case Western Reserve, in Cleveland for two years, with the Toronto Argonauts of the CFL for four years, and he spent a year at the University of New Hampshire before coming to Dallas. He also served as a physical therapy officer in the Air Force for two years.

Ken Locker, Assistant Trainer

Following four years as assistant trainer and interim head trainer at North Texas State, Ken Locker came to the Cowboys in 1973 as assistant trainer.

Locker received his master's degree in physical education from Texas Woman's University. He served two years as trainer for World Championship Tennis, making the men's tour in 1975 and '76. Last winter Ken was trainer for NBC's "Survival of the Fittest" competition in New Zealand.

Buck Buchanan, Equipment Manager

William T. "Buck" Buchanan joined the Cowboys in 1973 after supervising athletic programs in the Air Force for 20 years.

SMSgt. Buchanan was a non-commissioned officer in charge of Athletics and Programs at the U.S. Air Force Academy Prep School in Colorado Springs for four years. He was awarded the Bronze Star for his performance during a 1968-69 tour of duty in Thailand.

PART V

The All-Time Dallas Cowboys Profiles, Roster, Records and Statistics

You could view it this way: that the Dallas Cowboys never let themselves get into a position where they are forced to rebuild. Instead, the philosophy is to constantly rearm, adding good young players every year in a never-ending effort to keep the team's foundation strong.

Perhaps that plus a few other key factors (Tom Landry, for one) best explains the Cowboys' record of achievement over the past 16 years. For despite the constant turnover in player personnel that sends most NFL clubs through cycles of ups and downs, the Cowboys have fielded championship-caliber teams for the past 16 years, all of them winning seasons, 15 resulting in playoff appearances.

The Cowboys can set a league record in 1982 with their 17th straight winning season. They have won two Super Bowls, five NFC Championships (for a record five Super Bowl appearances), 12 division championships and they've appeared in a record 31 playoff games. The Cowboys also are the NFL's winningest team since 1960.

As someone once said about the Cowboys, "They are like a mighty river. You can scoop out a gallon or two, but it just keeps on rolling."

Cowboys Club Directory

CLINT W. MURCHISON, JR. . . . . Chairman of the Board
TEXAS E. SCHRAMM . . . . President and General Manager
GIL BRANDT . . . . Personnel Development (Vice President)
DON WILSON . . . . Treasurer (Vice President)
JOE BAILEY . . . . Administration (Vice President)
DOUG TODD . . . . Public Relations Director
DAN WERNER . . . . Business Manager
GREG AIELLO . . . . Assistant Public Relations Director
KAY LANG . . . . Ticket Manager
DICK BESTWICK, PETE CORDELLI, BOB GRIFFIN,
MIKE HAGEN, RON HILL, CHARLIE MACKEY,
JOHN WOOTEN, WALT YOWARSKY . . . . Scouts
DON COCHREN . . . . Trainer
KEN LOCKER . . . . Assistant Trainer
WILLIAM T. "BUCK" BUCHANAN . . . . Equipment Manager
BOB FRIEDMAN . . . . Director of Photography
DR. MARVIN P. KNIGHT . . . . Team Physician
DR. JAMES PAT EVANS . . . . Team Physician
SUZANNE MITCHELL . . . . Cowboys Cheerleaders Director
JIM SKINNER . . . . Entertainment Director
BILL LIVELY . . . . Cowboys Band Director

COACHING STAFF

Head Coach: TOM LANDRY. Assistant Coaches: JIM MYERS (Assistant Head Coach), ERMAL ALLEN (Special Assistant), NEILL ARMSTRONG (Research and Development), AL LAVAN, ALAN LOWRY, JOHN MACKOVIC, DICK NOLAN, GENE STALLINGS, ERNIE STAUTNER, JERRY TUBBS, BOB WARD

BENNY BARNES * 31

CORNERBACK-SAFETY STANFORD
HT: 6-1 * WT: 195 BORN: 3/3/51
11th YEAR FA FOR '72

Benny was the Cowboys' starting left cornerback from 1976-79. He has been moved to safety, the position he played in college, and entered training camp as the leading candidate to replace retired strong safety Charlie Waters. Barnes, a top special teams performer, has two career touchdowns, both scored on returns of fumbles.

LARRY BETHEA * 76

DEFENSIVE TACKLE MICHIGAN STATE
HT: 6-5 * WT: 254 BORN: 7/21/56
5th YEAR D-1 FOR '78

Bethea is the team's most experienced backup defensive lineman. He has the size, speed and versatility to play any position in the defensive line. The former No. 1 draft pick was named the Big Ten's most valuable player in 1977.

BOB BREUNIG * 53

LINEBACKER ARIZONA STATE
HT: 6-2 * WT: 225 BORN: 7/4/53
8th YEAR D-3 FOR '75

One of only three middle linebackers in club history, Breunig anchors the defense from the middle spot and calls the defensive signals. An excellent leader, Bob was named to the Pro Bowl in 1979 and 1980. He is very active in civic affairs and works for Roger Staubach's real estate company in the off season.

GUY BROWN * 59

LINEBACKER HOUSTON
HT: 6-4 * WT: 228 BORN: 6/1/55
6th YEAR D-4 FOR '77

An outstanding all-around athlete, Guy entered the 1982 season as one of the top candidates to replace retired D.D. Lewis as the starting right linebacker. Brown started six games last year at left linebacker for injured Mike Hegman. Guy has excellent size and speed.

GLENN CARANO * 18

QUARTERBACK NEVADA-LAS VEGAS
HT: 6-3 * WT: 202 BORN: 11/18/55
6th YEAR D-2 FOR '77

Getting his first chance to play under pressure, Glenn was instrumental in two victories last year. He replaced injured Danny White against Chicago and rallied the Cowboys to victory on Thanksgiving Day. The next week he directed a 37-13 win at Baltimore.

DEXTOR CLINKSCALE * 47

SAFETY SOUTH CAROLINA STATE
HT: 5-11 * WT: 189 BORN: 4/13/58
3rd YEAR FA FOR '80

A 1980 free agent, Dextor played regularly his rookie year on passing downs. He injured an Achilles tendon in training camp last year and spent the season on injured reserve. He began this season as a candidate for the strong safety position vacated by retired Charlie Waters.

JIM COOPER * 61

TACKLE TEMPLE
HT: 6-5 * WT: 260 BORN: 9/28/55
6th YEAR D-6 FOR '77

Considered by Tom Landry one of the team's most underrated players, Cooper has been the starting right tackle since 1979 when he took over for All-Pro Rayfield Wright. Jim was released near the end of his rookie training camp, but was recalled due to an injury situation in the offensive line. He has played all the positions in the offensive line.

DOUG COSBIE * 84

TIGHT END SANTA CLARA
HT: 6-6 * WT: 230 BORN: 3/27/56
4th YEAR D-3 FOR '79

Doug helps make tight end one of the Cowboys' strongest positions. He began to emerge last year when he got more playing time, catching a career-high 17 passes, including a team co-leading five touchdown receptions.

ANTHONY DICKERSON *51

LINEBACKER SOUTHERN METHODIST
HT: 6-2 * WT: 214 BORN: 6/9/57
3rd YEAR FA FOR '80

Another of the Cowboys' free agent finds, Dickerson played regularly on passing downs his first two seasons because of his excellent speed. He was a top candidate to replace retired D.D. Lewis as the starting weakside linebacker. Anthony is the club's swiftest and quickest linebacker.

DOUG DONLEY * 83

WIDE RECEIVER OHIO STATE
HT: 6-0 * WT: 175 BORN: 2/6/59
2nd YEAR D-2 FOR '81

Donley adds tremendous speed to the passing attack. That's the reason for the nickname "White Lightning" he earned at Ohio State, where he led his team in receiving three straight years and set career records for receiving yards and touchdowns. Doug served his apprenticeship last year behind Pearson, Hill and Johnson, but Tom Landry said he expected to use Donley more in 1982.

PAT DONOVAN * 67

TACKLE STANFORD
HT: 6-5 * WT: 256 BORN: 7/1/53
8th YEAR D-4A FOR '75

One of the top offensive tackles in the NFL, Donovan has been voted to three straight Pro Bowls and UPI All-NFC teams. Pat is one of many Cowboys who have successfully converted from college defensive lineman to offensive lineman. Pat works as a mechanical engineer in the off-season.

TONY DORSETT * 33

RUNNING BACK PITTSBURGH
HT: 5-11 * WT: 190 BORN: 4/7/54
6th YEAR D-1 FOR '77

TD had his best season yet as a pro last year when he set a team rushing record of 1,646 yards, second best in the NFL, and became the Cowboys' all-time leading rusher with 6,270 yards. Tony has rushed for more than 1,000 yards in each of his first five seasons, an NFL record, and counting college and high school he's surpassed 1,000 yards in each of the past 11 seasons.

MICHAEL DOWNS * 26

SAFETY RICE
HT: 6-3 * WT: 198 BORN: 6/9/59
2nd YEAR FA FOR '81

In a matter of weeks last year, Downs went from unknown free agent rookie to starting free safety. He opened and closed the season as the starter and helped solidify what was considered a trouble spot. He intercepted seven passes. Downs is a native of Dallas who attended the same high school as teammate Harvey Martin, South Oak Cliff.

BILLY JOE DuPREE * 89

TIGHT END MICHIGAN STATE
HT: 6-4 * WT: 229 BORN: 3/7/50
10th YEAR D-1 FOR '73

BJ had played in 134 consecutive games through '81, tops among current Cowboys, and he started 92 straight at tight end from '76-'81. Strong, dependable and unselfish, DuPree was the NFC's starting tight end in the Pro Bowl in '76, '77 and '78. His best season was '76 when he caught 42 passes, a club record for tight ends.

JOHN DUTTON * 78

DEFENSIVE TACKLE NEBRASKA
HT: 6-7 * WT: 265 BORN: 2/6/51
9th YEAR TRADE, BALT., '79

Dutton emerged as a solid force in the defense last year, his first as the starting left tackle. John entered the '81 season in sole possession of the left tackle spot he shared with Cole in 1980. The Cowboys acquired Dutton from Baltimore in 1979 for two draft choices. John was a three-time Pro Bowl choice and an All-Pro at defensive end with the Colts.

RON FELLOWS * 27

CORNERBACK MISSOURI
HT: 6-0 * WT: 170 BORN: 11/7/58
2nd YEAR D-7A FOR '81

Tom Landry considers Fellows "a definite cornerback prospect. He has the ability to cover people." A converted wide receiver (he led Missouri in receiving as a senior), Ron made the squad by showing a flair in preseason for returning kicks. By the end of the season he had earned a spot as a defensive back on the special pass defenses.

ANDY FREDERICK * 71

TACKLE NEW MEXICO
HT: 6-6 * WT: 255 BORN: 7/25/54
6th YEAR D-5 FOR '77

Andy is one of many Cowboys who successfully made the transition from college defensive lineman to NFL offensive lineman. He is the team's most experienced reserve tackle. He started five games during the '78 Super Bowl season when Rayfield Wright was injured.

MIKE HEGMAN * 58

LINEBACKER TENNESSEE STATE
HT: 6-1 * WT: 225 BORN: 1/17/53
7th YEAR D-7 FOR '75

An underrated player, Hegman has performed well at strongside (left) linebacker since taking over for Thomas Henderson in 1979. Mike has fine instincts and has a knack for big plays, such as the 37-yard touchdown he scored in Super Bowl XIII by stealing the ball from Terry Bradshaw. Mike missed the first five games last year due to a broken bone in his arm.

TONY HILL * 80

WIDE RECEIVER STANFORD
HT: 6-2 * WT: 198 BORN: 6/23/56
6th YEAR D-3A FOR '77

"Thrill" is the Cowboys' most feared receiver because of his speed and ability to catch the long pass. Tony caught 1,000 yards worth of passes in 1979 and '80 and would have last year except for a leg injury early in the season (he finished with 953 yards). He's been named to the Pro Bowl twice.

GARY HOGEBOOM * 14

QUARTERBACK CENTRAL MICHIGAN
HT: 6-4 * WT: 201 BORN: 8/21/58
3rd YEAR D-5 FOR '80

Hogeboom gives the Cowboys great depth at quarterback. Although he hasn't had a chance to play in the regular season, Gary has impressed his coaches with his work in practice. "He has good size, a quick release, a very strong arm and a good feel for delivering the ball," Tom Landry says.

BUTCH JOHNSON * 86

WIDE RECEIVER CAL-RIVERSIDE
HT: 6-1 * WT: 192 BORN: 5/28/54
7th YEAR D-3C FOR '76

A clutch receiver who knows how to make the key play, Butch turned in his best season last year, including tying for the club lead in touchdown catches with five. Johnson owns one of the greatest catches in Super Bowl history, a diving 45-yard touchdown reception in the end zone that helped Dallas beat Denver in Super Bowl XII.

ED JONES * 72

DEFENSIVE END TENNESSEE STATE
HT: 6-9 * WT: 270 BORN: 2/23/51
7th YEAR D-1A FOR '74

The No. 1 pick in the NFL draft in 1974, Too Tall had his best season last year and earned the All-Pro recognition that has long been due. A dominating force from his left end spot, Jones had eight quarterback traps, three fumble recoveries and 10 batted-down passes. Too Tall spent 1979 as a professional boxer but returned to the Cowboys in '80.

JAMES JONES * 23

RUNNING BACK MISSISSIPPI STATE
HT: 5-10 * WT: 201 BORN: 12/6/58
3rd YEAR D-3B FOR '80

Jones was the team's leading kick returner in 1980 and '81 while also serving as Tony Dorsett's backup at running back. He broke loose for a 59-yard touchdown run against Baltimore last year. In '80 he set club records for punt returns and punt return yardage. Tom Landry has considered trying him at fullback.

ANGELO KING * 57

LINEBACKER SOUTH CAROLINA STATE
HT: 6-1 * WT: 220 BORN: 2/10/58
2nd YEAR FA FOR '81

Released toward the end of training camp last year, King was re-signed after Mike Hegman broke a bone in his arm in the first game. Angelo made a strong impression the remainder of the year with his special teams work. He's exceptionally quick and has the ability to make key plays.

HARVEY MARTIN * 79

DEFENSIVE END EAST TEXAS STATE
HT: 6-5 * WT: 250 BORN: 11/16/50
10th YEAR D-3 FOR '73

Harvey has led the team in quarterback traps every year he's been with the Cowboys, the past nine in a row. Last year's 10 sacks increased his career total to 114. A four-time Pro Bowl selection and unanimous All-Pro in 1977, Martin was co-MVP of Super Bowl XII with Randy White. Harvey was born and raised in Dallas.

ROBERT NEWHOUSE * 44

FULLBACK HOUSTON
HT: 5-10 * WT: 215 BORN: 1/9/50
11th YEAR D-2 FOR '72

The fourth-leading rusher in team history, 'House has moved to a backup role in the twilight of his career after starting at fullback from 1974-80. His best season was in 1975 when he gained 930 yards. His biggest play was the 29-yard touchdown pass he threw to Golden Richards to seal the Cowboys' Super Bowl XII victory over Denver.

TIMMY NEWSOME * 30

FULLBACK WINSTON-SALEM
HT: 6-1 * WT: 227 BORN: 5/17/58
3rd YEAR D-6 FOR '80

Newsome was a candidate for the starting fullback position last year, but a pulled hamstring early in training camp kept him from winning the job. He's the club's biggest fullback and he also possesses fine running instincts and pass-catching ability.

DREW PEARSON * 88

WIDE RECEIVER TULSA
HT: 6-0 * WT: 183 BORN: 1/12/51
10th YEAR FA FOR '73

Signed by the Cowboys as a free agent after being passed over in the 1973 draft by all 26 NFL teams, Drew has become the team's all-time leading receiver. Known as one of football's top clutch receivers, Pearson owns some of the most memorable catches in Cowboys' history, including last-minute touchdown receptions to beat Minnesota in the '75 playoffs and Atlanta in the '80 playoffs.

KURT PETERSEN * 65

GUARD MISSOURI
HT: 6-4 * WT: 260 BORN: 6/17/57
3rd YEAR D-4 FOR '80

Petersen, another converted college defensive lineman, has all the tools to become a top NFL guard. Last year, in only his second season, Kurt became a starter at right guard when an injury to center Robert Shaw forced Tom Rafferty to move to center. Petersen is one of the team's strongest players.

TOM RAFFERTY * 64

GUARD PENN STATE
HT: 6-3 * WT: 250 BORN: 8/2/54
7th YEAR D-4 FOR '76

The versatile Rafferty made an emergency switch to center last year after the team lost both its centers, John Fitzgerald and Robert Shaw, to injuries. Tom had been the starting right guard since 1977. A quiet man outwardly, Rafferty is an intense competitor.

HOWARD RICHARDS * 70

TACKLE-GUARD MISSOURI
HT: 6-6 * WT: 248 BORN: 8/7/59
2nd YEAR D-1 FOR '81

The Cowboys' No. 1 draft choice last year, Richards has the size, speed and strength to play either tackle or guard. The team's depth at offensive line permitted Howard to learn his position last year and contribute on special teams. He's got vast potential and is expected to be a solid performer for years.

BILL ROE * 56

LINEBACKER COLORADO
HT: 6-3 * WT: 230 BORN: 2/6/58
3rd YEAR D-3A FOR '80

An intense player who made his mark on special teams as a rookie in 1980, Roe spent last season on injured reserve due to a training camp ankle injury. His size makes him a candidate at strongside (left) linebacker. Bill was the team's first 1980 draft choice since the first two picks had been dealt to Baltimore for John Dutton.

JAY SALDI * 87

TIGHT END SOUTH CAROLINA
HT: 6-3 * WT: 227 BORN: 10/8/54
7th YEAR FA FOR '76

Jay is the club's most versatile receiver, with the size to play tight end and the speed and moves to play wide receiver. He has been used most effectively in special situations, double and triple tight end formations and on passing downs. Jay runs outstanding pass routes and has fine hands. He made the club as a free agent rookie in 1976.

HERBERT SCOTT * 68

GUARD VIRGINIA UNION
HT: 6-2 * WT: 252 BORN: 1/18/53
8th YEAR D-13 FOR '75

Scott has been the team's most honored offensive lineman in recent years. He has played in the past three Pro Bowls, received All-NFC honors the past four seasons and earned All-Pro recognition the past two. The Cowboys' best open field blocker, Herbert was only a 13th-round draft choice in 1975 from obscure Virginia Union College.

RAFAEL SEPTIEN * 1

KICKER SOUTHWEST LOUISIANA
HT: 5-9 * WT: 171 BORN: 12/12/53
6th YEAR FA FOR '78

Last season Septien put together the best season ever by a Cowboys field goal kicker. The Mexican-born sidewinder set team records for points scored (122), field goals in a season (27 of 35) and career field goals (73). He tied the club mark twice of four field goals in a game. Rafael's performance earned him his first Pro Bowl berth and All-Pro honors.

ROBERT SHAW * 52

CENTER TENNESSEE
HT: 6-4 * WT: 260 BORN: 10/15/56
4th YEAR D-1 FOR '79

The Cowboys' 1979 No. 1 draft choice, the ever-improving Shaw earned the starting center position in training camp last year but injured a knee in the second game and missed the rest of the season. Shaw was the first center ever drafted in the first round by Dallas. He's exceptionally aggressive and competitive.

DON SMEREK * 60

DEFENSIVE END NEVADA-RENO
HT: 6-7 * WT: 256 BORN: 12/20/57
2nd YEAR FA FOR '80

An impressive physical specimen who plays aggressively, Smerek has been plagued by injuries since catching his coaches' attention as a free agent rookie in 1980. He has spent most of the past two years on injured reserve with a rib injury and a knee injury.

DANNY SPRADLIN * 55

LINEBACKER TENNESSEE
HT: 6-1 * WT: 221 BORN: 3/3/59
2nd YEAR D-5 FOR '81

Spradlin earned a spot on the team last year in training camp by showing the hard-hitting, aggressive qualities the Cowboys look for in a middle linebacker. He played a key role on special teams while learning the difficult middle spot as Bob Breunig's backup.

RON SPRINGS * 20

FULLBACK OHIO STATE
HT: 6-1 * WT: 210 BORN: 11/4/56
4th YEAR D-5C FOR '79

Ron won the starting fullback position in training camp last year, then rushed for 625 yards and gained another 359 on a team co-leading 46 receptions. He also led the team in touchdowns with 12, 10 rushing and two on pass receptions. Springs broke in as Tony Dorsett's backup. He was switched to fullback in order to take advantage of his multi-talents, especially his receiving ability.

BRUCE THORNTON * 77

DEFENSIVE END ILLINOIS
HT: 6-5 * WT: 266 BORN: 2/14/58
4th YEAR D-8 FOR '79

A fine natural pass-rusher, Thornton provides quality depth at defensive end behind Jones and Martin. He also can fill in at defensive tackle. Bruce led the Big 10 in quarterback traps in 1977 with 10.

DENNIS THURMAN * 32

SAFETY SOUTHERN CAL
HT: 5-11 * WT: 180 BORN: 4/13/56
5th YEAR D-11 FOR '78

Dennis played one of the key roles last year in helping the Cowboys regain the NFC East title when he moved from free safety to right corner. He played splendidly, intercepting nine passes, which tied for third in the NFL. He picked off three in the division-clinching victory over Philadelphia. Thurman was the starting free safety in 1980.

GLEN TITENSOR * 63

GUARD BRIGHAM YOUNG
HT: 6-4 * WT: 257 BORN: 2/21/58
2nd YEAR D-3 FOR '81

Another successfully converted college defensive lineman, Titensor showed great promise both at guard and center in addition to contributing on special teams. He possesses outstanding quickness for a big man. Glen began his college career at UCLA, then transferred to BYU.

EVERSON WALLS * 24

CORNERBACK GRAMBLING
HT: 6-1 * WT: 189 BORN: 12/28/59
2nd YEAR FA FOR '81

The biggest surprise of 1981 was Walls, a free agent rookie who ended up leading the NFL in interceptions and winning a spot in the Pro Bowl. Everson, a Dallas native, stole a team-record 11 passes. He added two more in the NFC title game and another two in the Pro Bowl.

NORM WELLS * 66

GUARD NORTHWESTERN
HT: 6-5 * WT: 261 BORN: 9/8/57
2nd YEAR D-12 FOR '80

One of the surprises of 1980 training camp was Norm Wells, a 12th-round draft choice who not only made the squad but also survived a mid-camp switch from defense to offense. He missed the final 13 games of that season and all of last year, however, due to a knee injury.

DANNY WHITE * 11

QUARTERBACK ARIZONA STATE
HT: 6-2 * WT: 192 BORN: 2/9/52
7th YEAR D-3A FOR '74

Danny has led the Cowboys to a pair of 12-4 records, a division championship and back-to-back appearances in the NFC title game in his two seasons as the starting quarterback. In '80 he set a team record by throwing 28 touchdown passes and last year he was the No. 2-rated passer in the NFC. Danny backed up Roger Staubach from 1976-79. He has been the Cowboys' punter since 1976.

RANDY WHITE * 54

DEFENSIVE TACKLE MARYLAND
HT: 6-4 * WT: 250 BORN: 1/15/53
8th YEAR D-1A FOR '75

The premier defensive tackle in the game, Randy has been named All-Pro the past four years and has been voted to the Pro Bowl the past five years. Randy was the Super Bowl XII co-MVP with Harvey Martin. "His performances range anywhere from spectacular to spectacular," says Tom Landry.

STEVE WILSON * 45

WIDE RECEIVER HOWARD
HT: 5-10 * WT: 192 BORN: 8/24/57
4th YEAR FA FOR '79

The Cowboys took advantage of Steve's athletic ability two years ago by moving him from wide receiver to cornerback to shore up a lack of depth in the defensive backfield. Steve started 11 games in 1980 while receiving on-the-job training. He was moved back to receiver this year.

STEVE WRIGHT * 73

TACKLE NORTHERN IOWA
HT: 6-5 * WT: 250 BORN: 4/8/59
2nd YEAR FA FOR '81

A longshot free agent rookie last year, Wright made the squad because of the potential he showed in training camp. A fine all-around athlete, Steve played tight end in college in addition to offensive tackle.

The Rookies

ROD HILL

CORNERBACK-KICK RETURNER KENTUCKY STATE
HT: 6-0 * WT: 182
BORN: 3/4/59 D-1

The 25th player selected overall and the first Kentucky State player ever taken in the first round, Rod was a nationally ranked kick return specialist at Kentucky State in addition to intercepting eight passes for 213 yards and a touchdown in his career.

JEFF ROHRER

LINEBACKER YALE
HT: 6-3 * WT: 228
BORN: 12/23/57 D-2

Jeff was the highest NFL draft choice from Yale since 1969 when the Cowboys made halfback Calvin Hill a stunning first-round selection. Exceptionally aggressive and intelligent, Rohrer was selected to the Coaches All-Ivy League and the Coaches All-New England first teams after leading Ivy co-champ Yale in tackles with a school-record 136 stops.

JIM ELIOPULOS

LINEBACKER WYOMING
HT: 6-2 * WT: 224
BORN: 4/18/59 D-3

This gifted and dedicated athlete earned first team All-Western Athletic Conference and AP honorable mention All-America honors. His best game came against Colorado State when he had 10 tackles, an interception, and six sacks for 54 yards in losses, earning Jim WAC player of the week honors.

BRIAN CARPENTER

CORNERBACK MICHIGAN
HT: 5-11 * WT: 166
BORN: 11/27/60 D-4A

Brian was considered Michigan's best man-to-man pass defender the past two seasons when he was a starting cornerback. He had six career interceptions, but all came at opportune moments, including one at Michigan's eight-yard line during the Wolverines' 1981 Rose Bowl victory over Washington.

MONTY HUNTER

SAFETY SALEM COLLEGE (W. VA.)
HT: 6-0 * WT: 201
BORN: 1/21/59 D-4B

Monty intercepted a school-record 19 passes in four years as a starting cornerback. In 1981 he earned All-West Virginia Intercollegiate Athletic Conference and honorable mention Little All-America honors after leading Salem in interceptions with five and finishing second in tackles with 76.

PHIL POZDERAC

TACKLE NOTRE DAME
HT: 6-8 * WT: 264
BORN: 12/19/59 D-5

Phil was chosen by his teammates as Notre Dame's offensive most valuable player for 1981. He won AP honorable mention All-America honors last year and he drew favorable notices in the 1982 East-West Shrine Game and the Japan Bowl. He also was selected to play in the Olympia Gold Bowl in San Diego.

KEN HAMMOND

GUARD VANDERBILT
HT: 6-3 * WT: 270
BORN 12/7/59 D-6A

A second team All-Southeastern Conference and honorable mention All-America choice by AP after his junior season, Ken was a consensus All-SEC choice and honorable mention All-America pick in 1981. He earned a starting position as offensive guard in his sophomore year.

CHARLES DAUM

DEFENSIVE LINEMAN CAL POLY-SAN LUIS OBISPO
HT: 6-6 * WT: 229
BORN: 11/3/59 D-6B

Charles, a two-year starter, was the only California Collegiate Athletic Association player selected to the American Football Coaches Association Kodak College Division All-America first team last year.

BILL PURIFOY

DEFENSIVE LINEMAN TULSA
HT: 6-8 * WT: 248
BORN: 11/15/79 D-7

Bill used his exceptional size and mobility to fashion a fine career at Tulsa, capping it with appearances in the 1982 Blue-Gray Game and Senior Bowl. Bill had his best game against Kansas with nine tackles, three quarterback traps and a blocked punt.

GEORGE PEOPLES

FULLBACK AUBURN
HT: 6-0 * WT: 202
BORN: 8/25/61 D-8A

A two-year starter, George rushed for 442 yards on 104 carries (4.2-yard average) in 1981, including a 63-yard touchdown run against Alabama on national television. He capped his career with an appearance in the Senior Bowl.

DWIGHT SULLIVAN

FULLBACK NORTH CAROLINA STATE
HT: 5-9 * WT: 204
BORN: 4/24/59 D-8B

Dwight assumed a different role last season in North Carolina State's new "I" running attack — that of blocking back. In 1979, operating out of the veer, Sullivan led Wolfpack rushers with 665 yards and six touchdowns on 150 carries (4.4 average). He caught 10 passes for 51 yards.

JOE GARY

DEFENSIVE LINEMAN UCLA
HT: 6-4 * WT: 262
BORN: 5/13/59 D-9

Joe possesses the size, strength and quickness that attracts the attention of pro scouts. Gary intercepted a pass in a victory over Ohio State his junior year. He made three tackles and picked off a pass in the final minutes of a win over Arizona State last year.

TODD ECKERSON

TACKLE NORTH CAROLINA STATE
HT: 6-4 * WT: 268
BORN: 1/24/60 D-10

An explosive, powerful blocker who plays with exceptional enthusiasm, Todd won a starting tackle berth his sophomore season. "He's the kind of player who can dominate you on the line of scrimmage," says Dick Kupec, N.C. State's offensive line coach.

GEORGE THOMPSON

WIDE RECEIVER ALBANY STATE (GEORGIA)
HT: 6-3 * WT: 211
BORN: 3/12/59 D-11A

George caught 60 passes for 885 yards and four touchdowns in three seasons at Albany State. George was a two-time All-Southern Intercollegiate Athletic Conference selection.

MICHAEL WHITING

FULLBACK FLORIDA STATE
HT: 6-0 * WT: 214
BORN: 1/11/60 D-11B

Michael finished his career with 1,485 yards and 12 touchdowns rushing on 355 carries (4.1-yard average) plus 74 receptions for 575 yards and two touchdowns. A two-year starter at fullback, he gained 461 yards on 111 carries and caught 29 passes for 211 yards in 1981.

RICH BURTNESS

OFFENSIVE LINEMAN MONTANA
HT: 6-4 * WT: 235
BORN: 6/25/60 D-12

A versatile athlete, Rick played fullback, tight end and offensive tackle at Montana before settling at offensive guard his senior year when he won a starting berth.

86
41

Historical Highlights

1960

NFL FRANCHISE — Clint Murchison, Jr., and Bedford Wynne were awarded an expansion franchise in the NFL at the annual league meeting in Miami Beach, Fla. The Cowboys were to play as a "swing" team, playing every other team one time during the first season, although listed in the Western Conference standings (January 28).

COWBOYS STOCKED — A player pool was set up in a league meeting at L.A., with each of 12 NFL teams freezing 25 names on its roster and the Cowboys allowed to pick three from each team for a total of 36 veterans. Dallas, once given the list, had to select its 36 players within 24 hours (March 13).

TRAINING STARTS — Rookies report to first Cowboys camp at Pacific U., in Forest Grove, Oregon (July 9).

FIRST PRE-SEASON GAME — The Cowboys, less than six months in existence, get their first test and drop a 10-16 pre-season game to San Francisco in Seattle (August 6).

FIRST HOME GAME — In their Dallas debut, in the Salesmanship Club pre-season game, the Cowboys led the World Champion Baltimore Colts into the final minute before a 62-yard pass from Johnny Unitas to Lenny Moore gave the Colts a 14-10 victory (August 19).

FIRST VICTORY — In a pre-season game at Louisville, Ky., the Cowboys beat New York's Giants, 14-3, with Frank Clarke catching touchdown passes of 73 yards (Eddie LeBaron) and 74 yards (Don Meredith) (August 27).

FIRST LEAGUE GAME — In their first league game, Dallas fell to Pittsburgh, 35-28, with Bobby Layne leading a fourth period Steeler rally (Sept. 24, Saturday night).

STREAK SNAPPED — Dallas snaps a 10-game loss streak by tying New York, 31-31, at Yankee Stadium (Dec. 4).

1961

TRAINING STARTS — Rookies launch training at new campsite — St. Olaf College in Northfield, Minn. (July 9).

FIRST LEAGUE WIN — Scoring ten points in the final 56 seconds, the Cowboys score their first NFL victory, 27-24, over Pittsburgh in the '61 league opener in the Cotton Bowl. Allen Green's 27-yard field goal on the game's final play won it before 23,500 (Sept. 17).

1962

TRAINING STARTS — Team begins training at new campsite — Northern Michigan College in Marquette, Mich. (July 13).

PENALTY HISTORY — For the first time in anyone's memory in an NFL game, points were awarded for a penalty. The Cowboys were detected holding in the end zone on a 99-TD pass from LeBaron to Clarke, and Pittsburgh was awarded a safety. The Steelers eventually won, 30-28 (Sept. 23).

100-YARD FIRSTS — Cowboys Amos Marsh returned a kickoff 101 yards and Mike Gaechter returned a pass interception 100 yards, both plays for fourth quarter TD's in a 41-19 win over Philadelphia in Dallas. It was the first time in NFL history that two 100-yard runs had been made in the same game, much less by the same team in the same quarter (Oct. 14).

1963

SHIFT TO KANSAS CITY — The rival Dallas Texans of the AFL announce they are moving the franchise to Kansas City (Feb. 8).

CALIFORNIA TRAINING SITE — The Cowboys open training at California Lutheran College in Thousand Oaks, Calif. (July 12).

HOWTON SETS RECORD — Bill Howton broke Don Hutson's all-time receiving mark with a 14-yard catch against Washington (there). Hutson's record was 7,991 yards and the catch gave Howton an even 8,000 yards (Sept. 29).

1964

LANDRY CONTRACT — With one year to go on his original contract, Tom Landry is signed to a ten-year extension, in effect giving him an 11-year pact, possibly the longest in major pro sports history (Feb. 5).

1965

FIRST SELLOUT — An overflow crowd of 76,251 jams the Cotton Bowl for the Cleveland game, notching the team's first home sellout. Cleveland won, 24-17 (Nov. 21).

1966

PLAYOFF BOWL — After defeating New York, 38-20, in the season finale (and winning five of their last seven games) to get into the Playoff Bowl at Miami, the Cowboys fall to Baltimore, 35-3 (Jan. 15).

MERGER — Peace comes to pro football with Cowboys GM Tex Schramm completing two months of negotiations with AFL's Lamar Hunt, merging the two leagues under the NFL banner (June 8).

SCHRAMM ELEVATED — Texas E. Schramm, Vice-President and General Manager of the Cowboys from the beginning, was named President of the club by owner Clint Murchison, Jr., who retained the title of Chairman of the Board.

NEELY CASE SOLVED — Dallas and Houston reached agreement in the Ralph Neely case. Neely remained with Dallas with Houston receiving the Cowboys' Nos. 1, 2 and two fifth place picks in the 1967 draft (Nov. 17).

THE CHAMPIONSHIP — The Cowboys won their first championship, capturing the Eastern Conference title with a 10-3-1 record, but lost the NFL Championship Game to Green Bay, 34-27.

1967

TEXAS STADIUM — On Dec. 23, owner Clint Murchison, Jr., formally announced plans to build Texas Stadium in suburban Irving. The stadium, to be financed through a bond-option plan, would be ready for the 1970 season. The stadium would seat a minimum of 58,000.

SECOND CHAMPIONSHIP — Under the NFL's new format, the Cowboys easily won the Capitol Division and defeated Cleveland, Century Division winner, 52-14, in the Cotton Bowl for the Eastern conference championship. However, on Dec. 31 in Green Bay, the Cowboys lost their second bid for an NFL title, falling to the Packers, 21-17, in the 13 degree below weather.

1968

WIN CAPITOL — For the second straight year the Cowboys won the Capitol Division, but for the first time in three years the Cowboys did not win the Eastern Championship, being upset at Cleveland, 31-20, on December 21st. Dallas won the Runner-Up Bowl over Minnesota, 17-13.

1969

TEXAS STADIUM — Ground was broken for Texas Stadium in suburban Irving on January 25, and on June 29 Bert Rose was named general manager of the stadium.

ORIGINALS RETIRE — An era ended for the Cowboys in July. On July 5th at a press conference in Dallas, quarterback Don Meredith, the last of the original Cowboys, announced his retirement. Then, on July 18th, the day the veterans were to report to training camp, all-time rushing great Don Perkins officially retired.

REPEAT CAPITOL WINS — Once again the Cowboys rolled to the Capitol Division Championship with an 11-2-1 season. However, the Cowboys failed to win the Eastern Championship when on Dec. 28, the Cowboys lost to Cleveland, 38-14, in the Cotton Bowl.

1970

FIVE STRAIGHT PLAYOFFS — The Cowboys won their last five games to finish 10-4, claim the Eastern Division championship and make the play-offs, for the fifth year in a row. They defeated Detroit, 5-0, in the opening round to get a shot at the National Conference championship.

FIRST NFC TITLE — The Cowboys captured the biggest prize of their 11-year history on Jan. 3 when they downed San Francisco, 17-10, for the NFC crown. A 16-13 loss to Baltimore in the Super Bowl Jan. 17 left Dallas with one major goal still unrealized.

1971

TEXAS STADIUM — The Cowboys opened a new era in their sparkling Irving, Tex., home with a 44-21 victory over the New England Patriots on October 24. Duane Thomas scored the first touchdown in the new stadium, a 56-yard run just two minutes and 16 seconds after the opening kickoff. Attendance was 65,708.

SIX STRAIGHT PLAYOFFS — The Cowboys won their last seven games to finish 11-3, claim the Eastern Division championship and make the playoffs for the sixth year in a row. They defeated Minnesota 20-12, in the opening round.

SECOND NFC TITLE — For the second consecutive year, the Cowboys met the San Francisco 49ers in the National Conference showdown. This time Dallas won, 14-3, to qualify for its second straight Super Bowl.

FIRST WORLD CHAMPIONSHIP — The Cowboys downed the Miami Dolphins, 24-3, to win Super Bowl VI in New Orleans on Jan. 16. It was the 10th victory in a row for Dallas as Roger Staubach passed for two touchdowns and was named the game's Most Valuable Player.

1972

FIRST 1,000-YARD BACK — Calvin Hill became the first Dallas player to rush for 1,000 yards when he gained 111 on Dec. 9 against the Washington Redskins in Texas Stadium. Hill wound up with 1,036 yards for the season on a record 245 carries.

SEVEN STRAIGHT PLAYOFFS — The Cowboys qualified for the NFL playoffs a record seventh consecutive year, their 10-4 record earning them the National Conference Wild Card berth. Roger Staubach passed for two touchdowns in the last 1½ minutes to give the Cowboys a 30-28 victory at San Francisco in the first round. Then, at Washington on New Year's Eve, Dallas was foiled in its bid for a third straight NFL title when the Redskins won, 26-3.

1973

100 VICTORIES — The Cowboys and Coach Tom Landry recorded their 100th victory with a 40-3 Texas Stadium win over the New Orleans Saints on Sept. 24. Landry, the only head coach the Cowboys have had, ended the season with a career mark of 108-80-6 to rank ninth on the list of the NFL's all-time winningest coaches.

EIGHT STRAIGHT PLAYOFFS — The Cowboys regained the NFC Eastern Division title with a 10-4 record and broke their own NFL record by reaching the playoffs for the eighth year in a row. Dallas defeated Western Division champion Los Angeles in the first round, 27-16, but fell to Central Division winner Minnesota in the NFC Championship Game, 27-10.

1974

FIRST TOP DRAFT CHOICE — For the first time in their history, the Cowboys had the very first choice in the NFL college draft. The No. 1 pick came to Dallas from Houston in exchange for Tody Smith and Billy Parks. The Cowboys selected Ed "Too Tall" Jones, a 6-9, 260-pound defensive end from Tennessee State.

PLAYOFFS MISSED — The Cowboys' record-breaking string of eight straight years in the NFL playoffs was broken when the club's 8-6 record failed to qualify.

1975

LILLY HONORED — "Mr. Cowboy" was honored on Bob Lilly Day at Texas Stadium at halftime of the Philadelphia game on Nov. 23. It was the first such recognition ever given to a Dallas player. Lilly never missed a game in 14 years with the Cowboys, earning All-Pro honors seven times at defensive tackle before retiring prior to the '75 season.

TEN STRAIGHT WINNING SEASONS — The Cowboys' 10-4 record earned them the NFC Wild Card berth in the playoffs. The composite record over 10 straight winning seasons was 101-37-2.

THIRD NFC TITLE — After shocking Minnesota in the first round, 17-14 on Roger Staubach's 50-yard "Hail Mary" pass to Drew Pearson, the Cowboys traveled to Los Angeles for the NFC showdown. Staubach threw four touchdown passes, three to Preston Pearson, and Dallas won, 37-7. Pittsburgh won Super Bowl X on Jan. 18 in Miami, 21-17.

1976

ELEVEN STRAIGHT WINNING SEASONS — The Cowboys won the NFC Eastern Division title after their 11-3 record, giving them their 11th straight winning season and 10th playoff berth in that period. A 14-12 first round loss to Los Angeles — the first time Dallas had lost in the first round under the current playoff setup — ended the season.

MEREDITH, PERKINS HONORED — Former Cowboys greats Don Meredith and Don Perkins joined Bob Lilly in the "Ring of Honor" at Texas Stadium during halftime ceremonies at the New York Giants game on Nov. 7.

1977

HOWLEY HONORED — Former All-Pro linebacker Chuck Howley, a Cowboy from 1961 through 1973, became the fourth member of the Ring of Honor. Howley was honored during ceremonies at halftime of the Detroit Lions game on Oct. 30.

TWELVE STRAIGHT WINNING SEASONS — Getting off to an 8-0 start, their best ever, the Cowboys rolled to a 12-2 record, the championship of the NFC East, and their 12th consecutive winning season. They opened their 11th visit to the playoffs in those 12 years with a 37-7 first-round victory over the Chicago Bears at Texas Stadium.

FOURTH NFC TITLE — Dallas crushed the Minnesota Vikings at Texas Stadium, 23-6, for National Conference crown No. 4 and the right to meet the Denver Broncos in Super Bowl XII.

SECOND WORLD CHAMPIONSHIP — The Cowboys stopped the Denver Broncos, 27-10, to win Super Bowl XII in New Orleans on January 15, 1978. In the process, Dallas tied Minnesota for most Super Bowl appearances (four) and Green Bay, Miami and Pittsburgh for most Super Bowl victories (two). Defensive linemen Harvey Martin and Randy White were named co-Most Valuable Players in the game.

1978

THIRTEEN STRAIGHT WINNING SEASONS — After a mediocre 6-4 start, the Cowboys won six straight games to finish the expanded regular season with a 12-4 record and their 10th Division crown. It marked the Cowboys' 13th consecutive winning season and 12th trip to the playoffs in that span. Dallas rallied to beat Atlanta 27-20 in a divisional playoff at Texas Stadium, sending the Cowboys to their seventh NFC championship game in the last nine years.

FIFTH NFC TITLE — Dallas shut out the Rams in Los Angeles 28-0 in the National Conference title game to advance to the Super Bowl a record fifth time, including three of the last four. In the first Super Bowl rematch, Pittsburgh edged the Cowboys 35-31 for the NFL championship on Jan. 21 in Miami's Orange Bowl.

1979

TWENTIETH ANNIVERSARY — The Cowboys celebrated their 20th anniversary season at halftime of the St. Louis Cardinals game at Texas Stadium on Oct. 21. Stars from each of those 20 seasons plus Coach Tom Landry were introduced during the halftime ceremonies.

FOURTH STRAIGHT NFC EAST TITLE — Rallying from a mid-season slump, the Cowboys won their final three games to finish with an 11-5 record, their 11th division championship, including the past four NFC East titles, and 14th consecutive winning season. The Cowboys made their 13th trip to the playoffs in those 14 years, but were eliminated by Los Angeles 21-19 in a divisional playoff at Texas Stadium.

1980

LILLY ENTERS HALL OF FAME — Bob Lilly, a seven-time all-pro defensive tackle in his 14-year career with the Cowboys from 1961-74, became the first Cowboys-only player to be inducted into the Pro Football Hall of Fame. Enshrined along with Lilly on Aug. 2 at Canton, Ohio, were Herb Adderley, who played for the Cowboys from 1970-72, Jim Otto and Deacon Jones.

STAUBACH RETIRES — At a press conference at Texas Stadium on March 31, Roger Staubach announced his retirement after 11 record-breaking years as the Cowboys' quarterback. Staubach held all major Cowboys passing records and was the all-time leading NFL passer.

FIFTEEN STRAIGHT WINNING SEASONS — Behind new starting quarterback Danny White, the Cowboys rolled to their 15th consecutive winning season with a surprising 12-4 record, tied for best in the league with Philadelphia and Atlanta. The Cowboys lost the NFC East title to Philadelphia on a tie-breaker, but entered the playoffs for the 14th time in 15 years, this time as a wild card team. The Cowboys beat Los Angeles 34-13 at Texas Stadium in the NFC wild card playoff and rallied past the Falcons at Atlanta 30-27 to advance to the NFC championship game at Philadelphia. But the Cowboys lost 20-7 in their bid for a sixth Super Bowl appearance.

LANDRY'S 200th VICTORY — Tom Landry joined George Halas and Curly Lambeau as the only coaches with 200 NFL victories when the Cowboys beat Los Angeles 34-13 on Dec. 28 at Texas Stadium in the NFC wild card playoff, raising Landry's record to 200-119-6, counting regular-season and playoff games.

1981

RENFRO HONORED — Former All-Pro defensive back Mel Renfro, the Cowboys' all-time leading pass interceptor, became the fifth member of the Cowboys' Ring of Honor. Renfro, who played for Dallas from 1964 through 1977, was honored during halftime ceremonies of the Cowboys-Miami Dolphins game at Texas Stadium Oct. 25.

TWELFTH DIVISION CHAMPIONSHIP — The Cowboys regained the NFC Eastern Division Championship, their 12th division title since 1966, with a 12-4 record and tied Oakland's NFL mark of 16 consecutive winning seasons. Entering the playoffs for the 15th time in that span, the Cowboys advanced to the NFC Championship Game for the ninth time in 12 years by routing Tampa Bay 38-0 at Texas Stadium. But for the second year in a row Dallas lost the conference title game. San Francisco scored a last minute touchdown at Candlestick Park to edge the Cowboys 28-27 for a berth in Super Bowl XVI.

Cowboys 1981 Awards

Tony Dorsett (RB)

— All-Pro (AP, PFWA, NEA, Sporting News)
All-NFC (UPI)
Pro Bowl
UPI NFC Player of the Year

Pat Donovan (T)

— All-Pro (2nd team — AP, 2nd team — NEA)
All-NFC (2nd team — UPI)
Pro Bowl

Ed Jones (DE)

— All-Pro (NEA, 2nd team — AP)
All-NFC (UPI)
Pro Bowl

Herb Scott (G)

— All-Pro (AP, Sporting News, 2nd team — NEA)
All-NFC (UPI)
Pro Bowl

Rafael Septien (K)

— All-Pro (AP, PFWA, Sporting News)
All-NFC (UPI)
Pro Bowl

Dennis Thurman (CB)

— All-NFC (2nd team — UPI)

Everson Walls (CB)

— All-Rookie (PFWA, UPI)
Pro Bowl

Danny White (QB)

— All-NFC (2nd team — UPI)

Randy White (DT)

— All-Pro (AP, PFWA, NEA, Sporting News)
All-NFC (UPI)
Pro Bowl

Dallas Cowboys 1982 Veteran Roster

NO	NAME	POS	HT	WT	BIRTHDATE	COLLEGE	NFL EXP
31	Barnes, Benny	CB	6-1	203	3/3/51	Stanford	11
76	Bethea, Larry	DT	6-5	249	7/21/56	Michigan State	5
53	Breunig, Bob	LB	6-2	223	7/4/53	Arizona State	8
59	Brown, Guy	LB	6-4	228	6/1/55	Houston	6
18	Carano, Glenn	QB	6-3	198	11/18/55	Nevada-Las Vegas	6
47	Clinkscale, Dextor	S	5-11	189	4/13/58	South Carolina St.	2
61	Cooper, Jim	T	6-5	263	9/28/55	Temple	6
84	Cosbie, Doug	TE	6-6	226	2/27/56	Santa Clara	4
51	Dickerson, Anthony	LB	6-2	222	6/9/57	SMU	3
83	Donley, Doug	WR	6-0	175	2/6/59	Ohio State	2
67	Donovan, Pat	T	6-4	259	7/1/53	Stanford	8
33	Dorsett, Tony	RB	5-11	185	4/7/54	Pittsburgh	6
26	Downs, Michael	S	6-3	198	6/9/59	Rice	2
89	DuPree, Billy Joe	TE	6-4	228	3/7/50	Michigan State	10
78	Dutton, John	DT	6-7	263	2/6/51	Nebraska	9
27	Fellows, Ron	CB	6-0	170	11/7/58	Missouri	2
71	Frederick, Andy	T	6-6	265	7/25/54	New Mexico	6
58	Hegman, Mike	LB	6-1	225	1/17/53	Tennessee State	7
80	Hill, Tony	WR	6-2	206	6/23/56	Stanford	6
14	Hogeboom, Gary	QB	6-4	200	8/21/58	Central Michigan	3
86	Johnson, Butch	WR	6-1	180	5/28/54	UC-Riverside	7
72	Jones, Ed	DE	6-9	272	2/23/51	Tennessee State	7
23	Jones, James	RB	5-10	196	12/6/58	Mississippi State	3
57	King, Angelo	LB	6-1	220	2/10/58	South Carolina St.	2
79	Martin, Harvey	DE	6-5	252	11/16/50	East Texas State	10
44	Newhouse, Robert	FB	5-10	220	1/9/50	Houston	11
30	Newsome, Timmy	FB	6-1	232	5/17/58	Winston-Salem St.	3
88	Pearson, Drew	WR	6-0	190	1/12/51	Tulsa	10
65	Petersen, Kurt	G	6-4	266	6/17/57	Missouri	3
64	Rafferty, Tom	G	6-3	258	8/2/54	Penn State	7
70	Richards, Howard	T	6-6	248	8/7/59	Missouri	2
56	Roe, Bill	LB	6-3	230	2/6/58	Colorado	2
87	Saldi, Jay	TE	6-3	223	10/8/54	South Carolina	7
68	Scott, Herbert	G	6-2	258	1/18/53	Virginia Union	8
1	Septien, Rafael	K	5-9	174	12/12/53	SW Louisiana	6
52	Shaw, Robert	C	6-4	260	10/15/56	Tennessee	4
60	Smerek, Don	DT	6-7	256	12/20/57	Nevada-Reno	2
75	Spears, Ron	DE	6-6	252	11/23/59	San Diego State	1
20	Springs, Ron	FB	6-1	216	11/1/56	Ohio State	4
55	Spradlin, Danny	LB	6-1	221	3/3/59	Tennessee	2
77	Thornton, Bruce	DE	6-5	262	2/14/58	Illinois	4
32	Thurman, Dennis	CB	5-11	178	4/13/56	So. California	5
63	Titensor, Glen	G	6-4	257	2/21/58	Brigham Young	2
24	Walls, Everson	CB	6-1	189	12/28/59	Grambling	2
66	Wells, Norm	G	6-5	261	9/8/57	Northwestern	2
11	White, Danny	QB	6-2	196	2/9/52	Arizona State	7
54	White, Randy	DT	6-4	262	1/15/53	Maryland	8
45	Wilson, Steve	WR	5-10	193	8/24/57	Howard	4
73	Wright, Steve	T	6-5	250	4/8/59	Northern Iowa	2

How the Cowboys Were Built

There were 47 players active with the Cowboys in 1981. Here's a look at how they came to Dallas:

FROM THE DRAFT:

1968 — D. D. Lewis (6th, Mississippi State).
1970 — Charlie Waters (3rd, Clemson).
1972 — Robert Newhouse (2nd, Houston).
1973 — Billy Joe DuPree (1st, Michigan State); Harvey Martin (3rd, East Texas State).
1974 — Ed Jones (1st, Tennessee State); Danny White (3rd, Arizona State).
1975 — Randy White (1st, Maryland); Bob Breunig (3rd, Arizona State); Pat Donovan (4th, Stanford); Mike Hegman (7th, Tennessee State); Herbert Scott (13th, Virginia Union).
1976 — Butch Johnson (3rd, Cal-Riverside); Tom Rafferty (4th, Penn State).
1977 — Tony Dorsett (1st, Pittsburgh); Glenn Carano (2nd, Nevada-Las Vegas); Tony Hill (3rd, Stanford); Guy Brown (4th, Houston); Andy Frederick (5th, New Mexico); Jim Cooper (6th, Temple).
1978 — Larry Bethea (1st, Michigan State); Dennis Thurman (11th, Southern California).
1979 — Robert Shaw (1st, Tennessee); Doug Cosbie (3rd, Santa Clara); Ron Springs (5th, Ohio State); Bruce Thornton (8th, Illinois).
1980 — James Jones (3rd, Mississippi State); Kurt Petersen (4th, Missouri); Gary Hogeboom (5th, Central Michigan); Timmy Newsome (6th, Winston-Salem).
1981 — Howard Richards (1st, Missouri); Doug Donley (2nd, Ohio State); Glen Titensor (3rd, Brigham Young); Danny Spradlin (5th, Tennessee); Ron Fellows (7th, Missouri).

SIGNED AS FREE AGENTS:

1972 — Benny Barnes (Stanford).
1973 — Drew Pearson (Tulsa).
1976 — Jay Saldi (South Carolina).
1978 — Rafael Septien (SW Louisiana, after pre-season release by Los Angeles Rams).
1979 — Steve Wilson (Howard).
1980 — Anthony Dickerson (Southern Methodist); Don Smerek (Nevada-Reno).
1981 — Michael Downs (Rice); Angelo King (South Carolina State); Everson Walls (Grambling); Steve Wright (Northern Iowa).

OBTAINED IN TRADES:

1979 — John Dutton (Nebraska, from Baltimore for Cowboys' 1st and 2nd round draft choices in 1980).

Cowboys All-Time Roster

ASSISTANT COACHES

Allen, Ermal, 1962-81
Berry, Raymond, 1968
Dahms, Tom, 1960-62
Dimancheff, Babe, 1960-62
Ditka, Mike, 1973-81
Ecklund, Brad, 1960-63
Franklin, Bobby, 1968-72
Gillman, Sid, 1972
Hickey, Red, 1964
Hughes, Ed, 1973-76
Lavan, Al, 1980-81
Mackovic, John, 1981
Myers, Jim, 1962-81
Nolan, Dick, 1962-67
Reeves, Dan, 1970-80
Renfro, Ray, 1968-72
Roy, Alvin, 1973
Stallings, Gene, 1972-81
Stautner, Ernie, 1966-81
Tubbs, Jerry, 1966-81
Ward, Bob, 1976-81

PLAYERS

Adderley, Herb, CB, Mich. St., 1970-72
Adkins, Margene, WR, Henderson J.C., 1970-71
Alworth, Lance, WR, Arkansas, 1971-72
Andrie, George, DE, Marquette, 1962-72
Arneson, Jim, G-C, Arizona, 1973-74
Asher, Bob, T, Vanderbilt, 1970
Babb, Gene, LB-RB, Austin College, 1960-61
Babinecx, John, LB, Villanova, 1972-73
Baker, Sam, P-K, Oregon State, 1962-63
Barnes, Benny, CB, Stanford, 1972-81
Barnes, Gary, WR, Clemson, 1963
Barnes, Rodrigo, LB, Rice, 1973-74
Bateman, Marv, P, Utah, 1972-74
Baynham, Craig, RB, Georgia Tech, 1967-69
Belden, Bob, QB, Notre Dame, 1969-70
Bercich, Bob, S, Michigan State, 1960-61
Bethea, Larry, DE, Michigan St. 1978-81
Bielski, Dick, TE, Maryland, 1960-61
Bishop, Don, CB, CCLA, 1960-65
Blackwell, Alois, RB, Houston, 1978-79
Boeke, Jim, T, Heidelberg, 1964-67
Borden, Nate, DE, Indiana, 1960-61
Braatz, Tom, LB, Marquette, 1960
Bradfute, Byron, T, So. Miss., 1960-61
Breunig, Bob, LB, Arizona State, 1975-81
Brinson, Larry, RB, Florida, 1977-79
Brock, Clyde, DT, Utah State, 1962-63
Brown, Guy, LB, Houston, 1977-81
Brown, Otto, CB-S, Prairie View, 1969
Bullocks, Amos, RB, So. Ill., 1962-64
Burkett, Jackie, LB, Auburn, 1968-69
Butler, Bill, S, Chattanooga, 1960
Caffey, Lee Roy, LB, Texas A&M, 1971
Capone, Warren, LB, Louisiana State, 1975
Carano, Glenn, QB, Nevada-Las Vegas, 1977-81
Carrell, Duane, P, Florida State, 1974
Clark, Mike, K, Texas A&M, 1968-71, 1973
Clark, Monte, T, Southern California, 1962
Clark, Phil, CB-S, Northwestern, 1967-69
Clarke, Frank, TE-WR, Colorado 1960-67
Clinkscale, Dextor, S, South Carolina St., 1980
Cole, Larry, DE-DT, Hawaii, 1968-80
Coleman, Ralph, LB, N. Car., A&T, 1972
Colvin, Jim, DT, Houston 1964-66
Cone, Fred, K, Clemson, 1960
Connelly, Mike, C, Utah State, 1960-67
Conrad, Bobby Joe, WR, Texas A&M, 1969
Cooper, Jim, C-G, Temple, 1977-81
Cosbie, Doug, TE, Santa Clara, 1979-81
Cronin, Gene, DE, Pacific, 1960
Cvercko, Andy, G, Northwestern, 1961-62
Daniels, Dick, S, Pacific (Ore.), 1966-68
Davis, Donnie, WR, Southern, 1962
Davis, Kyle, C, Oklahoma, 1975
Davis, Sonny, LB, Baylor, 1961
Dennison, Doug, RB, Kutztown State, 1974-78
Deters, Harold, K, North Carolina St., 1967
Dial, Buddy, WR, Rice, 1964-66
Dickerson, Anthony, LB, SMU, 1980-81
Dickson, Paul, T, Baylor, 1960
Diehl, John, DT, Virginia, 1965
Ditka, Mike, TE, Pittsburgh, 1969-72
Doelling, Fred, S, Pennsylvania, 1960
Donley, Doug, WR, Ohio State, 1981
Donohue, Leon, G, San Jose State, 1965-67
Donovan, Pat, T, Stanford, 1975-81
Doran, Jim, WR, Iowa State, 1960-61
Dorsett, Tony, RB, Pittsburgh, 1977-81
Douglas, Merrill, RB, Utah, 1961
Dowdle, Mike, RB-LB, Texas, 1960-62
Downs, Michael, S, Rice, 1981
Dugan, Fred, WR, Dayton, 1960
Dunn, Perry Lee, RB, Mississippi, 1964-65
Dupre, L. G., RB, Baylor, 1960-61
DuPree, Billy Joe, TE, Michigan St., 1973-81
Dutton, John, DE, Nebraska, 1979-81
East, Ron, DT, Montana State, 1967-70
Edwards, Dave, LB, Auburn, 1963-75
Eidson, Jim, G-C, Miss. State, 1976
Falls, Mike, G, Minnesota, 1960-61
Fellows, Ron, CB, Missouri, 1981
Fisher, Ray, T, Eastern Illinois, 1960
Fitzgerald, John, G-C, Bost. Coll., 1971-80
Folkins, Lee, TE, Washington, 1962-64
Flowers, Richmond, S, Tennessee, 1969-71
Franckhauser, Tom, CB, Purdue, 1960-61
Frank, Bill, T, Colorado, 1964
Frederick, Andy, T, New Mexico, 1977-81
Fritsch, Toni, K, Vienna, Austria, 1971-73, 1975
Frost, Ken, DT, Tennessee, 1961-62
Fry, Bob, T, Kentucky, 1960-64
Fugett, Jean, TE, Amherst, 1972-75
Gaechter, Mike, S, Oregon, 1962-69
Garrison, Walt, RB, Okla. St., 1966-74
Gent, Pete, WR-TE, Mich. St., 1964-68
Gibbs, Sonny, QB, Texas Christian, 1963
Gonzaga, John, DE, no college, 1960
Granger, Charlie, T, Southern, 1961
Green, Allen, P-K, Mississippi, 1961
Green, Cornell, CB-S, Utah State, 1962-74
Gregg, Forrest, G-T, SMU, 1971
Gregory, Bill, DT-DE, Wisconsin, 1971-77
Gregory, Glynn, WR-CB-S, SMU, 1961-62
Grottkau, Bob, G, Oregon, 1961
Guy, Buzz, G, Duke, 1960
Hagen, Halvor, C-G, Weber State, 1969-70
Hansen, Wayne, LB, Texas Western, 1960
Harris, Cliff, S, Ouachita, 1970-79
Harris, Jim, S, Oklahoma, 1961
Hayes, Bob, WR, Florida A&M, 1965-74
Hayes, Wendell, RB, Humboldt State, 1963
Hays, Harold, LB, So. Miss., 1963-67
Healy, Don, DT, Maryland, 1960-61
Hegman, Mike, LB, Tennessee State, 1976-81
Heinrich, Don, QB, Washington, 1960
Henderson, Thomas, LB, Langston, 1975-79
Herchman, Bill, DT, Texas Tech, 1960-61
Herrera, Efren, K, UCLA, 1974, 1976-77
Hill, Calvin, RB, Yale, 1969-74
Hill, Tony, WR, Stanford, 1977-81
Hogeboom, Gary, QB, Central Michigan, 1980-81
Homan, Dennis, WR, Alabama, 1968-70
Hoopes, Mitch, P, Arizona, 1975
Houser, John, C-G, Redlands, 1960-61
Houston, Bill, WR, Jackson State, 1974
Howard, Percy, WR, Austin Peay, 1975
Howard, Ron, TE, Seattle, 1974-75
Howley, Chuck, LB, West Virginia, 1961-73
Howton, Bill, WR, Rice, 1960-63
Hoyem, Lynn, C-G, Long Beach, 1962-63
Hughes, Randy, S, Oklahoma, 1975-80
Humphrey, Buddy, QB, Baylor, 1961
Hunt, Eric, CB, San Jose St., 1980
Husmann, Ed, DT, Nebraska, 1960
Hutcherson, Ken, LB, Livingston State, 1974
Huther, Bruce, LB, New Hampshire, 1977-80
Isbell, Joe Bob, G, Houston, 1962-65
Jensen, Jim, RB, Iowa, 1976
Johnson, Butch, WR, Cal-Riverside, 1976-81
Johnson, Mike, CB, Kansas, 1966-69
Johnson, Mitch, G, UCLA, 1965
Jones, Ed, DE, Tennessee State, 1974-78, 1980-81
Jones, James, RB, Miss. State, 1980-81
Jordan, Lee Roy, LB, Alabama, 1963-76
Keller, Mike, LB, Michigan, 1972
Killian, Gene, G, Tennessee, 1974
Kiner, Steve, LB, Tennessee, 1970
King, Angelo, LB, South Carolina St., 1981
Klein, Dick, T, Iowa, 1960
Kowalczyk, Walt, RB, Michigan State, 1960
Kupp, Jake, G, Washington, 1964-65
Kyle, Aaron, CB, Wyoming, 1976-79
Laidlaw, Scott, RB, Stanford, 1975-79
Lawless, Burton, G, Florida, 1975-79
LeBaron, Eddie, QB, Pacific, 1960-63
Lewis, D. D., LB, Miss. State, 1968-81
Lewis, Woodley, WR, Oregon, 1960
Lilly, Bob, DE-DT, Texas Christian, 1961-74
Liscio, Tony, T, Tulsa, 1963-64, 1966-71
Livingston, Warren, CB, Arizona, 1961-66
Lockett, J. W., RB, Central Okla., 1961-62
Logan, Obert, S, Trinity (Tex.), 1965-66
Long, Bob, LB, UCLA, 1962
Longley, Clint, QB, Abilene Christian, 1974-75
Lothridge, Billy, P-QB, Georgia Tech, 1964
Manders, Dave, C, Mich. State, 1964-66, 1968-74
Manning, Wade, CB, Ohio State, 1979
Marsh, Amos, RB, Oregon State, 1961-64
Martin, Harvey, DE, East Texas St., 1973-81
Mathews, Ray, WR, Clemson, 1960
McCreary, Bob, T, Wake Forest, 1961
McDaniels, David, WR, Miss. Val., 1968
McDonald, Tommy, WR, Oklahoma, 1964
McIlhenny, Don, RB, SMU, 1960-61
Memmelaar, Dale, G, Wyoming, 1962-63
Meredith, Don, QB, SMU, 1960-68
Meyers, John, DT, Washington, 1962-63
Mitchell, Aaron, CB, Nevada-Las Vegas, 1979-80
Moegle, Dick, S, Rice, 1961
Montgomery, Mike, RB-WR, Kans. St., 1972-73
Mooty, Jim, CB, Arkansas, 1960
Morgan, Dennis, RB, Western Illinois, 1974
Morton, Craig, QB, California, 1965-74
Murchison, Ola Lee, WR, Pacific, 1961
Neely, Ralph, G-T, Oklahoma, 1965-77
Newhouse, Robert, RB, Houston, 1972-81
Newsome, Timmy, RB, Winston-Salem, 1980-81
Niland, John, G, Iowa, 1966-74
Nolan, Dick, S, Maryland, 1962
Norman, Pettis, TE, J. C. Smith, 1962-70
Norton, Jerry, S, SMU, 1962
Nutting, Ed, T, Georgia Tech, 1963
Nye, Blaine, G, Stanford, 1968-76
Overton, Jerry, S, Utah, 1963
Parks, Billy, WR, Long Beach State, 1972
Patera, Jack, LB, Oregon, 1960-61
Pearson, Drew, WR, Tulsa, 1973-81
Pearson, Preston, RB, Illinois, 1975-80
Percival, Mac, K, Texas Tech, 1974
Perkins, Don, RB, New Mexico, 1961-68
Petersen, Kurt, G, Missouri, 1980-81
Peterson, Calvin, LB, UCLA, 1974-75
Pinder, Cyril, RB, Illinois, 1973
Poimboeuf, Lance, K, SW La., 1963
Porterfield, Garry, DE, Tulsa, 1965
Pugh, Jethro, DT, Eliz. City St., 1965-78
Putnam, Duane, G, Pacific, 1960
Rafferty, Tom, G-C, Penn State, 1976-81
Randall, Tom, DG, Iowa State, 1978
Randle, Sonny, WR, Virginia, 1968
Reece, Beasley, CB-WR, N. Texas St., 1976
Reese, Guy, DT, SMU, 1962-63
Reeves, Dan, RB-QB, S. Car., 1965-72
Renfro, Mel, CB-RB-S, Oregon, 1964-77
Rentzel, Lance, WR, Oklahoma, 1967-70
Rhome, Jerry, QB, Tulsa, 1965-68
Richards, Golden, WR, Hawaii, 1973-78
Richards, Howard, T, Missouri, 1981
Richardson, Gloster, WR, Jack. St., 1971
Ridgway, Colin, P-K, Lamar Tech, 1965
Ridlon, Jim, S, Syracuse, 1963-64
Roach, John, QB, SMU, 1964
Robinson, Larry, RB, Tennessee, 1973
Roe, Bill, LB, Colorado, 1980
Rucker, Reggie, WR, Boston U., 1970-71
Saldi, Jay, TE, South Carolina, 1976-81
Sandeman, Bill, DT, Pacific, 1966
Schaum, Greg, DE, Michigan State, 1976
Schoenke, Ray, T, SMU, 1963-64
Scott, Herbert, G, Virginia Union, 1975-81
Sellers, Ron, WR, Florida State, 1972
Septien, Rafael, K, SW Louisiana, 1978-81
Shaw, Robert, C, Tennessee 1979-81
Sherer, Dave, P, SMU, 1960
Shy, Les, RB, Long Beach State, 1966-69
Simmons, Dave, LB, Georgia Tech, 1968
Smerek, Don, DL, Nevada Reno, 1981
Smith, J. D., RB, N. Car. A&T, 1965-66
Smith, Jackie, TE, NW Louisiana 1978
Smith, Jim Ray, G-T, Baylor, 1963-64
Smith, Tody, DE-DT, USC, 1971-72
Solomon, Roland, S, Utah, 1980
Spradlin, Danny, LB, Tennessee, 1981
Springs, Ron, RB, Ohio State, 1979-81
Stalls, Dave, DE, Northern Colorado, 1977-79
Staubach, Roger, QB, Navy, 1969-79
Steele, Robert, WR, N. Alabama, 1978
Stephens, Larry, DE, Texas, 1963-67
Stiger, Jim, RB, Washington, 1963-65
Stincic, Tom, LB, Michigan, 1969-71
Stokes, Sim, WR, Northern Arizona, 1967
Stowe, Otto, WR, Iowa State, 1973
Strayhorn, Les, RB, East Carolina, 1973-74
Stynchula, Andy, DE, Penn State, 1968
Talbert, Don, DE-T, Texas, 1962, 1965, 1971
Thomas, Bill, RB, Boston College, 1972
Thomas, Duane, RB, W. Texas St., 1970-71
Thomas, Ike, CB, Bishop, 1971
Thornton, Bruce, DE-DT, Illinois, 1979-81
Thurman, Dennis, CB, USC, 1978-81
Titensor, Glen, G, Brigham Young, 1981
Toomay, Pat, DE, Vanderbilt, 1970-74
Townes, Willie, DE, Tulsa, 1966-68
Truax, Billy, TE, Louisiana State, 1971-73
Tubbs, Jerry, LB, Oklahoma, 1960-67
Van Raaphorst, Dick, K, Ohio State, 1964
Villanueva, Danny, P-K, New Mex. St., 1965-67
Walker, Louie, LB, Colorado State, 1974
Walker, Malcolm, C, Rice, 1966-69
Wallace, Rodney, G-T, New Mex., 1971-73
Walls, Everson, CB, Grambling, 1981
Walton, Bruce, G, UCLA, 1973-75
Washington, Mark, CB, Morgan St., 1970-78
Waters, Charlie, S-CB, Clemson, 1970-78, 1980-81
Wayt, Russell, LB, Rice, 1965
Welch, Claxton, RB, Oregon, 1969-71
Wells, Norm, G, Northwestern, 1980
White, Danny, QB-P, Arizona State, 1976-81
White, Randy, LB-DE, Maryland, 1975-81
Whitfield, A. D., RB, N. Texas St., 1965
Whittingham, Fred, LB, Cal. Poly, 1969
Widby, Ron, P, Tennessee, 1968-71
Wilbur, John, T, Stanford, 1966-69
Williams, Joe, RB, Wyoming, 1971
Wilson, Steve, WR, Howard, 1979-81
Wisener, Gary, WR, Baylor, 1960
Woolsey, Rolly, CB-S, Boise State, 1975
Wright, Rayfield, TE-T, Ft. Valley St., 1967-79
Wright, Steve, T, Northern Iowa, 1981
Youmans, Maury, DE, Syracuse, 1964-65
Young, Charles, RB, N.C. State, 1974-76

54
54

Cowboys All-Time Draft

1961
(Drafted 2nd)

1. **(A) NO CHOICE**
Choice traded along with sixth choice to Washington for EDDIE LeBARON.
1. **(B) BOB LILLY**
T, Texas Christian University, 6-5, 242 — Choice from Cleveland for first round pick in 1962.
2. **E. J. HOLUB**
LB, Texas Tech, 6-4, 218 (went to AFL).
3. **STEW BARBER**
G, Penn State, 6-3, 230 (went to AFL).
4. **SONNY DAVIS**
E, Baylor, 6-2, 210.
5. **NO CHOICE**
Choice traded to San Francisco for GENE BABB.
6. **NO CHOICE**
Choice traded, along with first choice to Washington for LeBARON.
7. **ART GILMORE**
HB, Oregon State, 6-0, 200.
8. **DON TALBERT**
T, Texas, 6-5, 220.
9. **GLENN GREGORY**
HB, SMU, 6-2, 195.
10. **NO CHOICE**
Choice traded to Green Bay for FRED CONE.
11. **NORRIS STEVENSON**
HB, Missouri, 6-1, 205.
12. **LOWNDES SHINGLER**
QB, Clemson, 6-1, 205.
13. **DON GOODMAN**
HB, Florida, 6-0, 200.
14. **BILL SHAW**
T, Georgia Tech, 6-3, 222 (went to AFL).
15. **JULIUS VARNADO**
T, San Francisco State, 6-4, 220 (went to AFL).
16. **JERRY STEFFEN**
HB, Colorado, 6-10, 190.
17. **EVERETT CLOUD**
HB, Maryland, 6-0, 190.
18. **RANDY WILLIAMS**
HB, Indiana, 6-3, 208.
19. **LYNN HOYEM**
C, Long Beach State, 6-4, 225.
20. **JERRY MORGAN**
QB, Iowa State, 6-3, 195.

1962
(Drafted 4th)

1. **NO CHOICE**
Choice traded to Cleveland for first round pick in 1961 when Cowboys picked BOB LILLY.
2. **SONNY GIBBS***
QB, TCU, 6-7, 225.
3. **(A) NO CHOICE**
Choice to Chicago for DON MEREDITH.
3. **(B) BOBBY PLUMMER**
G, TCU, 6-2, 235 — Choice from Cleveland for DUANE PUTNAM.
4. **NO CHOICE**
Choice to San Francisco for BILL HERCHMAN.
5. **NO CHOICE**
Choice to Los Angeles for JIMMY HARRIS.
6. **(A) DONNIE DAVIS**
E, Southern University, 6-2, 235.
6. **(B) GEORGE ANDRIE**
E, Marquette, 6-7, 247 — Choice and ALLEN GREEN from New York for FRED DUGAN.
7. **NO CHOICE**
Choice to Los Angeles for JOHN HOUSER.
8. **KEN TUREAUD**
B, Michigan, 6-1, 198.
9. **NO CHOICE**
Choice to Baltimore for DON PERKINS.
10. **JOHN M. LONGMEYER**
G, Southern Illinois, 6-3, 230.
11. **LARRY HUDAS**
E, Michigan State, 6-4, 208.
12. **NO CHOICE**
Choice to Green Bay for STEVE MEILINGER.
13. **ROBERT MOSES**
E, Texas, 6-3, 211.
14. **HAROLD HAYS***
G, Southern Mississippi, 6-3, 218.
15. **GUY REESE**
T, SMU, 6-5, 238.
16. **ROBERT JOHNSTON**
T, Rice, 6-4, 215.
17. **RAY JACOBS**
T, Howard Payne, 6-3, 265 (went to AFL).
18. **DAVE CLOUTIER***
B, Maine, 6-0, 195 (went to AFL).
19. **PAUL HOLMES**
T, Georgia, 6-5, 220.
20. **AMOS BULLOCKS**
B, Southern Illinois, 6-1, 197.

1963
(Drafted 6th)

1. **LEE ROY JORDAN**
LB, Alabama, 6-2, 210.
2. **NO CHOICE**
Choice traded, along with ninth choice, to Chicago for CHUCK HOWLEY.
3. **JIM PRICE**
LB, Auburn, 6-3, 225.
4. **WHALEY HALL***
G, Mississippi, 6-3, 230.
5. **NO CHOICE**
Choice traded to New York for DICK NOLAN.
6. **NO CHOICE**
Choice traded to Green Bay for JOHN SUTRO.
7. **MARV CLOTHIER**
G, Kansas, 6-4, 220.
8. **NO CHOICE**
Choice traded to Green Bay for LEE FOLKINS.
9. **NO CHOICE**
Choice traded to Chicago.
10. **ROD SCHEYER**
T, Washington, 6-2, 220.
11. **RAY SCHOENKE**
C, SMU, 6-3, 225.
12. **BILL PERKINS**
B, Iowa, 6-2, 218.
13. **PAUL WICKER***
T, Fresno State, 6-5, 248.
14. **LOU CIOCI**
LB, Boston College, 6-2, 225.
15. **JERRY OVERTON**
B, Utah, 6-2, 192.
16. **DENNIS GOLDEN**
T, Holy Cross, 6-4, 235.
17. **ERNEST PARKS***
G, McMurry, 6-4, 230 (went to AFL).
18. **BILL FRANK**
T, Colorado, 6-4, 250.
19. **JIM STIGER**
B, Washington, 5-11, 195.
20. **TOMMY LUCAS**
E, Texas, 6-3, 218.

1964
(Drafted 4th)

1. **NO CHOICE**
Choice traded to Pittsburgh for BUDDY DIAL.
2. **MEL RENFRO**
B, Oregon, 6-0, 195.
3. **NO CHOICE**
Choice traded to Los Angeles for BOB LONG and JOHN MEYERS.
4. **PERRY LEE DUNN**
B, Mississippi, 6-2, 205.
5. **NO CHOICE**
Choice traded to Green Bay for GARY BARNES.
6. **(A) BILLY LOTHRIDGE**
QB, Georgia Tech, 6-1, 188.
6. **(B) JIM CURRY**
E, Cincinnati, 6-4, 215 — Choice from Cleveland for ANDY CVERCKO.
6. **(C) JIMMY EVANS**
E, Texas Western, 6-1, 194 — Choice from Green Bay for JERRY NORTON.
7. **BOB HAYES***
WR, Florida A&M, 5-11, 189.
8. **AL GEVERINK**
B, UCLA, 6-2, 190.
9. **JAKE KUPP**
E, Washington, 6-3, 215.
10. **ROGER STAUBACH***
QB, Navy, 6-2, 190.
11. **BOBBY CRENSHAW**
G, Baylor, 6-3, 230 (went to AFL).
12. **JOHNNY NORMAN**
E, Northwestern Louisiana, 6-1, 185.
13. **JERRY RHOME**
QB, Tulsa, 6-0, 185.
14. **JIM WORDEN**
LB, Wittenberg, 6-1, 230.
15. **BILL VAN BURKLEO**
B, Tulsa, 5-11, 185.
16. **PAUL CERCEL**
C, Pittsburgh, 6-2, 222.
17. **HARRY ABELL**
E, Missouri, 6-3, 212 (went to AFL).
18. **NO SELECTION**
Player chosen not eligible.
19. **H. D. MURPHY**
B, Oregon, 6-0, 190.
20. **JOHN HUGHES**
LB, SMU, 6-2, 220.

1965
(Drafted 5th)

1. **CRAIG MORTON**
QB, California, 6-4, 215.
2. **MALCOLM WALKER**
LB, Rice, 6-4, 245.
3. **NO CHOICE**
Choice traded to Green Bay (who traded it to New York) for JOHN ROACH.
4. **(A) JIM SIDLE**
B, Auburn, 6-2, 215.
4. **(B) BOB SVIHUS**
T, USC, 6-4, 240 (went to AFL) — Choice from Detroit for SONNY GIBBS.
5. **ROGER PETTEE**
LB, Florida, 6-4, 230.
6. **SONNY UTZ**
RB, VPI, 5-11, 215.
7. **BRIG OWENS**
B, Cincinnati, 5-11, 183.
8. **RUSSELL WAYT**
LB, Rice, 6-4, 235.
9. **JIM ZANIOS**
FB, Texas Tech, 6-0, 215.
10. **GAYLON McCOLLOUGH**
C, Alabama, 6-3, 215.
11. **JETHRO PUGH**
T, Elizabeth City State, 6-6, 255.
12. **ERNIE KELLERMAN**
QB, Miami (Ohio), 6-0, 175.
13. **JACK SCHRAUB**
E, California, 6-6, 210.
14. **GARRY PORTERFIELD**
E, Tulsa, 6-3, 235.
15. **GENE FOSTER**
B, Arizona State, 6-0, 195 (went to AFL).
16. **DOUG McDOUGAL**
E, Oregon State, 6-4, 228.
17. **MITCH JOHNSON**
T, UCLA, 6-4, 245.
18. **MARTIN AMSLER**
T, Evansville, 6-5, 250.
19. **MARV RETTENMUND**
HB, Ball State, 5-10, 195.
20. **RON BARLOW***
T, Kansas State, 6-2, 230.

1966
(Drafted 5th)

1. **JOHN NILAND**
G, Iowa, 6-3, 245.
2. **WILLIE TOWNES***
DE, Tulsa, 6-5, 265.
3. **NO CHOICE**
Choice to San Francisco for LEON DONOHUE.
4. **NO CHOICE**
Choice to Baltimore for RALPH NEELY.
5. **(A) NO CHOICE**
Choice to San Francisco for J. D. SMITH.
5. **(B) WALT GARRISON**
RB, Oklahoma State, 6-0, 209 — Choice from Baltimore thru Detroit for AMOS MARSH.
6. **BOB DUNLEVY**
E, West Virginia, 6-4, 195.
7. **ART ROBINSON**
E, Florida A&M, 6-0, 208.
8. **DON KUNIT**
RB, Penn State, 6-2, 200.
9. **DARRELL ELAM**
FL, West Virginia Tech, 6-2, 189.
10. **MASON MITCHELL**
RB, Washington, 6-1, 170.
11. **AUSTIN DENNEY***
E, Tennessee, 6-2, 225.
12. **(A) LES SHY**
RB, Long Beach State, 6-1, 200 — Choice from Pittsburgh for LEE FOLKINS.
12. **(B) CRAIG BAYNHAM***
RB, Georgia Tech, 6-1, 200.
13. **RONNIE LAMB**
B, South Carolina, 6-2, 216.
14. **LEWIS TURNER**
RB, Norfolk State, 6-2, 183.
15. **MARK GARTUNG***
DT, Oregon State, 6-4, 255.
16. **TOM PIGGEE**
RB, San Francisco State, 5-11, 200.
17. **GEORGE ALLEN**
T, West Texas State, 6-7, 245 (went to AFL).
18. **STEVE ORR**
DT, Washington, 6-4, 230.
19. **BYRON JOHNSON**
E, Central Washington State, 6-5, 255.
20. **LOU HUDSON**
FL, Minnesota, 6-5, 220.

1967
(Drafted 23rd)

1. **NO CHOICE**
Choice given along with second and two fifths, to Houston for RALPH NEELY.
2. **NO CHOICE**
NEELY trade.
3. **PHIL CLARK**
DB, Northwestern, 6-2, 207.
4. **CURTIS MARKER**
G, Northern Michigan, 6-2, 253.
5. **(A) NO CHOICE**
Choice and JIM STEFFEN from Washington for BRIG OWENS, MITCH JOHNSON and JAKE KUPP; NEELY trade.
5. **(B) NO CHOICE**
Choice from Cleveland for JOE BOB ISBELL; NEELY trade.
5. **(C) NO CHOICE**
Choice to Green Bay for HENRY GREMMINGER.
6. **SIMS STOKES**
E, Northern Arizona, 6-1, 198.
7. **RAYFIELD WRIGHT**
T, Ft. Valley State, 6-7, 235.
8. **STEVE LAUB**
QB, Illinois Wesleyan, 6-1, 190.
9. **BYRON MORGAN**
DB, Findlay (Ohio), 6-3, 212.
10. **EUGENE BOWEN**
RB, Tennessee A&I, 5-8, 210.
11. **PAT RILEY**
E, Kentucky, 6-2, 205.
12. **HAROLD DETERS**
K, North Carolina State, 6-0, 200.
13. **AL KERKIAN**
DE, Akron, 6-6, 235.
14. **TOM BOYD**
G, Tarleton State, 6-3, 250.
15. **LEAVIE DAVIS**
DB, Edward Waters College (Florida), 6-4, 210.
16. **PAUL BROTHERS**
HB, Oregon State, 6-1, 195.
17. **GEORGE ADAMS**
LB, Morehead State (Kentucky), 6-2, 218.

1968
(Drafted Alternately 20th, 19th, 21st)

1. **DENNIS HOMAN**
FL, Alabama, 6-1, 181.
2. **DAVID McDANIELS**
E, Mississippi Valley, 6-4, 200.
3. **(A) NO CHOICE**
Choice to Minnesota for LANCE RENTZEL.
3. **(B) ED HARMON**
LB, Louisville, 6-4, 246 — Choice from Chicago for AUSTIN DENNEY and MAC PERCIVAL.
4. **(A) NO CHOICE**
Choice to New Orleans for LARRY STEPHENS.
4. **(B) JOHN DOUGLAS**
LB, Missouri, 6-2, 215 — Choice from New York for JIM COLVIN.
5. **BLAINE NYE**
G, Stanford, 6-4, 255.
6. **D. D. LEWIS**
LB, Mississippi State, 6-1, 210.
7. **BOB TAUCHER**
T, Nebraska, 6-4, 251.
8. **FRANK BROWN**
DE, Albany (Ga.) State, 6-3, 249.

9. **KEN KMIEC**
DB, Illinois, 6-2, 187.
10. **BEN OLISON**
FL, Kansas, 6-1, 170.
11. **RON SHOTTS**
RB, Oklahoma, 6-0, 206.
12. **WILSON WHITTY**
LB, Boston University, 6-3, 224.
13. **CARTER LORD**
TE, Harvard, 6-2, 214.
14. **RON WILLIAMS**
DB, West Virginia, 6-2, 190.
15. **TOMMY LUNCEFORD**
P, Auburn, 6-2, 202.
16. **LARRY COLE**
DE, Hawaii, 6-5, 250.
17. **GEORGE NORDGREN**
RB, Houston, 6-0, 200.

1969
(Drafted Alternately 24th, 23rd, 22nd)

1. **CALVIN HILL**
RB, Yale, 6-3, 230.
2. **RICHMOND FLOWERS**
WR, Tennessee, 6-0, 183.
3. **(A) TOM STINCIC**
LB, Michigan, 6-2, 226.
3. **(B) HALVOR HAGEN**
DE, Weber State, 6-5, 250 — Choice from San Francisco for HAROLD HAYS.
4. **NO CHOICE**
Choice to New Orleans for DAVE SIMMONS.
5. **(A) NO CHOICE**
Choice to Baltimore for ANDY STYNCHULA.
5. **(B) CHUCK KYLE**
LB, Purdue, 6-1, 220 — Choice from Los Angeles for COY BACON.
6. **RICH SHAW**
FL, Arizona State, 6-4, 205.
7. **LARRY BALES**
WR, Emory & Henry, 5-11, 185.
8. **ELMER BENHARDT**
LB, Missouri, 6-2, 200.
9. **CLAXTON WELCH**
RB, Oregon, 5-11, 200.
10. **STUART GOTTLIEB**
G, Weber State, 6-5, 250.
11. **CLARENCE WILLIAMS**
DT, Prairie View A&M, 6-5, 250.
12. **BOB BELDEN**
QB, Notre Dame, 6-2, 210.
13. **RENE MATISON**
WR, New Mexico, 6-0, 185.
14. **GERALD LUTRI**
T, Northern Michigan, 6-4, 256.
15. **BILL JUSTUS**
DB, Tennessee, 6-1, 180.
16. **FLOYD KERR**
DB, Colorado State, 6-3, 195.
17. **BILL BAILEY**
DT, Lewis & Clark, 6-4, 260.

1970
(Drafted 23rd)

1. **DUANE THOMAS**
RB, West Texas, 6-1, 220.
2. **(A) BOB ASHER**
T, Vanderbilt, 6-5, 250 — Choice from Chicago for CRAIG BAYNHAM and PHIL CLARK.
2. **(B) MARGENE ADKINS**
WR, Henderson, J.C., 5-10, 183.
3. **(A) CHARLIE WATERS**
CB, Clemson, 6-1, 193 — Choice from Houston through Cleveland for JERRY RHOME.
3. **(B) STEVE KINER**
LB, Tennessee, 6-1, 220 — Choice from Cleveland for JERRY RHOME.
3. **(C) DENTON FOX**
S, Texas Tech, 6-2, 205.
4. **JOHN FITZGERALD**
T, Boston College, 6-4, 265.
5. **NO CHOICE**
Choice to St. Louis for BOBBY JOE CONRAD.
6. **PAT TOOMAY**
DE, Vanderbilt, 6-5, 230.
7. **DON ABBEY**
LB, Penn State, 6-2, 252.
8. **JERRY DOSSEY**
G, Arkansas, 6-4, 244.
9. **ZENON ANDRUSYSHYN**
K, UCLA, 6-2, 212.
10. **PETE ATHAS**
S, Dade J.C. 6-0, 186.
11. **IVAN SOUTHERLAND**
DT, Clemson, 6-4, 246.
12. **JOE WILLIAMS**
RB, Wyoming, 6-1, 193.
13. **MARK WASHINGTON**
CB, Morgan State, 5-11, 183.
14. **JULIAN MARTIN**
WR, North Carolina Central, 6-3, 190.
15. **KEN DeLONG**
TE, Tennessee, 6-2, 223.
16. **SEABERN HILL**
CB, Arizona State, 6-2, 195.
17. **GLENN PATTERSON**
C, Nebraska, 6-3, 220.

1971
(Drafted 25th)

1. **TOBY SMITH**
DE, Southern California, 6-5, 250.
2. **ISAAC THOMAS**
CB, Bishop, 6-2, 190.
3. **(A) SAM SCARBER**
RB, New Mexico, 6-2, 235 — Choice from St. Louis for JOHN WILBUR.
3. **(B) BILL GREGORY**
DE, Wisconsin, 6-5, 240.
4. **(A) JOE CARTER**
TE, Grambling, 6-3, 219 — Choice from New Orleans for WILLIE TOWNES.
4. **(B) BUDDY MITCHELL**
T, Mississippi, 6-5, 232.
5. **RON KADZIEL**
LB, Stanford, 6-3, 215.
6. **STEVE MAIER**
WR, Northern Arizona, 6-3, 192.
7. **BILL GRIFFIN**
T-G, Catawba, 6-5, 250.
8. **RON JESSIE**
WR, Kansas, 6-0, 183.
9. **HONOR JACKSON**
WR, Pacific, 6-2, 190.
10. **RODNEY WALLACE**
DT, New Mexico, 6-5, 260.
11. **ERNEST BONWELL**
LB, Lane College, 6-4, 225.
12. **STEVE GOEPEL**
QB, Colgate, 6-1½, 200.
13. **JAMES FORD**
RB, Texas Southern, 6-0, 200.
14. **TYRONE COUEY**
DB, Utah State, 6-1½, 194.
15. **BOB YOUNG**
TE, Delaware, 6-5, 250.
16. **JOHN BRENNAN**
T, Boston College, 6-2½, 260.
17. **JOHN BOMER**
C, Memphis State, 6-3, 230.

1972
(Drafted 26th)

1. **BILL THOMAS**
RB, Boston College, 6-2, 225.
2. **(A) ROBERT NEWHOUSE**
RB, Houston, 5-10, 202 — Choice from New England for HALVOR HAGEN and HONOR JACKSON.
2. **(B) JOHN BABINECZ**
LB, Villanova, 6-1, 222 — Choice from New Orleans for MARGENE ADKINS.
2. **(C) CHARLES McKEE**
WR, Arizona, 6-2, 199.
3. **(A) MIKE KELLER**
LB, Michigan, 6-4, 221 — Choice from New England for HALVOR HAGEN and HONOR JACKSON.
3. **(B) MARV BATEMAN**
P-K, Utah, 6-4, 213.
4. **(A) TIM KEARNEY**
LB, Northern Michigan, 6-2, 225 — Choice from New Orleans for JOE WILLIAMS.
4. **(B) ROBERT WEST**
WR, San Diego State, 6-4, 218 — Choice from New England for STEVE KINER.
4. **(C) CHARLES ZAPIEC**
LB, Penn State, 6-2, 222 — Choice from Detroit for RON JESSIE.
4. **(D) NO CHOICE**
Choice to New Orleans for DON TALBERT.
5. **NO CHOICE**
Choice to San Diego for TONY LISCIO.
6. **CHARLES BOLDEN**
DB, Iowa, 6-3, 195.
7. **NO CHOICE**
Choice to Chicago for LEE ROY CAFFEY.
8. **RALPH COLEMAN**
LB, North Carolina A&T, 6-4, 216.
9. **ROY BELL**
RB, Oklahoma, 5-10, 208.
10. **RICHARD AMMAN**
DE, Florida State, 6-5, 234.
11. **LONNIE LEONARD**
T-G, North Carolina A&T, 6-4, 244.
12. **JIMMY HARRIS**
WR, Ohio State, 5-10, 180.
13. **JEAN FUGETT**
TE, Amherst, 6-3, 219.
14. **ALAN THOMPSON**
RB, Wisconsin, 6-0, 225.
15. **CARLOS ALVAREZ**
WR, Florida 5-10, 184.
16. **GORDON LONGMIRE**
QB, Utah, 6-1, 205.
17. **ALFONSO CAIN**
DT, Bethune-Cookman, 6-3, 271.

1973
(Drafted Alternately 20th, 22nd and 21st)

1. **BILLY JOE DuPREE**
TE, Michigan State, 6-4, 225.
2. **(A) GOLDEN RICHARDS**
WR, Hawaii, 6-0, 172 — Choice from Green Bay for RON WIDBY and IKE THOMAS.
2. **(B) NO CHOICE**
Choice to Chicago as compensation for signing JACK CONCANNON.
3. **(A) HARVEY MARTIN**
DT, East Texas State, 6-5, 262 — Choice from Houston through New Orleans for TOM STINCIC.
3. **(B) NO CHOICE**
Choice to New England for RON SELLERS.
4. **DRANE SCRIVENER**
DB, Tulsa, 6-0, 176.
5. **BRUCE WALTON**
T, UCLA, 6-6, 251.
6. **BOB LEYEN**
G, Yale, 6-4, 256.
7. **RODRIGO BARNES**
LA, Rice, 6-1, 215.
8. **DAN WERNER**
QB, Michigan State, 6-4, 195.
9. **MIKE WHITE**
CB, Minnesota, 6-0, 196.

10. **CARL JOHNSON**
LB, Tennessee, 6-1, 225.
11. **GERALD CASWELL**
G, Colorado State, 6-4, 250.
12. **JIM ARNESON**
G, Arizona, 6-3, 236.
13. **JOHN SMITH**
WR, UCLA, 6-1, 187.
14. **BOB THORNTON**
G-C, North Carolina, 6-3, 234.
15. **WALT BAISY**
LB, Grambling, 6-2, 222.
16. **JOHN CONLEY**
TE, Hawaii, 6-2, 228.
17. **LES STRAYHORN**
RB, East Carolina, 5-10, 205.

1974
(Drafted Alternately 22nd, 21st, 20th and 23rd)

1. **(A) ED JONES**
DE, Tennessee State, 6-8, 260 — Choice from Houston for TODY SMITH and BILLY PARKS.
1. **(B) CHARLES YOUNG**
RB, North Carolina State, 6-1, 215.
2. **NO CHOICE**
Choice and RON SELLERS to Miami for OTTO STOWE.
3. **(A) DANNY WHITE**
QB, Arizona State, 6-2, 180 — Choice from Houston for TODY SMITH and BILLY PARKS.
3. **(B) CALVIN PETERSON**
LB, UCLA, 6-3, 218.
4. **(A) KEN HUTCHERSON**
LB, Livingston State, 6-1, 214 — Choice from Oakland for GLOSTER RICHARDSON.
4. **(B) ANDY ANDRADE**
RB-DB, Northern Michigan, 5-11, 193.
5. **JOHN KELSEY**
T, Missouri, 6-6, 226.
6. **JIM BRIGHT**
DB, UCLA, 6-1, 210.

7. **RAYMOND NESTER**
LB, Michigan State, 6-2, 224.
8. **MIKE HOLT**
DB, Michigan State, 5-11, 176.
9. **BILL DULIN**
T, Johnson C. Smith, 6-6, 244.
10. **DENNIS MORGAN**
DB, Western Illinois, 5-11, 203.
11. **HARVEY McGEE**
WR, Southern Mississippi, 6-2, 209.
12. **KEITH BOBO**
QB, Southern Methodist, 6-3, 196.
13. **FRED LIMA**
K, Colorado, 5-9, 202.
14. **DOUG RICHARDS**
DB, Brigham Young, 6-4, 185.
15. **BRUCE CRAFT**
DT, Geneva, Pa., 6-4, 232.
16. **GENE KILLIAN**
T, Tennessee, 6-4, 225.
17. **LAWRIE SKOLROOD**
T, North Dakota, 6-5, 230.

1975
(Drafted 18th)

1. **(A) RANDY WHITE**
DE, Maryland, 6-4, 250 — Choice from N.Y. Giants for CRAIG MORTON.
1. **(B) THOMAS HENDERSON**
LB, Langston, 6-2, 214.
2. **BURTON LAWLESS**
G, Florida, 6-4, 253.
3. **BOB BREUNIG**
LB, Arizona State, 6-2, 236.
4. **(A) PAT DONOVAN**
DE, Stanford, 6-5, 240 — Choice from Houston for MIKE MONTGOMERY.
4. **(B) RANDY HUGHES**
DB, Oklahoma, 6-4, 209.
5. **(A) KYLE DAVIS**
C, Oklahoma, 6-3, 240 — Choice from Green Bay for JACK CONCANNON.
5. **(B) NO CHOICE**
Choice to Cincinnati for CLINT LONGLEY.
6. **ROLLY WOOLSEY**
DB, Boise State, 6-1, 175.
7. **MICHAEL HEGMAN**
LB, Tennessee State, 6-4, 220.
8. **MITCH HOOPES**
P, Arizona, 6-0, 210.
9. **ED JONES**
DB, Rutgers, 6-0, 193.
10. **DENNIS BOOKER**
RB, Millersville State, 6-1, 235.
11. **GREG KRPALEK**
C, Oregon State, 6-5, 242.
12. **CHUCK BLAND**
DB, Cincinnati, 5-11, 188.
13. **HERBERT SCOTT**
G, Virginia Union, 6-2, 248.
14. **SCOTT LAIDLAW**
RB, Stanford, 6-0, 206.
15. **WILLIE HAMILTON**
RB, Arizona, 5-11, 182.
16. **PETE CLARK**
TE, Colorado State, 6-4, 234.
17. **JIM TESTERMAN**
TE, Dayton, 6-5, 225.

1976
(Drafted 27th)

1. **AARON KYLE**
DB, Wyoming, 5-11, 183.
2. **(A) JIM JENSEN**
RB, Iowa, 6-4, 226 — Choice from N.Y. Giants for CRAIG MORTON.
2. **(B) JIM EIDSON**
G, Mississippi St., 6-4, 253.
3. **(A) DUKE FERGERSON**
WR, San Diego St., 6-1, 186 — Choice from San Francisco for BOB HAYES.
3. **(B) JOHN SMITH**
RB, Boise State, 6-0, 191 — Choice from Denver for OTTO STOWE.
3. **(C) BUTCH JOHNSON**
WR, UC-Riverside, 6-1, 175.
4. **TOM RAFFERTY**
G, Penn State, 6-3, 248.
5. **WALLY PESUIT**
T, Kentucky, 6-4, 260.
6. **GREG McGUIRE**
T, Indiana, 6-3, 265.
7. **(A) GREG SCHAUM**
DT, Michigan State, 6-4, 246 — Choice from San Diego for KEN HUTCHERSON.
7. **(B) DAVID WILLIAMS**
RB, Colorado, 6-2, 210.
8. **HENRY LAWS**
DB, South Carolina, 5-10, 171.
9. **BEASLEY REECE**
DB, North Texas, 6-1, 193.
10. **LEROY COOK**
DE, Alabama, 6-4, 212.
11. **CORNELIUS GREEN**
QB, Ohio, 5-11, 170.
12. **CHARLES McSHANE**
LB, Cal Lutheran, 6-2, 211.
13. **MARK DRISCOLL**
QB, Colorado St., 6-1, 184.
14. **LARRY MUSHINSKIE**
TE, Nebraska, 6-3, 217.
15. **DALE CURRY**
LB, UCLA, 6-2, 222.
16. **RICH COSTANZO**
T, Nebraska, 6-4, 260.
17. **STAN WOODFILL**
K, Oregon, 6-0, 190.

1977
(Drafted Alternately 24th, 25th and 26th)

1. **TONY DORSETT**
RB, Pittsburgh, 5-11, 192 — Choice from Seattle for Cowboys' first-round choice and three second-round choices.
2. **GLENN CARANO**
QB, Nevada-Las Vegas, 6-3, 195 — Choice from Seattle for DUKE FERGERSON.
3. **(A) TONY HILL**
WR, Stanford, 6-2,196 — Choice from Philadelphia for JOHN NILAND.
3. **(B) VAL BELCHER**
G, Houston, 6-3, 250.
4. **GUY BROWN**
LB, Houston, 6-4, 215.
5. **ANDY FREDERICK**
OL, New Mexico, 6-6, 241.
6. **JIM COOPER**
T, Temple, 6-5, 252.
7. **DAVID STALLS**
DT, Northern Colorado, 6-4, 236.
8. **(A) AL CLEVELAND**
DL, Pacific, 6-4, 246 — Choice from San Diego for MITCH HOOPES.
8. **(B) FRED WILLIAMS**
RB, Arizona State, 5-10, 189.
9. **MARK CANTRELL**
C, North Carolina, 6-3, 252.
10. **STEVE DeBERG**
QB, San Jose State, 6-2, 205.
11. **DON WARDLOW**
TE, Washington, 6-6, 230.
12. **GREG PETERS**
OL, California, 6-5, 257.

1978
(Drafted 28th)

1. **LARRY BETHEA**
DL, Michigan State, 6-5, 258.
2. **TODD CHRISTENSEN**
RB-TE, Brigham Young, 6-3, 224.
3. **DAVID HUDGENS**
OL, Oklahoma, 6-5, 245.
4. **ALOIS BLACKWELL**
RB, Houston, 5-11, 194.
5. **RICH ROSEN**
G, Syracuse, 6-3, 242.
6. **HAROLD RANDOLPH**
LB, East Carolina, 6-1, 191.
7. **TOM RANDALL**
DT, Iowa State, 6-5, 248.
8. **HOMER BUTLER**
WR, UCLA, 6-1, 184.
9. **RUSS WILLIAMS**
DB, Tennessee, 6-1, 197.
10. **BARRY TOMASETTI**
OL, Iowa, 6-3, 249.
11. **DENNIS THURMAN**
S, Southern Cal, 5-11, 172.
12. **LEE WASHBURN**
OL, Montana State, 6-6, 253.

1979
(Drafted 27th)

1. **ROBERT SHAW**
C, Tennessee, 6-4, 252.
2. **AARON MITCHELL**
CB, Nevada-Las Vegas, 6-1, 196.
3. **DOUG COSBIE**
TE, Santa Clara, 6-6, 230. Swapped choices with Seattle in BILL GREGORY trade.
4. **RALPH DeLOACH**
DE, California, 6-5, 254.
5. **(A) BOB HUKILL**
OL, North Carolina, 6-5, 250. Choice from Chicago for GOLDEN RICHARDS.
5. **(B) CURTIS ANDERSON**
DE, Central State (O), 6-6, 240. Choice from Seattle for EFREN HERRERA.
5. **(C) RON SPRINGS**
RB, Ohio State, 6-0, 197.
6. **(A) TIM LAVENDER**
CB, So. California, 6-3, 187. Choice from Seattle for BILL GREGORY.
6. **(B) MIKE SALZANO**
OL, North Carolina, 6-3, 242. Choice from Denver for JIM JENSEN.
6. **(C) CHRIS DeFRANCE**
WR, Arizona St., 6-1, 205.
7. **GREG FITZPATRICK**
LB, Youngstown, 6-2, 227.
8. **BRUCE THORNTON**
DT, Illinois, 6-5, 266.
9. **GARRY COBB**
LB, So. California, 6-2, 209.
10. **MIKE CALHOUN**
DT, Notre Dame, 6-4, 228.
11. **NO CHOICE**
Choice to Detroit for SKIP BUTLER
12. **QUENTIN LOWRY**
LB, Youngstown, 6-2, 225.

1980
(Drafted Alternately 23rd, 24th and 25th)

1. **NO CHOICE**
Choice given along with second-round choice to Baltimore for JOHN DUTTON.
2. **NO CHOICE**
Choice given along with first-round choice to Baltimore for JOHN DUTTON.
3. **(A) BILL ROE**
LB, Colorado, 6-3, 220 — Choice from Chicago for GOLDEN RICHARDS.
3. **(B) JAMES JONES**
RB, Mississippi State, 5-10, 200.
4. **KURT PETERSEN**
DL, Missouri, 6-5, 255.
5. **GARY HOGEBOOM**
QB, Central Michigan, 6-4, 195.
6. **TIMMY NEWSOME**
RB, Winston-Salem St., 6-1, 228.
7. **LESTER BROWN**
CB, Clemson, 5-11, 176.
8. **LARRY SAVAGE**
LB, Michigan State, 6-3, 225.
9. **JACKIE FLOWERS**
WR, Florida State, 6-0, 194.
10. **MATTHEW TEAGUE**
DE, Prairie View A&M, 6-4, 238.
11. **GARY PADJEN**
LB, Arizona State, 6-1, 238.
12. **NORM WELLS**
DT, Northwestern, 6-5, 249.

1981
(Drafted Alternately 25th, 26th)

1. **HOWARD RICHARDS**
OT, Missouri, 6-5, 255.
2. **DOUG DONLEY**
WR, Ohio St., 6-0, 180.
3. **GLEN TITENSOR**
DL, Brigham Young, 6-4, 250.
4. **(A) SCOTT PELLUER**
LB, Wash. St., 6-1, 213 — Choice from San Francisco for THOMAS HENDERSON.
4. **(B) DERRIE NELSON**
LB, Nebraska, 6-2, 217.
5. **DANNY SPRADLIN**
LB, Tennessee, 6-1, 229.
6. **VINCE SKILLINGS**
DB, Ohio St., 5-11, 176.
7. **(A) RON FELLOWS**
DB, Missouri, 5-11, 165 — Choice from Tampa Bay for DAVE STALLS.
7. **(B) KEN MILLER**
DB, East. Michigan, 5-11, 180.
8. **PAUL PIUROWSKI**
LB, Florida St., 6-2, 219.
9. **MIKE WILSON**
WR, Wash. St., 6-3, 202.
10. **PAT GRAHAM**
DT, California, 6-3, 257.
11. **TIM MORRISON**
OG, Georgia, 6-3, 258.
12. **NATE LUNDY**
WR, Indiana, 6-0, 169.

1982
(Drafted 26th)

1. **ROD HILL**
CB, Kentucky State, 6-0, 182.
2. **JEFF ROHRER**
LB, Yale, 6-3, 228.
3. **JIM ELIOPULOS**
LB, Wyoming, 6-2, 224.
4. **(A) BRIAN CARPENTER**
CB, Michigan, 5-11, 166 — Choice from Tampa Bay for DAVE STALLS.
4. **(B) MONTY HUNTER**
S, Salem College, 6-0, 201.
5. **PHIL POZDERAC**
T, Notre Dame, 6-8, 264.
6. **(A) KEN HAMMOND**
G, Vanderbilt, 6-3, 270 — Choice from Cleveland for BRUCE HUTHER
6. **(B) CHARLES DAUM**
DL, Cal Poly-SLO, 6-6, 229.
7. **BILL PURIFOY**
DL, Tulsa, 6-8, 248.
8. **(A) GEORGE PEOPLES**
RB, Auburn, 6-0, 202 — Choice from Denver through Buffalo for WADE MANNING.
8. **(B) DWIGHT SULLIVAN**
RB, North Carolina State, 5-9, 204.
9. **JOE GARY**
DL, UCLA, 6-4, 262.
10. **TODD ECKERSON**
T, North Carolina State, 6-4, 268.
11. **(A) GEORGE THOMPSON**
WR, Albany State (Ga.), 6-3, 211 — Choice from Tampa Bay for AARON MITCHELL.
11. **(B) MICHAEL WHITING**
RB, Florida State, 6-0, 214.
12. **RICH BURTNESS**
G, Montana, 6-4, 235.

*Drafted as Future

Cowboys vs. NFL Opponents

Atlanta Falcons

(Dallas Leads Series, 7-1)

Year	Site	Winner-Score	Att.
1966	Atlanta	Dallas, 47-14	56,990
1967	Dallas	Dallas, 37-7	54,751
1969	Atlanta	Dallas, 24-17	54,833
1970	Dallas	Dallas, 13-0	53,611
1974	Atlanta	Dallas, 24-0	52,322
1976	Atlanta	Atlanta, 17-10	54,972
1978†	Dallas	Dallas, 27-20	60,338
1981†	Atlanta	Dallas, 30-27	60,022

†NFC Divisional Playoffs

Baltimore Colts

(Dallas Leads Series, 5-3)

Year	Site	Winner-Score	Att.
1960	Dallas	Balt., 45-7	25,500
1967	Balt.	Balt., 23-17	60,238
1969	Dallas	Dallas, 27-10	63,191
1970†	Miami	Balt., 16-13	80,055
1972	Balt.	Dallas, 21-0	58,992
1976	Dallas	Dallas, 30-27	64,237
1978	Dallas	Dallas, 38-0	64,224
1981	Balt.	Dallas, 37-13	54,871

†Super Bowl Jan. 17, 1971

Buffalo Bills

(Dallas Leads Series, 3-0)

Year	Site	Winner-Score	Att.
1971	Buffalo	Dallas, 49-37	46,206
1976	Dallas	Dallas, 17-10	51,779
1981	Dallas	Dallas, 27-14	62,583

Chicago Bears

(Dallas Leads Series, 7-3)

Year	Site	Winner-Score	Att.
1960	Chicago	Chicago, 17-7	39,951
1962	Dallas	Chicago, 34-33	12,692
1964	Chicago	Dallas, 24-10	47,527
1968	Chicago	Dallas, 34-3	46,667
1971	Chicago	Chicago, 23-19	55,049
1973	Chicago	Dallas, 20-17	55,701
1976	Dallas	Dallas, 31-21	61,346
1977*	Dallas	Dallas, 37-7	62,920
1979	Dallas	Dallas, 24-20	64,056
1981	Dallas	Dallas, 10-9	63,499

*NFC Divisional Playoffs

Cincinnati Bengals

(Dallas Leads Series, 2-0)

Year	Site	Winner-Score	Att.
1973	Dallas	Dallas, 38-10	58,802
1979	Dallas	Dallas, 38-13	63,179

1982 Oct. 24 at Cincinnati

Cleveland Browns

(Cleveland Leads Series, 15-7)

Year	Site	Winner-Score	Att.
1960	Dallas	Cleve., 48-7	28,500
1961	Cleve.	Cleve., 25-7	43,638
1961	Dallas	Cleve., 38-17	23,500
1962	Cleve.	Cleve., 19-10	44,040
1962	Dallas	Dallas, 45-21	24,226
1963	Dallas	Cleve., 41-24	28,710
1963	Cleve.	Cleve., 27-17	55,096

Year	Site	Winner-Score	Att.
1964	Cleve.	Cleve., 27-6	72,062
1964	Dallas	Cleve., 20-16	37,456
1965	Cleve.	Cleve., 23-17	80,451
1965	Dallas	Cleve., 24-17	76,251
1966	Cleve.	Cleve., 30-21	84,721
1966	Dallas	Dallas, 26-14	80,259
1967	Cleve.	Dallas, 21-14	81,039
1967*	Dallas	Dallas, 52-14	70,786
1968	Dallas	Dallas, 28-7	68,733
1968*	Cleve.	Cleve., 31-20	81,497
1969	Cleve.	Cleve., 42-10	84,850
1969*	Dallas	Cleve., 38-14	69,321
1970	Cleve.	Dallas, 6-2	75,458
1974	Dallas	Dallas, 41-17	48,754
1979	Cleve.	Cleve., 26-7	80,123

1982 Nov. 25 at Dallas
*Eastern Conference Championship Game

Denver Broncos
(Dallas Leads Series, 3-1)

Year	Site	Winner-Score	Att.
1973	Denver	Dallas, 22-10	51,706
1977	Dallas	Dallas, 14-6	63,752
1978*	New O.	Dallas, 27-10	76,400
1980	Denver	Denver, 41-20	74,919

*Super Bowl XII, Jan. 15, 1978

Detroit Lions
(Dallas Leads Series, 6-2)

Year	Site	Winner-Score	Att.
1960	Detroit	Detroit, 23-14	43,272
1963	Dallas	Dallas, 17-14	27,264
1968	Dallas	Dallas, 59-13	61,382
1970*	Dallas	Dallas, 5-0	73,167
1972	Dallas	Dallas, 28-24	65,378
1975	Detroit	Dallas, 36-10	79,784
1977	Dallas	Dallas, 37-0	63,160
1981	Detroit	Detroit, 27-24	79,694

*Divisional Playoff Game

Green Bay Packers
(Green Bay Leads Series, 8-3)

Year	Site	Winner-Score	Att.
1960	Gr. Bay	Gr. Bay, 41-7	32,294
1964	Dallas	Gr. Bay, 45-21	44,975
1965	Milw.	Gr. Bay, 13-3	48,311
1966*	Dallas	Gr. Bay, 34-27	75,504
1967*	Gr. Bay	Gr. Bay, 21-17	50,861
1968	Dallas	Gr. Bay, 28-17	74,604
1970	Dallas	Dallas, 16-3	67,182
1972	Milw.	Gr. Bay, 16-14	47,103
1975	Dallas	Gr. Bay, 19-17	64,934
1978	Milw.	Dallas, 42-14	55,256
1980	Milw.	Dallas, 28-7	54,776

*NFL Championship Game

Houston Oilers
(Dallas Leads Series, 2-1)

Year	Site	Winner-Score	Att.
1970	Dallas	Dallas, 52-10	50,504
1974	Houston	Dallas, 10-0	49,775
1979	Dallas	Houston, 30-24	63,897

1982 Dec. 13 at Houston

Kansas City Chiefs
(Series Tied, 1-1)

Year	Site	Winner-Score	Att.
1970	Kan. City	Dallas, 27-16	51,158
1975	Dallas	Kan. City, 34-31	63,539

Los Angeles Rams
(Dallas Leads Series, 9-8)

Year	Site	Winner-Score	Att.
1960	Dallas	L.A., 38-13	16,000
1962	L.A.	Dallas, 27-17	26,907
1967	Dallas	L.A., 35-13	75,229
1969	L.A.	L.A., 24-23	79,105
1971	Dallas	Dallas, 28-21	66,595
1973	L.A.	L.A., 37-31	81,428
1973†	Dallas	Dallas, 27-16	64,291
1975	Dallas	Dallas, 18-7	49,091
1975‡	L.A.	Dallas, 37-7	84,483
1976†	Dallas	L.A., 14-12	62,436
1978	L.A.	L.A., 27-14	65,749
1978‡	L.A.	Dallas, 28-0	67,470
1979	Dallas	Dallas, 30-6	64,462
1979†	Dallas	L.A., 21-19	64,792
1980	L.A.	L.A., 38-14	62,548
1980§	Dallas	Dallas, 34-13	64,533
1981	Dallas	Dallas, 29-17	64,649

§Wild Card Game
†Divisional Playoff Game
‡NFC Championship Game

Miami Dolphins
(Series Tied 2-2)

Year	Site	Winner-Score	Att.
1971*	New O.	Dallas, 24-3	81,035
1973	Dallas	Miami, 14-7	64,100
1978	Miami	Miami, 23-16	69,414
1981	Dallas	Dallas, 28-27	64,221

*Super Bowl VI, Jan. 16, 1972

Minnesota Vikings
(Dallas Leads Series, 9-4)

Year	Site	Winner-Score	Att.
1961	Dallas	Dallas, 21-7	20,500
1961	Minn.	Dallas, 28-0	33,070
1966	Dallas	Dallas, 28-17	64,116
1968	Dallas	Dallas, 20-7	47,644
1970	Minn.	Minn., 54-13	47,900
1971*	Minn.	Dallas, 20-12	49,100
1973†	Dallas	Minn., 27-10	64,524
1974	Dallas	Minn., 23-21	57,847
1975*	Minn.	Dallas, 17-14	48,341
1977	Minn.	Dallas, 16-10(OT)	47,678
1977†	Dallas	Dallas, 23-6	61,968
1978	Dallas	Minn., 21-10	61,848
1979	Minn.	Dallas, 36-20	47,572

1982 Sept. 26 at Minnesota
*Divisional Playoff Game
†NFC Championship Game

New England Patriots
(Dallas Leads Series, 4-0)

Year	Site	Winner-Score	Att.
1971	Dallas	Dallas, 44-21	65,708
1975	N. Eng.	Dallas, 34-31	60,905
1978	Dallas	Dallas, 17-10	63,263
1981	N. Eng.	Dallas, 35-21	60,311

New Orleans Saints
(Dallas Leads Series, 8-1)

Year	Site	Winner-Score	Att.
1967	Dallas	Dallas, 14-10	52,562
1967	N.O.	Dallas, 27-10	83,437
1968	N.O.	Dallas, 17-3	84,728
1969	N.O.	Dallas, 21-17	79,567
1969	Dallas	Dallas, 33-17	68,282
1971	N.O.	N.O., 24-14	83,088
1973	Dallas	Dallas, 40-3	53,972
1976	N.O.	Dallas, 24-6	61,413
1978	Dallas	Dallas, 27-7	57,920

1982 Dec. 19 at Dallas

New York Giants
(Dallas Leads Series, 28-11-2)

Year	Site	Winner-Score	Att.
1960	N.Y.	Tie, 31-31	55,033
1961	Dallas	N.Y., 31-10	41,500
1961	N.Y.	Dallas, 17-16	60,254
1962	Dallas	N.Y., 41-10	45,668
1962	N.Y.	N.Y., 41-31	62,694
1963	N.Y.	N.Y., 37-21	62,889
1963	Dallas	N.Y., 34-27	29,635
1964	Dallas	Tie, 13-13	33,225
1964	N.Y.	Dallas, 31-21	63,031
1965	Dallas	Dallas, 31-2	59,366
1965	N.Y.	Dallas, 38-20	62,871
1966	Dallas	Dallas, 52-7	60,010
1966	N.Y.	Dallas, 17-7	62,735
1967	Dallas	Dallas, 38-24	66,209
1968	Dallas	N.Y., 27-21	72,163
1968	N.Y.	Dallas, 28-10	62,617
1969	Dallas	Dallas, 25-3	58,964
1970	Dallas	Dallas, 28-10	57,236
1970	N.Y.	N.Y., 23-20	62,938
1971	Dallas	Dallas, 20-13	68,378
1971	N.Y.	Dallas, 42-14	62,815
1972	N.Y.	Dallas, 23-14	62,725
1972	Dallas	N.Y., 23-3	64,602
1973	Dallas	Dallas, 45-28	64,898
1973	N. Haven	Dallas, 23-10	70,128
1974	Dallas	N.Y., 14-6	46,353
1974	N. Haven	Dallas, 21-7	61,191
1975	N.Y.	Dallas, 13-7	56,511
1975	Dallas	Dallas, 14-3	53,329
1976	N.Y.	Dallas, 24-14	76,042
1976	Dallas	Dallas, 9-3	58,870
1977	Dallas	Dallas, 41-21	64,215
1977	N.Y.	Dallas, 24-10	74,532
1978	N.Y.	Dallas, 34-24	73,265
1978	Dallas	Dallas, 24-3	64,869
1979	N.Y.	Dallas, 16-14	76,490
1979	Dallas	Dallas, 28-7	63,787
1980	Dallas	Dallas, 24-3	59,126
1980	N.Y.	N.Y., 38-35	68,343
1981	Dallas	Dallas, 18-10	63,449
1981	N.Y.	N.Y., 13-10(OT)	73,009

1982 Oct. 3 at Dallas
1982 Oct. 31 at New York

New York Jets
(Dallas Leads Series, 3-0)

Year	Site	Winner-Score	Att.
1971	Dallas	Dallas, 52-10	66,689
1975	N.Y.	Dallas, 31-21	37,279
1978	N.Y.	Dallas, 30-7	52,532

Oakland Raiders
(Series Tied, 1-1)

Year	Site	Winner-Score	Att.
1974	Oakland	Oakland, 27-23	45,850
1980	Oakland	Dallas, 19-13	53,194

Philadelphia Eagles

(Dallas Leads Series, 29-15)

Year	Site	Winner-Score	Att.
1960	Dallas	Phil., 27-25	18,500
1961	Dallas	Phil., 43-7	25,000
1961	Phil.	Phil., 35-13	60,127
1962	Dallas	Dallas, 41-19	18,645
1962	Phil.	Phil., 28-14	58,070
1963	Phil.	Phil., 24-21	60,671
1963	Dallas	Dallas, 27-20	23,694
1964	Dallas	Phil., 17-14	55,972
1964	Phil.	Phil., 24-14	60,671
1965	Dallas	Phil., 35-24	56,249
1965	Phil.	Dallas, 21-19	54,714
1966	Dallas	Dallas, 56-7	69,372
1966	Phil.	Phil., 24-23	60,658
1967	Phil.	Phil., 21-14	60,740
1967	Dallas	Dallas, 38-17	55,834
1968	Phil.	Dallas, 45-13	60,858
1968	Dallas	Dallas, 34-14	72,083
1969	Phil.	Dallas, 38-7	60,658
1969	Dallas	Dallas, 49-14	71,509
1970	Phil.	Dallas, 17-7	59,728
1970	Dallas	Dallas, 21-17	55,736
1971	Phil.	Dallas, 42-7	65,358
1971	Dallas	Dallas, 20-7	60,178
1972	Dallas	Dallas, 28-6	55,850
1972	Phil.	Dallas, 28-7	65,720
1973	Phil.	Phil., 30-16	65,954
1973	Dallas	Dallas, 31-10	61,985
1974	Phil.	Phil., 13-10	64,088
1974	Dallas	Dallas, 31-24	43,586
1975	Phil.	Dallas, 20-17	64,889
1975	Dallas	Dallas, 27-17	57,893
1976	Dallas	Dallas, 27-7	54,052
1976	Phil.	Dallas, 26-7	55,072
1977	Phil.	Dallas, 16-10	65,507
1977	Dallas	Dallas, 24-14	60,289
1978	Dallas	Dallas, 14-7	60,525
1978	Phil.	Dallas, 31-13	64,667
1979	Dallas	Phil., 31-21	62,417
1979	Phil.	Dallas, 24-17	71,434
1980	Phil.	Phil., 17-10	70,696
1980	Dallas	Dallas, 35-27	62,548
1981†	Phil.	Phil., 20-7	70,696
1981	Phil.	Dallas, 17-14	72,111
1981	Dallas	Dallas, 21-10	64,955

1982 Oct. 17 at Philadelphia
1982 Dec. 26 at Dallas
†NFC Championship Game

Pittsburgh Steelers

(Pittsburgh Leads Series, 11-10)

Year	Site	Winner-Score	Att.
1960	Dallas	Pitts., 35-28	30,000
1961	Dallas	Dallas, 27-24	23,500
1961	Pitts.	Pitts., 37-7	17,519
1962	Dallas	Pitts., 30-28	19,478
1962	Pitts.	Dallas, 42-27	23,106
1963	Pitts.	Pitts., 27-21	19,047
1963	Dallas	Pitts., 24-19	24,136
1964	Pitts.	Pitts., 23-17	35,594
1964	Dallas	Dallas, 17-14	35,271
1965	Pitts.	Pitts., 22-13	37,804
1965	Dallas	Dallas, 24-17	57,293
1966	Dallas	Dallas, 52-21	58,453
1966	Pitts.	Dallas, 20-7	42,185
1967	Pitts.	Dallas, 24-21	39,641
1968	Dallas	Dallas, 28-7	55,069
1969	Pitts.	Dallas, 10-7	24,990
1972	Dallas	Dallas, 17-13	65,682
1975*	Miami	Pitts., 21-17	80,187
1977	Pitts.	Pitts., 28-13	49,761
1978†	Miami	Pitts., 35-31	78,656
1979	Pitts.	Pitts., 14-3	50,199

1982 Sept. 13 at Dallas
*Super Bowl X, Jan. 18, 1976
†Super Bowl XIII, Jan. 21, 1979

St. Louis Cardinals

(Dallas Leads Series, 24-15-1)

Year	Site	Winner-Score	Att.
1960	St. Louis	St. Louis, 12-10	23,128
1961	Dallas	St. Louis, 31-17	20,500
1961	St. Louis	St. Louis, 31-13	15,384
1962	Dallas	St. Louis, 28-24	16,027
1962	St. Louis	St. Louis, 52-20	14,201
1963	Dallas	St. Louis, 34-7	36,432
1963	St. Louis	Dallas, 28-24	12,695
1964	Dallas	St. Louis, 16-6	36,605
1964	St. Louis	Dallas, 31-13	28,253
1965	St. Louis	St. Louis, 20-13	32,034
1965	Dallas	Dallas, 27-13	38,499
1966	St. Louis	Tie, 10-10	50,673
1966	Dallas	Dallas, 31-17	76,965
1967	Dallas	Dallas, 46-21	68,787
1968	Dallas	Dallas, 27-10	48,296
1969	Dallas	Dallas, 24-3	62,134
1970	St. Louis	St. Louis, 20-7	50,780
1970	Dallas	St. Louis, 38-0	69,323
1971	St. Louis	Dallas, 16-13	50,486
1971	Dallas	Dallas, 31-12	66,672
1972	Dallas	Dallas, 33-24	65,218
1972	St. Louis	Dallas, 27-6	49,787
1973	Dallas	Dallas, 45-10	64,729
1973	St. Louis	Dallas, 30-3	43,946
1974	St. Louis	St. Louis, 31-28	49,885
1974	Dallas	Dallas, 17-14	64,146
1975	Dallas	Dallas, 37-31	52,417
1975	St. Louis	St. Louis, 31-17	49,701
1976	St. Louis	St. Louis, 21-17	50,317
1976	Dallas	Dallas, 19-14	62,498
1977	St. Louis	Dallas, 30-24	50,129
1977	Dallas	St. Louis, 24-17	64,038
1978	Dallas	Dallas, 21-12	62,760
1978	St. Louis	Dallas, 24-21 OT	48,991
1979	St. Louis	Dallas, 22-21	50,855
1979	Dallas	Dallas, 22-13	64,300
1980	St. Louis	Dallas, 27-24	50,701
1980	Dallas	Dallas, 31-21	52,567
1981	Dallas	Dallas, 30-17	63,602
1981	St. Louis	St. Louis, 20-17	49,777

1982 Sept. 19 at St. Louis
1982 Nov. 7 at Dallas

San Diego Chargers

(Dallas Leads Series, 2-0)

Year	Site	Winner-Score	Att.
1972	San D.	Dallas, 34-28	54,476
1980	Dallas	Dallas, 42-31	60,639

San Francisco 49ers

(Dallas Leads Series, 8-6-1)

Year	Site	Winner-Score	Att.
1960	Dallas	San Fran., 26-14	10,000
1963	San Fran.	San Fran., 31-24	29,563
1965	Dallas	Dallas, 39-31	39,677
1967	San Fran.	San Fran., 24-16	27,182
1969	Dallas	Tie, 24-24	62,348
1970*	San Fran.	Dallas, 17-10	59,625
1971†	Dallas	Dallas, 14-3	66,311
1972	Dallas	San Fran., 31-10	65,124
1972*	San Fran.	Dallas, 30-28	61,214
1974	Dallas	Dallas, 20-14	50,018
1977	San Fran.	Dallas, 42-35	55,848
1979	San Fran.	Dallas, 21-13	56,728
1980	Dallas	Dallas, 59-14	63,39
1981	San Fran.	San Fran., 45-14	57,57
1981†	San Fran.	San Fran., 28-27	60,52

1982 Nov. 14 at San Francisco
*Divisional Playoff Game
†NFC Championship Game

Seattle Seahawks

(Dallas Leads Series, 2-0)

Year	Site	Winner-Score	Att.
1976	Seattle	Dallas, 28-13	62,02
1980	Dallas	Dallas, 51-7	57,54

Tampa Bay Buccaneers

(Dallas Leads Series, 3-0)

Year	Site	Winner-Score	Att.
1977	Dallas	Dallas, 23-7	55,31
1980	Dallas	Dallas, 28-17	62,75
1981*	Dallas	Dallas, 38-0	64,84

1982 Nov. 21 at Dallas
*Divisional Playoff Game

Washington Redskins

(Dallas Leads Series, 26-16-2)

Year	Site	Winner-Score	Att.
1960	Wash.	Wash., 26-14	21,14
1961	Dallas	Tie, 28-28	17,50
1961	Wash.	Wash., 34-24	21,45
1962	Dallas	Tie, 35-35	15,73
1962	Wash.	Dallas, 38-10	49,88
1963	Wash.	Wash., 21-17	40,10
1963	Dallas	Dallas, 35-20	18,83
1964	Dallas	Dallas, 24-18	25,15
1964	Wash.	Wash., 28-16	49,21
1965	Dallas	Dallas, 27-7	61,57
1965	Wash.	Wash., 34-31	50,20
1966	Wash.	Dallas, 31-30	50,92
1966	Dallas	Wash., 34-31	64,19
1967	Wash.	Dallas, 17-14	50,56
1967	Dallas	Wash., 27-20	75,53
1968	Wash.	Dallas, 44-24	50,81
1968	Dallas	Dallas, 29-20	66,07
1969	Wash.	Dallas, 41-28	50,47
1969	Dallas	Dallas, 20-10	56,92
1970	Wash.	Dallas, 45-21	50,41
1970	Dallas	Dallas, 34-0	57,93
1971	Dallas	Wash., 20-16	72,00
1971	Wash.	Dallas, 13-0	53,04
1972	Wash.	Wash., 24-20	53,03
1972	Dallas	Dallas, 34-24	65,13
1972*	Wash.	Wash., 26-3	53,12
1973	Wash.	Wash., 14-7	54,31
1973	Dallas	Dallas, 27-7	64,45
1974	Wash.	Wash., 28-21	54,39
1974	Dallas	Dallas, 24-23	63,24
1975	Wash.	Wash., 30-24 (OT)	55,00
1975	Dallas	Dallas, 31-10	61,09
1976	Wash.	Dallas, 20-7	55,00
1976	Dallas	Wash., 27-14	59,91
1977	Dallas	Dallas, 34-16	62,11
1977	Wash.	Dallas, 14-7	55,03
1978	Wash.	Wash., 9-5	55,03
1978	Dallas	Dallas, 37-10	64,90
1979	Wash.	Wash., 34-20	55,03
1979	Dallas	Dallas, 35-34	62,86
1980	Wash.	Dallas, 17-3	55,04
1980	Dallas	Dallas, 14-10	58,80
1981	Wash.	Dallas, 26-10	55,04
1981	Dallas	Dallas, 24-10	64,58

1982 Oct. 10 at Dallas
1982 Dec. 5 at Washington
*NFC Championship Game

1981 Season at a Glance

COWBOYS 26, REDSKINS 10
at Washington, September 6

DALLAS	0	14	6	6	— 26
WASHINGTON	0	7	3	0	— 10

COWBOYS — DuPree 33 pass from D. White (Septien Kick)
REDSKINS — Washington 15 pass from Theisman (Moseley Kick)
COWBOYS — Pearson 42 pass from White (Septien Kick)
COWBOYS — F.G. Septien 29
REDSKINS — F.G. Moseley 42
COWBOYS — F.G. Septien 42
COWBOYS — F.G. Septien 23
COWBOYS — F.G. Septien 18
Attendance — 55,045

	COWBOYS	REDSKINS
First Downs	20	20
Total Net Yards	346	324
Net Yards Rushing	206	44
Net Yards Passing	140	280
Passes	12-24	23-49
Passes Intercepted By	4	0
Punts — Average	6-44.1	5-41
Fumbles — Lost	2-1	5-2
Penalties — Yards	10-87	7-89

COWBOYS 30, CARDINALS 17
at Dallas, September 13

ST. LOUIS	7	7	0	3	— 17
DALLAS	14	13	3	0	— 30

COWBOYS — Springs 1 run (Septien Kick)
CARDINALS — Harrell 62 pass from Lomax (O'Donoghue Kick)
COWBOYS — Springs 4 run (Septien Kick)
COWBOYS — F.G. Septien 47
COWBOYS — Springs 1 run (Septien Kick)
CARDINALS — Brown 11 run (O'Donoghue Kick)
COWBOYS — F.G. Septien 32
COWBOYS — F.G. Septien 25
CARDINALS — F.G. O'Donoghue 24
Attendance — 63,602

	CARDINALS	COWBOYS
First Downs	18	24
Total Net Yards	404	391
Net Yards Rushing	142	181
Net Yards Passing	262	210
Passes	14-41-2	21-29-1
Passes Intercepted By	1	2
Punts — Average	4-36.0	4-43.2
Fumbles — Lost	0-0	2-1
Penalties — Yards	11-84	6-35

COWBOYS 35, PATRIOTS 21
at New England, September 21

DALLAS	7	10	7	11	— 35
NEW ENGLAND...	7	7	7	0	— 21

COWBOYS — Johnson 28 pass from White (Septien Kick)
PATRIOTS — Calhoun 4 run (Smith Kick)
COWBOYS — F.G. Septien 26
COWBOYS — Dorsett 75 run (Septien Kick)
PATRIOTS — Collins 3 run (Smith Kick)
PATRIOTS — Tatupu 38 run (Smith Kick)
COWBOYS — DuPree 1 pass from White (Septien Kick)
COWBOYS — F.G. Septien 36
COWBOYS — Safety — Intentional Grounding in E.Z.
COWBOYS — F.G. Septien 27
COWBOYS — F.G. Septien 25
Attendance — 60,311

	COWBOYS	PATRIOTS
First Downs	22	16
Total Net Yards	455	333
Net Yards Rushing	237	108
Net Yards Passing	218	225
Passes	24-34	14-27
Passes Intercepted By	4	0
Punts — Average	4-36.3	2-34.0
Fumbles — Lost	4-1	3-3
Penalties — Yards	7-75	5-38

COWBOYS 18, GIANTS 10
at Dallas, September 27

NEW YORK	0	3	0	7	— 10
DALLAS...........	3	7	0	8	— 18

COWBOYS — F.G. Septien 36
GIANTS — F.G. Danelo 42
COWBOYS — Johnson 41 pass from White (Septien Kick)
COWBOYS — F.G. Septien 20
COWBOYS — Giants covered own fumble in E.Z.
COWBOYS — F.G. Septien 21
GIANTS — Perkins 20 pass from Simms (Danelo Kick)
Attendance — 63,449

	GIANTS	COWBOYS
First Downs	16	16
Total Net Yards	343	317
Net Yards Rushing	85	124
Net Yards Passing	258	193
Passes	18-35	14-27
Passes Intercepted By	0	3
Punts — Average	5-45.4	7-43.2
Fumbles — Lost	3-0	1-0
Penalties — Yards	7-52	3-25

CARDINALS 20, COWBOYS 17
at St. Louis, October 4

DALLAS	7	3	7	0	— 17
ST. LOUIS	10	0	7	3	— 20

CARDINALS — Morris 9 run (O'Donoghue Kick)
COWBOYS — Dorsett 7 run (Septien Kick)
CARDINALS — F.G. O'Donoghue 19
COWBOYS — F.G. Septien 26
CARDINALS — R. Green 30 pass from Hart (O'Donoghue Kick)
COWBOYS — Dorsett 11 pass from White (Septien Kick)
CARDINALS — F.G. O'Donoghue 37
Attendance — 49,777

	COWBOYS	CARDINALS
First Downs	17	18
Total Net Yards	306	299
Net Yards Rushing	140	115
Net Yards Passing	166	184
Passes	15-28	16-29
Passes Intercepted By	1	1
Punts — Average	7-37.7	6-45.2
Fumbles — Lost	3-1	3-2
Penalties — Yards	5-45	5-41

49ers 45, COWBOYS 14
at San Francisco, October 11

DALLAS	0	7	0	7	— 14
SAN FRANCISCO	21	3	14	7	— 45

49ers — Solomon 1 pass from Montana (Wersching Kick)
49ers — Hofer 4 run (Wersching Kick)
49ers — Davis 1 run (Wersching Kick)
49ers — F.G. Wersching 18
COWBOYS — Hill 22 pass from Pearson (Septien Kick)
49ers — Clark 78 pass from Montana (Wersching Kick)
49ers — Lott 41 INT Return (Wersching Kick)
49ers — Lawrence 1 run (Wersching Kick)
COWBOYS — Barnes 72 Fumble Return (Septien Kick)
Attendance — 57,574

	COWBOYS	49ers
First Downs	10	23
Total Net Yards	192	440
Net Yards Rushing	83	150
Net Yards Passing	109	290
Passes	12-29	20-33
Passes Intercepted By	0	2
Punts — Average	8-39.5	6-46.2
Fumbles — Lost	3-2	4-1
Penalties — Yards	5-40	4-28

COWBOYS 29, RAMS 17
at Dallas, October 18

LOS ANGELES	0	10	7	0	— 17
DALLAS	12	14	0	3	— 29

COWBOYS — Springs 1 run (Septien Kick)
COWBOYS — F.G. Septien 40
COWBOYS — Safety (Martin tackle Haden in E.Z.)
COWBOYS — Dorsett 44 run (Septien Kick)
RAMS — Tyler 2 run (Corral Kick)
RAMS — F.G. Corral 40
COWBOYS — Hill 63 pass from White (Septien Kick)
RAMS — Hill 43 pass from Haden (Corral Kick)
COWBOYS — F.G. Septien 39
Attendance — 64,649

	RAMS	COWBOYS
First Downs	22	24
Total Net Yards	374	496
Net Yards Rushing	171	221
Net Yards Passing	203	275
Passes	13-30	15-33
Passes Intercepted By	2	3
Punts — Average	5-48.0	5-42.6
Fumbles — Lost	1-0	2-1
Penalties — Yards	10-78	15-108

COWBOYS 28, DOLPHINS 27
at Dallas, October 25

MIAMI	0	6	7	14	— 27
DALLAS	7	7	0	14	— 28

COWBOYS — Springs 5 run (Septien Kick)
DOLPHINS — Nathan 5 pass from Woodley (Kick failed)
COWBOYS — Johnson 21 pass from White (Septien Kick)
DOLPHINS — Cefelo 69 pass from Woodley (Von Schamman Kick)
DOLPHINS — Nathan 10 run (Von Schamman Kick)
DOLPHINS — Rose 4 pass from Woodley (Von Schamman Kick)
COWBOYS — Cosbie 5 pass from White (Septien Kick)
COWBOYS — Springs 32 pass from White (Septien Kick)
Attendance — 64,221

	DOLPHINS	COWBOYS
First Downs	25	23
Total Net Yards	540	466
Net Yards Rushing	148	139
Net Yards Passing	392	327
Passes	21-37	22-32
Passes Intercepted By	1	5
Punts — Average	5-41.6	6-36.3
Fumbles — Lost	3-0	2-1
Penalties — Yards	2-11	3-20

GO
80
THE
KiAUNE'S
Billy

COWBOYS 17, EAGLES 14
at Philadelphia, November 1

DALLAS	0	3	0	14	— 17
PHILADELPHIA	0	7	7	0	— 14

COWBOYS — F.G. Septien 31
EAGLES — Montgomery 2 run (Franklin Kick)
EAGLES — Carmichael 85 pass from Jaworski (Franklin Kick)
COWBOYS — Cosbie 17 pass from White (Septien Kick)
COWBOYS — Dorsett 9 run (Septien Kick)
Attendance — 72,111

	COWBOYS	EAGLES
First Downs	19	17
Total Net Yards	317	291
Net Yards Rushing	141	94
Net Yards Passing	176	197
Passes	13-24	12-27
Passes Intercepted By	1	2
Punts — Average	4-45.0	5-40.8
Fumbles — Lost	4-1	1-0
Penalties — Yards	4-42	10-76

COWBOYS 27, BILLS 14
at Dallas, November 9

BUFFALO	7	7	0	0	— 14
DALLAS	7	0	20	0	— 27

BILLS — Butler 16 pass from Ferguson (Mike-Mayer Kick)
COWBOYS — Cosbie 12 pass from White (Septien Kick)
BILLS — Brown 9 pass from Cribbs (Mike-Mayer Kick)
COWBOYS — Dorsett 73 pass from White (Septien Kick)
COWBOYS — Hill 37 pass from White (Septien Kick)
COWBOYS — F.G. Septien 47
COWBOYS — F.G. Septien 31
Attendance — 62,583

	BILLS	COWBOYS
First Downs	18	21
Total Net Yards	365	398
Net Yards Rushing	58	196
Net Yards Passing	307	202
Passes	20-43	9-17
Passes Intercepted By	1	4
Punts — Average	7-35.1	4-43.2
Fumbles — Lost	3-1	3-2
Penalties — Yards	10-89	7-50

LIONS 27, COWBOYS 24
at Detroit, November 15

DALLAS	7	10	0	7	— 24
DETROIT	0	7	10	10	— 27

COWBOYS — Pearson 10 pass from White (Septien Kick)
COWBOYS — F.G. Septien 43
COWBOYS — Pearson 12 pass from White (Septien Kick)
LIONS — Sims 3 run (Murray Kick)
LIONS — Nichols 6 pass from Hipple (Murray Kick)
LIONS — F.G. Murray 37
COWBOYS — Saldi 14 pass from White (Septien Kick)
LIONS — Sims 81 pass from Hipple (Murray Kick)
LIONS — F.G. Murray 47
Attendance — 79,694

	COWBOYS	LIONS
First Downs	19	23
Total Net Yards	323	429
Net Yards Rushing	98	198
Net Yards Passing	225	231
Passes	20-30	14-24
Passes Intercepted By	1	2
Punts — Average	5-43	4-41.3
Fumbles — Lost	1-0	3-2
Penalties — Yards	3-20	6-51

COWBOYS 24, REDSKINS 10
at Dallas, November 22

WASHINGTON	0	7	3	0	— 10
DALLAS	7	3	7	7	— 24

COWBOYS — Johnson 28 pass from White (Septien Kick)
COWBOYS — F.G. Septien 25
REDSKINS — Giaquinto 7 pass from Theismann (Moseley Kick)
REDSKINS — F.G. Moseley 26
COWBOYS — Cosbie 10 pass from White (Septien Kick)
COWBOYS — Springs 1 run (Septien Kick)
Attendance — 64,583

	REDSKINS	COWBOYS
First Downs	17	27
Total Net Yards	256	470
Net Yards Rushing	125	258
Net Yards Passing	131	212
Passes	14-34	13-27
Passes Intercepted By	0	1
Punts — Average	5-41.4	3-39.0
Fumbles — Lost	2-0	3-2
Penalties — Yards	3-22	12-94

26

COWBOYS 10, BEARS 9
at Dallas, November 26

CHICAGO	0	3	0	6	— 9
DALLAS	3	0	0	7	— 10

COWBOYS — F.G. Septien 41
BEARS — F.G. Roveto 43
BEARS — Evans 2 run (Kick Blocked)
COWBOYS — Springs 6 run (Septien Kick)
Attendance — 63,499

	BEARS	COWBOYS
First Downs	15	11
Total Net Yards	272	273
Net Yards Rushing	229	95
Net Yards Passing	43	178
Passes	6-19	9-23
Passes Intercepted By	1	1
Punts — Average	7-37.7	6-44.0
Fumbles — Lost	4-2	3-2
Penalties — Yards	5-29	4-45

COWBOYS 37, COLTS 13
at Baltimore, December 6

DALLAS	17	10	0	10	— 37
BALTIMORE	6	0	7	0	— 13

COWBOYS — Springs 1 run (Septien Kick)
COWBOYS — F.G. Septien 42
COWBOYS — Springs 2 run (Septien Kick)
COLTS — Dickey 67 run (Kick Failed)
COWBOYS — Springs 2 pass from Carano (Septien Kick)
COWBOYS — F.G. Septien 35
COLTS — Dickey 20 run (Wood Kick)
COWBOYS — F.G. Septien 31
COWBOYS — J. Jones 59 run (Septien Kick)
Attendance — 54,871

	COWBOYS	COLTS
First Downs	29	9
Total Net Yards	464	238
Net Yards Rushing	354	156
Net Yards Passing	110	82
Passes	8-19	7-24
Passes Intercepted By	2	1
Punts — Average	2-30.0	7-39.1
Fumbles — Lost	3-1	2-1
Penalties — Yards	6-33	11-87

COWBOYS 21, EAGLES 10
at Dallas, December 13

PHILADELPHIA	3	7	0	0	— 10
DALLAS	0	7	7	7	— 21

EAGLES — F.G. Franklin 50
EAGLES — Russell 1 run (Franklin Kick)
COWBOYS — Hill 8 pass from White (Septien Kick)
COWBOYS — Johnson 36 pass from White (Septien Kick)
COWBOYS — Springs 12 run (Septien Kick)
Attendance — 64,955

	EAGLES	COWBOYS
First Downs	14	23
Total Net Yards	225	412
Net Yards Rushing	90	148
Net Yards Passing	135	264
Passes	11-32	17-30
Passes Intercepted By	0	4
Punts — Average	2-44.5	3-36.0
Fumbles — Lost	2-1	4-2
Penalties — Yards	3-20	5-50

GIANTS 13, COWBOYS 10
at New York, December 19

					OT	
DALLAS	0	0	0	10	0	— 10
NEW YORK	0	0	7	3	3	— 13

GIANTS — Mullady 20 pass from Brunner (Danelo Kick)
COWBOYS — Cosbie 3 pass from White (Septien Kick)
COWBOYS — F.G. Septien 36
GIANTS — F.G. Danelo 40
GIANTS — F.G. Danelo 35 (O.T.)
Attendance — 73,009

	COWBOYS	GIANTS
First Downs	16	15
Total Net Yards	254	297
Net Yards Rushing	90	139
Net Yards Passing	164	158
Passes	17-33	13-27
Passes Intercepted By	1	1
Punts — Average	7-39.7	5-40.0
Fumbles — Lost	5-2	4-1
Penalties — Yards	8-70	5-42

Divisional Playoff

DALLAS, Jan. 2 — Led by their best defensive showing of the season, the NFC East champion Cowboys advanced to their ninth NFC Championship Game in 12 years by blanking NFC Central champ Tampa Bay 38-0 at Texas Stadium.

The margin of victory tied an NFC Divisional playoff record set by the Cowboys in their 52-14 win over Cleveland in 1967. It was Dallas' first shutout victory since a 28-0 rout of Los Angeles for the 1978 NFC title.

The Cowboys' defense dominated the contest, sacking Bucs' quarterback Doug Williams four times and intercepting four of his passes, two by Dennis Thurman.

Tony Dorsett rushed for 86 yards on 16 carries and caught four passes for 48 yards. Danny White completed 15-of-26 passes for 143 yards, including a nine-yard touchdown pass to Tony Hill in the first quarter.

Dallas led 10-0 at the half, then broke open the game with three touchdowns in the third quarter on a one-yard run by Ron Springs and five-yard runs by Tony Dorsett and James Jones.

The Cowboys outgained Tampa Bay 345 yards to 222 and ran 73 plays to the Bucs' 55. The victory ran the Cowboys' Texas Stadium winning streak to 18.

COWBOYS 38, BUCCANEERS 0
at Dallas, January 2

TAMPA BAY	0	0	0	0	— 0
DALLAS	0	10	21	7	— 38

COWBOYS — Hill 9 pass from White (Septien Kick)
COWBOYS — F.G. Septien 32
COWBOYS — Springs 1 run (Septien Kick)
COWBOYS — Dorsett 5 run (Septien Kick)
COWBOYS — J. Jones 5 run (Septien Kick)
COWBOYS — Newsome 1 run (Septien Kick)
Attendance — 64,848

	BUCCANEERS	COWBOYS
First Downs	12	26
Total Net Yards	222	345
Net Yards Rushing	74	212
Net Yards Passing	148	133
Passes	10-29	15-26
Passes Intercepted By	0	4
Punts — Average	5-38.4	4-30.0
Fumbles — Lost	2-0	0-0
Penalties — Yards	10-105	5-40

Rushing

Buccaneers — Owens, 12 for 40; Wilder, 4 for 23; Williams, 2 for 9; Eckwood, 4 for 2.

Cowboys — Dorsett, 16 for 86, 1 touchdown; Springs, 15 for 70, 1 touchdown; J. Jones, 9 for 32, 1 touchdown; Newhouse, 4 for 23; Newsome, 1 for 1, 1 touchdown; Cosbie, 1 for 0.

Passing

Buccaneers — Williams, 10 of 29 for 187 yards, 4 interceptions.

Cowboys — White, 15 of 26 for 143 yards, 1 touchdown.

Receiving

Buccaneers — T. Bell, 3 for 36; Owens, 3 for 32; Giles, 2 for 98; Wilder, 1 for 11; House, 1 for 10.

Cowboys — Dorsett, 4 for 48; DuPree, 3 for 22; Pearson, 2 for 21; Hill, 2 for 18; J. Jones, 2 for 15; Donley, 1 for 14; Cosbie, 1 for 5.

N.F.C. Championship

SAN FRANCISCO, Jan. 10 — For the second year in a row the Cowboys saw their quest for a record sixth Super Bowl berth stopped one victory shy of the goal. And this time the ending was especially frustrating, San Francisco capturing the conference title with a touchdown in the last minute of play.

The Cowboys had taken a 27-21 lead with 10:41 remaining on Danny White's 21-yard scoring pass to Doug Cosbie. Following Everson Walls' second interception and a 26-yard drive, White's punt pinned the 49ers to their 11-yard-line with 4:54 left.

But quarterback Joe Montana continued the unlikely story of the 1981 49ers by driving his team 89 yards in 13 plays to take the lead. The touchdown came on third down from the Dallas six, Montana rolling to his right and lofting a pass in the back of the end zone for a leaping Dwight Clark with 51 seconds to go.

With their final opportunity, the Cowboys moved to the 49ers' 44 on White's 31-yard pass to Drew Pearson. But on the next play White's fumble caused by Lawrence Pillers was recovered by Jim Stuckey, ending Dallas' comeback bid.

49ers 28, COWBOYS 27
at San Francisco, January 10

DALLAS	10	7	0	10	— 27
SAN FRANCISCO	7	7	7	7	— 28

49ers — Solomon 8 pass from Montana (Wersching Kick)
COWBOYS — F.G. Septien 44
COWBOYS — Hill 26 pass from White (Septien Kick)
49ers — Clark 20 pass from Montana (Wersching Kick)
COWBOYS — Dorsett 5 run (Septien Kick)
49ers — Davis 2 run (Wersching Kick)
COWBOYS — F.G. Septien 22
COWBOYS — Cosbie 21 pass from White (Septien Kick)
49ers — Clark 6 pass from Montana (Wersching Kick)
Attendance — 60,525

	COWBOYS	49ers
First Downs	16	26
Total Net Yards	250	393
Net Yards Rushing	115	127
Net Yards Passing	135	266
Passes	16-24	22-35
Passes Intercepted By	3	1
Punts — Average	6-39.3	3-35.7
Fumbles — Lost	4-2	3-3
Penalties — Yards	5-39	7-106

Rushing

Cowboys — Dorsett, 22 for 91, 1 touchdown; J. Jones, 4 for 14; Springs, 5 for 10; White, 1 for 0.

49ers — Elliott, 10 for 48; Cooper, 8 for 35; Ring, 6 for 27; Solomon, 1 for 14; Easley, 2 for 6; Davis, 1 for 2; Montana, 3 for -5.

Passing

Cowboys — White, 16 of 24 for 173 yards, 2 touchdowns, 1 interception.

49ers — Montana, 22 of 35 for 286 yards, 3 touchdowns, 3 interceptions.

Receiving

Cowboys — J. Jones, 3 for 17; DuPree, 3 for 15; Springs, 3 for 13; Hill, 2 for 43, 1 touchdown; Pearson, 1 for 31; Cosbie, 1 for 21, 1 touchdown; Johnson, 1 for 20; Saldi, 1 for 9; Donley, 1 for 4.

49ers — Clark, 8 for 120, 2 touchdowns; Solomon, 6 for 75, 1 touchdown; Young, 4 for 45; Cooper, 2 for 11; Elliott, 1 for 24; Shumann, 1 for 11.

Cowboys Final Official 1981 Statistics

RESULTS AND ATTENDANCE				(12-4)	
(W)	26	@ Washington	55,045	10	(SO)
(W)	30	ST. LOUIS	63,602	17	(SO)
(W)	35	@ New England	60,311	21	(SO)
(W)	18	N.Y. GIANTS	63,449	10	(SO)
(L)	17	@ St. Louis	49,777	20	(SO)
(L)	14	@ S.F. 49ers	57,574	45	(SO)
(W)	29	L.A. RAMS	64,649	17	(SO)
(W)	28	MIAMI	64,221	27	(SO)
(W)	17	@ Philadelphia	72,111	14	(SO)
(W)	27	BUFFALO BILLS	62,583	14	(SO)
(L)	24	@ Detroit	79,694	27	(SO)
(W)	24	WASHINGTON	64,583	10	(SO)
(W)	10	CHICAGO	63,499	9	(SO)
(W)	37	@ Baltimore	54,871	13	(SO)
(W)	21	PHILADELPHIA	64,955	10	(SO)
(L)	10	@ N.Y. Giants	73,009	13	(SO)

TEAM STATISTICS	DALLAS	OPP.
TOTAL FIRST DOWNS	321	286
Rushing	137	107
Passing	158	160
Penalty	26	18
Third Down-Made/Att.	99/244	72/211
Third Down Efficiency	40.6	34.1
TOTAL NET YARDS	5880	5419
Avg. Per Game	367.5	338.7
Total Plays	1100	1021
Avg. Per Play	5.3	5.3
NET YARDS RUSHING	2711	2049
Avg. Per Game	169.4	128.0
Total Rushes	630	468
Avg. Per Rush	4.3	4.4
NET YARDS PASSING	3169	3370
Avg. Per Game	198.1	210.6
Tackled/Yards Lost	31/245	42/347
Gross Yards	3414	3717
Attempts/Completions	439/241	511/236
Pct. of Completions	54.9	46.2
Had Intercepted	15	37
PUNTS/AVERAGE	83/40.3	80/41.1
Net Punting Average	37.5	36.4
PUNT RET./AVG.	45/5.2	38/6.1
KICKOFF RET./AVG.	54/18.2	71/21.2
INTERCEPTIONS/AVG. RET.	37/13.0	15/8.3
PENALTIES/YARDS	103/839	104/837
FUMBLES/BALL LOST	45/20	43/16
TOUCHDOWNS	40	34
Rushing	15	16
Passing	24	17
Returns	1	1
EXTRA POINTS/ATTEMPTS	40/40	31/34
FIELD GOAL ATTEMPTS	27/35	14/29
TOTAL POINTS	367	277
TIME OF POSSESSION	8:37:29	7:29:24

SCORING	TDR	TDP	TDRt	FG	PAT	TP
Septien	0	0	0	27/35	40/40	121
Springs	10	2	0	0	0	72
Dorsett	4	2	0	0	0	36
Johnson	0	5	0	0	0	30
Cosbie	0	5	0	0	0	30
Hill	0	4	0	0	0	24
Pearson	0	3	0	0	0	18
DuPree	0	2	0	0	0	12
Saldi	0	1	0	0	0	6
Barnes	0	0	1	0	0	6
J. Jones	1	0	0	0	0	6
Team	0	0	0	0	0	6
COWBOY TOTAL	15	24	1	27/35	40/40	367
Opponents	16	17	1	14/29	31/34	276

RUSHING	ATT	YDS	AVG	LG	TD
Dorsett	342	1646	4.8	75T	4
Springs	172	625	3.6	16	10
J. Jones	34	183	5.3	59T	1
D. White	38	104	2.7	17	0
Newhouse	14	33	2.3	6	0
Cosbie	4	33	8.3	15	0
Pearson	3	31	10.3	25	0
DuPree	1	12	12.0	12	0
Newsome	13	38	2.9	7	0
Carano	8	9	1.1	0	0
Hill	1	3	3.0	3	0
COWBOY TOTAL	630	2711	4.3	75T	15
Opponents	468	2049	4.4	38T	16

RECEIVING	NO	YDS	AVG	LG	TD
Hill	46	953	20.7	63T	4
Springs	46	359	7.8	32T	2
Pearson	38	614	16.2	42T	3
Dorsett	32	325	10.2	73T	2
Johnson	25	552	22.1	55	5
DuPree	19	214	11.3	33T	2
Cosbie	17	225	13.2	28T	5
Saldi	8	82	10.2	14T	1
J. Jones	6	37	6.2	16	0
Donley	3	32	10.7	17	0
Newhouse	1	21	21.0	21	0
COWBOY TOTAL	241	3414	14.2	73T	24
Opponents	236	3717	15.8	81T	17

INTERCEPTIONS	NO	YDS	AVG	LG	TD
Walls	11	133	12.1	33	0
Thurman	9	187	20.8	96	0
Downs	7	81	11.6	21	0
Waters	3	21	7.0	21	0
Breunig	2	8	4.0	8	0
Brown	1	28	28.0	28	0
Lewis	1	0	0	0	0
Wilson	2	0	0	0	0
Barnes	1	24	24.0	24	0
COWBOY TOTAL	37	482	13.0	96	0
Opponents	15	124	8.3	41	0

PUNTING	NO	YDS	AVG	TB	In20	LG
D. White	81	3284	40.8	7	19	60
Septien	2	62	31.0	0	0	33
COWBOY TOTAL	83	3346	40.3	7	19	60
Opponents	80	3289	41.1	7	17	57

KICKOFF RETURNS	NO	YDS	AVG	LG	TD
J. Jones	27	517	19.1	33	0
Newsome	12	228	19.0	27	0
Fellows	8	170	21.3	31	0
Newhouse	3	34	10.4	12	0
Wilson	2	32	16.0	17	0
Cosbie	1	0	0	0	0
COWBOY TOTAL	54	981	18.2	33	0
Opponents	71	1508	21.2	65	0

PUNT RETURNS	NO	FC	YDS	AVG	LG	TD
J. Jones	33	2	188	5.7	17	0
Fellows	11	1	44	4.4	10	0
Donley	1	0	3	3.0	3	0
Thurman	0	1	0	0	0	0
Wilson	0	1	0	0	0	0
COWBOY TOTAL	45	5	235	5.2	17	0
Opponents	38	8	231	6.1	21	0

SCORE BY QUARTERS	1	2	3	4	OT	TP
COWBOYS	91	108	57	111	0	367
Opponents	61	81	79	53	3	277

FIELD GOALS	1-19	20-29	30-39	40-49	50+
COWBOYS	1-1	11-11	8-9	7-12	0-2
Opponents	2-2	2-5	3-6	7-14	1-2

Septien: (29, 42, 23, 18); (47, 32, 25); (26, 40M, 26, 26, 25); (36, 20, 21); (26); (NA); (40, 39); (48M); (39); (47, 31); (43); (25, 35M); (41, 50M, 42M); (42, 35, 31), (47M, 43M); (60M, 36)

PASSING	ATT	COMP	YDS	PCT	AATT	TD	PTD	INT	PINT	LG	LOST/ATT	RATING
D. White	391	223	3098	57.0	7.92	22	5.6	13	3.3	73T	30/234	87.5
Carano	45	16	235	35.5	5.22	1	2.2	1	2.2	21	1/10	51.6
Pearson	2	2	81	100	40.5	1	.5	0	0	59	—	121.0
Springs	1	-0-	-0-	-0-	-0-	-0-	-0-	1	-0-	-0-	-0-	-0-
COWBOY TOTAL	439	241	3414	54.9	7.78	24	5.5	15	3.4	73T	31/245	84.4
Opponents	511	236	3717	46.2	7.27	17	3.3	37	7.2	81T	42/347	51.9

1981 Cowboys Defensive Statistics

Sixteen Games
Tackles (Primary-Assists — Combined)

1. **Breunig**	63-51 — 114	11. **Hegman**	30-19 — 49
2. **Downs**	72-38 — 110	12. **Dickerson**	31- 8 — 39
3. **R. White**	61-33 — 94	13. **Brown**	20-18 — 38
4. **Walls**	65-18 — 83	14. **Barnes**	23-11 — 34
5. **E. Jones**	58-25 — 83	15. **Wilson**	19- 6 — 25
6. **Dutton**	44-37 — 81	16. **Bethea**	6- 2 — 8
7. **Waters**	52-28 — 80	17. **Fellows**	6- 1 — 7
8. **Thurman**	58-18 — 76	18. **King**	2- 2 — 4
9. **Lewis**	38-29 — 67	19. **Spradlin**	2- 0 — 2
10. **Martin**	31-19 — 50	20. **Thornton**	2- 0 — 2

QB Traps (42) — Martin 10, R. White 8½, E. Jones 8, Dutton 4½, Dickerson 4, Waters 3, Bethea 2, Barnes, Lewis.

Interceptions (37) — Walls 11, Thurman 9, Downs 7, Waters 3, Wilson 2, Breunig 2, Brown, Lewis, Barnes.

Passes Defensed (132) — Walls 37, Thurman 19, Downs 11, Wilson 10, E. Jones 10, Waters 9, Barnes 6, Breunig 6, Dutton 5, Dickerson 4, Lewis 4, Brown 3, Martin 3, R. White 2, Fellows 2, King.

Opp. Fumbles Recovered (17) — E. Jones 3, Dickerson 3, Barnes 2, Saldi, Thurman, Wilson, King, Titensor, Springs, Downs, Walls, Martin.

Forced Fumbles (21) — Martin 4, Lewis 3, Breunig 2, Barnes, E. Jones, Wilson, Brown, Dutton, Dickerson, Hegman, Spradlin, Newhouse, Petersen, Waters, R. White.

Cowboys All-Time Leaders

RUSHING

Player	Att.	Yds.	Avg.	Long	TD
1. Dorsett, Tony (1977-81)	1,368	6,270	4.6	84	40
2. Perkins, Don (1961-68)	1,500	6,217	4.1	59	42
3. Hill, Calvin (1969-74)	1,166	5,009	4.3	55	39
4. Newhouse, Robert (1972-81)	1,165	4,671	4.0	54	30
5. Garrison, Walt (1966-74)	899	3,886	4.3	41	30
6. Staubach, Roger (1969-79)	410	2,264	5.5	33	20
7. Marsh, Amos (1961-64)	427	2,065	4.8	71	14
8. Reeves, Dan (1965-72)	535	1,990	3.7	67	25
9. Thomas, Duane (1970-71)	326	1,596	4.9	56	16

PASSING

Player	Att.	Comp.	Pct.	Yds.	TD	Int.	Rating
1. Staubach, R. (1969-79)	2,958	1,685	57.0	22,700	153	109	83.5
2. White, Danny (1976-81)	930	539	58.0	7,112	53	44	81.5
3. Morton, C. (1965-74)	1,308	685	52.4	10,279	80	73	75.5
4. Meredith, D. (1960-68)	2,308	1,170	50.7	17,199	135	111	74.7
5. LeBaron, E. (1960-63)	692	359	51.9	5,331	45	52	67.8

RECEIVING

Player	No.	Yds.	Avg.	Long	TD
1. Pearson, Drew (1973-81)	416	6,895	16.6	67	40
2. Hayes, Bob (1965-74)	365	7,295	20.0	95	71
3. Clarke, Frank (1960-67)	281	5,214	18.6	80	50
4. DuPree, Billy Joe (1973-81)	248	3,382	13.6	42	38
5. Hill, Tony (1977-81)	214	3,914	18.3	75	28
6. Pearson, Preston (1975-80)	189	2,274	12.0	49	11
7. Rentzel, Lance (1967-70)	183	3,521	19.2	86	31
8. Garrison, Walt (1966-74)	182	1,794	9.9	53	9
9. Dorsett, Tony (1977-81)	177	1,614	9.1	91	6
10. Howton, Billy (1960-63)	161	2,368	14.7	69	17

PUNTING

Player	No.	Avg.	Long	Blk
1. Baker, Sam (1962-63)	128	45.1	72	
2. Sherer, Dave (1960)	57	42.5	67	
3. Widby, Ron (1968-71)	247	41.8	84	
4. White, Danny (1976-81)	454	40.3	73	
4. Villanueva, Danny (1965-67)	192	40.3	58	
4. Lothridge, Billy (1964)	62	40.3	75	
7. Carrell, Duane (1974)	40	39,8	59	
8. Hoopes, Mitch (1975)	68	39.4	55	
9. Bateman, Marv (1972-74)	139	39.3	62	
10. Green, Allen (1961)	61	36.7	53	

INTERCEPTIONS

Player	No.	Yds.	Avg.	Long	TD
1. Renfro, Mel (1964-77)	52	626	12.0	90	
2. Waters, Charlie (1970-78, 1980)	41	584	14.2	56	
3. Green, Cornell (1962-74)	34	552	16.2	59	
4. Jordan, Lee Roy (1963-76)	32	472	14.8	49	
5. Harris, Cliff (1970-79)	29	281	9.7	60	
6. Howley, Chuck (1961-73)	24	395	16.5	58	
7. Bishop, Don (1960-65)	22	364	16.5	57	
8. Gaechter, Mike (1962-69)	21	420	20.0	100	
9. Thurman, Dennis (1978-81)	17	336	19.8	96	
10. Tubbs, Jerry (1960-67)	15	176	11.7	44	

PUNT RETURNS (Min. 40 Returns)

Player	No.	Yds.	Avg.	Long	TD
1. Hayes, Bob (1965-74)	104	1,158	11.1	90	
2. Johnson, Butch (1976-81)	146	1,313	9.0	55	
3. Jones, James (1980-81)	87	736	8.5	52	
4. Richards, Golden (1973-78)	62	501	8.1	46	
5. Renfro, Mel (1964-77)	109	842	7.7	69	

KICKOFF RETURNS (Min. 40 Returns)

Player	No.	Yds.	Avg.	Long	TD
1. Renfro, Mel (1964-77)	85	2,246	26.4	100	
2. Harris, Cliff (1970-79)	63	1,622	25.7	77	
3. Marsh, Amos (1961-64)	65	1,561	24.0	101	
4. Johnson, Butch (1976-81)	79	1,832	23.2	74	
5. Jones, James (1980-81)	59	1,237	21.0	41	

SCORING

Player	TD	PAT	FG	Total
1. Hayes, Bob (1964-74)	76	—	—	45
2. Septien, Rafael (1978-81)	—	185	73	40
3. Clark, Mike (1968-71, 1973)	—	180	69	38
4. Fritsch, Toni (1971-73, 1975)	—	119	66	31
5. Clarke, Frank (1960-67)	51	—	—	30
6. Dorsett, Tony (1977-81)	47	—	—	28
7. Perkins, Don (1961-68)	45	—	—	27
8. Hill, Calvin (1969-74)	45	—	—	27
9. Villanueva, Danny (1965-67)	—	134	42	26
10. Reeves, Dan (1965-72)	42	1 (run)	—	25

FIELD GOALS

Player	Att.	Made	Pct.	Long
1. Septien, Rafael (1978-81)	107	73	.682	5
2. Clark, Mike (1968-71, 1973)	119	69	.580	5
3. Fritsch, Toni (1971-73, 75)	107	66	.617	5
4. Herrera, Efren (1974, 1976-77)	65	44	.677	5
5. Villanueva, Danny (1965-67)	81	42	.519	4
6. Baker, Sam (1962-63)	47	23	.489	5
7. Van Raaphorst, Dick (1964)	29	14	.483	4
8. Cone, Fred (1960)	13	6	.462	4
9. Bielski, Dick (1961)	9	6	.667	4
10. Percival, Mac (1974)	8	2	.250	3

12

11

Cowboys Leaders By Years

RUSHING

Year	Player	Att.	Yds.	Avg.	Long	TD	NFL/ NFC Rank
1960	Dupre, L. G.	104	362	3.5	18	3	20
1961	*Perkins, Don	200	815	4.1	47	4	6
1962	Perkins, Don	222	945	4.3	35	7	5
1963	Perkins, Don	149	614	4.1	19	7	10
1964	Perkins, Don	174	768	4.4	59	6	5
1965	Perkins, Don	177	690	3.9	43	0	7
1966	Reeves, Dan	175	757	4.3	67	8	6
1967	Perkins, Don	201	823	4.1	30	6	6
1968	Perkins, Don	191	836	4.4	28	4	6
1969	*Hill, Calvin	204	942	4.6	55	8	2
1970	*Thomas, Duane	151	803	5.3	47	5	8/5
1971	Thomas, Duane	175	793	4.5	56	11	11/7
1972	Hill, Calvin	245	1,036	4.2	26	6	7/3
1973	Hill, Calvin	273	1,142	4.2	21	6	3/2
1974	Hill, Calvin	185	844	4.6	27	7	8/3
1975	Newhouse, Robert	209	930	4.4	29	2	9/4
1976	Dennison, Doug	153	542	3.5	14	6	35/18
1977	*Dorsett, Tony	208	1,007	4.8	84	12	9/4
1978	Dorsett, Tony	290	1,325	4.6	63	7	3/2
1979	Dorsett, Tony	250	1,107	4.4	41	6	11/8
1980	Dorsett, Tony	278	1,185	4.3	56	11	6/6
1981	Dorsett, Tony	342	1,646	4.8	75	4	2/2

PASSING

Year	Player	Att.	Comp.	Pct.	Yds.	TD	Int.	Rating	NFL/ NFC Rank
1960	LeBaron, E.	225	111	49.3	1,736	12	25	53.4	8
1961	LeBaron, E.	236	120	50.8	1,741	14	16	66.5	9
1962	LeBaron, E.	166	95	57.2	1,436	16	9	95.3	3
1963	Meredith, D.	310	167	53.9	2,381	17	18	73.2	10
1964	Meredith, D.	323	158	48.9	2,143	9	16	67.3	15
1965	Meredith, D.	305	141	46.2	2,415	22	13	79.7	8
1966	Meredith, D.	344	177	51.5	2,805	24	12	87.7	4
1967	Meredith, D.	255	128	50.2	1,834	16	16	68.6	8
1968	Meredith, D.	309	171	55.3	2,500	21	12	88.3	2
1969	Morton, C.	302	162	53.6	2,619	21	15	85.4	5
1970	Morton, C.	207	102	49.3	1,819	15	7	89.7	5/4
1971	Staubach, R.	211	126	59.7	1,882	15	4	104.8	1/1
1972	Morton, C.	339	185	54.6	2,396	15	21	65.9	15/7
1973	Staubach, R.	286	179	62.6	2,428	23	15	94.6	1/1
1974	Staubach, R.	360	190	52.8	2,552	11	15	68.5	14/7
1975	Staubach, R.	348	198	56.9	2,666	17	16	78.6	8/2
1976	Staubach, R.	369	208	56.4	2,715	14	11	79.9	8/5
1977	Staubach, R.	361	210	58.2	2,620	18	9	87.1	2/1
1978	Staubach, R.	413	231	55.9	3,190	25	16	84.9	1/1
1979	Staubach, R.	461	267	57.9	3,586	27	11	92.4	1/1
1980	White, D.	436	260	59.6	3,287	28	25	80.8	9/7
1981	White, D.	391	223	57.0	3,098	22	13	87.5	5/2

RECEIVING

Year	Player	No.	Yds.	Avg.	Long	TD	NFL/ NFC Rank
1960	Doran, Jim	31	554	17.9	15	3	21
1961	Howton, Billy	56	785	14.0	53	4	6
1962	Howton, Billy	49	706	14.4	69	6	15
1963	Clarke, Frank	43	833	19.4	75	10	3
1964	Clarke, Frank	65	973	15.0	49	5	3
1965	*Hayes, Bob	46	1,003	21.8	82	12	13
1966	Hayes, Bob	64	1,232	19.3	95	13	4
1967	Rentzel, Lance	58	996	17.2	74	8	6
1968	Rentzel, Lance	54	1,009	18.7	65	6	3
1969	Rentzel, Lance	43	960	22.3	75	12	20
1970	Hayes, Bob	34	889	26.1	89	10	45/26
1971	Garrison, Walt	40	396	9.9	36	1	23/10
1972	Hill, Calvin	43	364	8 5	33	3	18/9
1973	Hill, Calvin	32	290	9.1	29	0	36/21
1974	Pearson, Drew	62	1,087	17.9	50	2	3/2
1975	Pearson, Drew	46	822	17.9	46	8	16/9
1976	Pearson, Drew	58	806	13.9	40	6	4/1
1977	Pearson, Drew	48	870	18.1	67	2	9/3
1978	Pearson, Preston	47	256	11.2	34	0	26/15
1979	Hill, Tony	60	1,062	17.7	75t	10	12/6
1980	Hill, Tony	60	1,055	17.6	58t	8	16/9
1981	Hill, Tony	46	953	20.7	63	4	47/26
	Springs, Ron	46	359	7.8	32	2	47/26

PUNTING

Year	Player	No.	Avg.	Long	Had Blocked	NFL/ NFC Rank
1960	Sherer, Dave	57	42.5	67	1	7
1961	*Green, Allen	61	36.7	53	1	14
1962	Baker, Sam	57	45.4	72	0	3
1963	Baker, Sam	71	44.2	64	0	7
1964	*Lothridge, Billy	62	40.3	75	1	15
1965	Villanueva, Danny	60	41.8	58	0	10
1966	Villanueva, Danny	65	39.2	58	1	13
1967	Villanueva, Danny	67	40.4	57	0	9
1968	Widby, Ron	59	40.9	84	0	5
1969	Widby, Ron	63	43.3	62	0	2
1970	Widby, Ron	69	41.3	59	1	10/2
1971	Widby, Ron	56	41.6	59	1	8/3
1972	*Bateman, Marv	51	38.2	61	0	24/13
1973	Bateman, Marv	55	41.6	62	2	11/7
1974	*Carrell, Duane	40	39.8	59	0	11/5
1975	*Hoopes, Mitch	68	39.4	55	1	16/9
1976	*White, Danny	70	38.4	54	2	20/9
1977	White, Danny	80	39.6	57	1	12/8
1978	White, Danny	76	40.5	56	1	8/5
1979	White, Danny	76	41.7	73	0	4/2
1980	White, Danny	71	40.9	58	0	10/5
1981	White, Danny	81	40.8	60	0	14/8

SCORING

Year	Player	TD	PAT	FG	Tot.	NFL/ NFC Rank
1960	Cone, Fred	0	21	6	39	27
1961	Clarke, Frank	9	0	0	54	22
1962	Baker, Sam	0	50	14	92	6
1963	Baker, Sam	0	38	9	65	14
1964	*VanRaaphorst, Dick	0	28	14	70	13
1965	Villanueva, Danny	0	37	16	85	10
1966	Villanueva, Danny	0	56	17	107	2
1967	Hayes, Bob	11	0	0	66	T16
	Reeves, Dan	11	0	0	66	T16
1968	Clark, Mike	0	54	17	105	2
1969	Clark, Mike	0	43	20	103	2
1970	Clark, Mike	0	35	18	89	12/8
1971	Clark, Mike	0	47	13	86	13/7
1972	Fritsch, Toni	0	36	21	99	7/3
1973	Fritsch, Toni	0	43	18	97	11/7
1974	*Herrera, Efren	0	33	8	57	26/9
1975	Fritsch, Toni	0	38	22	104	3/2
1976	Herrera, Efren	0	34	18	88	6/4
1977	Herrera, Efren	0	39	18	93	3/2
1978	Septien, Rafael	0	46	16	94	5/2
1979	Septien, Rafael	0	40	19	97	8/3
1980	Septien, Rafael	0	59	11	92	13/6
1981	Septien, Rafael	0	40	27	122	1/1

KICKOFF RETURNS

Year	Player	No.	Yds.	Avg.	Long	TD	NFL/ NFC Rank
1960	Franckhauser, Tom	26	526	20.2	46	0	19
1961	*Marsh, Amos	26	667	25.7	79	0	13
1962	Marsh, Amos	29	725	25.0	101	1	10
1963	*Stiger, Jim	18	432	24.0	66	0	12
1964	*Renfro, Mel	40	1,017	25.4	65	0	7
1965	Renfro, Mel	21	630	30.0	100	1	4
1966	Renfro, Mel	9	487	25.6	87	1	9
1967	Garrison, Walt	20	366	18.3	36	0	23
1968	Baynham, Craig	23	590	25.7	40	0	7
1969	*Flowers, Richmond	11	283	25.7	30	0	29
1970	*Thomas, Duane	19	416	21.9	33	0	23/10
1971	Harris, Cliff	29	823	28.4	77	0	4/4
1972	Harris, Cliff	26	615	23.7	44	0	23/11
1973	**Montgomery, Mike	6	175	29.2	63	0	DNQ
1974	*Morgan, Dennis	35	823	23.5	43	0	21/11
1975	Pearson, Preston	16	391	24.4	42	0	13/7
1976	*Johnson, Butch	28	693	24.8	74	0	11/5
1977	Johnson, Butch	22	536	24.4	64	0	9/5
1978	Johnson, Butch	29	603	20.8	56	0	27/12
1979	*Springs, Ron	38	780	20.5	70	0	25/12
1980	*Jones, James	32	720	22.5	41	0	11/6
1981	Jones, James	27	517	19.1	33	0	36/17

FIELD GOALS

Year	Player	Att.	Made	Pct.	Long	NFL/ NFC Rank
1960	Cone, Fred	13	6	.462	45	
1961	Bielski, Dick	9	6	.667	42	
1962	Baker, Sam	27	14	.519	53	
1963	Baker, Sam	20	9	.450	53	
1964	*VanRaaphorst, Dick	9	14	.483	43	
1965	Villanueva, Danny	27	16	.593	41	
1966	Villanueva, Danny	31	17	.548	37	
1967	Villanueva, Danny	23	9	.391	34	
1968	Clark, Mike	29	17	.586	50	
1969	Clark, Mike	36	20	.555	47	
1970	Clark, Mike	27	18	.667	43	
1971	Clark, Mike	25	13	.520	48	1
1972	Fritsch, Toni	36	21	.583	54	1
1973	Fritsch, Toni	28	18	.643	37	1
1974	*Herrera, Efren	13	8	.615	39	1
1975	Fritsch, Toni	35	22	.629	43	1
1976	Herrera, Efren	23	18	.783	46	
1977	Herrera, Efren	29	18	.621	52	1
1978	Septien, Rafael	26	16	.615	48	1
1979	Septien, Rafael	29	19	.655	51	
1980	Septien, Rafael	17	11	.647	52	1
1981	Septien, Rafael	35	27	.771	47	

PUNT RETURNS

Year	Player	No.	Yds.	Avg.	Long	TD	NFL/ NFC Rank
1960	Butler, Bill	13	131	10.1	46	0	
1961	*Marsh, Amos	14	71	5.1	19	0	
1962	Lockett, J. W.	8	45	5.6	17	0	
1963	*Stiger, Jim	14	141	10.1	45	0	
1964	*Renfro, Mel	32	418	13.1	69	1	
1965	Renfro, Mel	24	145	6.0	35	0	
1966	Hayes, Bob	17	106	6.2	18	0	
1967	Hayes, Bob	24	276	11.5	69	1	
1968	Hayes, Bob	15	312	20.8	90	2	
1969	Hayes, Bob	18	179	9.9	50	0	
1970	Hayes, Bob	15	116	7.7	34	0	2
1971	Harris, Cliff	17	129	7.6	35	0	1
1972	Harris, Cliff	19	78	4.1	21	0	21
1973	*Richards, Golden	21	139	6.6	46	0	23
1974	*Morgan, Dennis	19	287	15.1	98	1	
1975	Richards, Golden	28	288	10.3	43	1	1
1976	*Johnson, Butch	45	489	10.9	55	0	
1977	Johnson, Butch	50	423	8.5	38	0	2
1978	Johnson, Butch	51	401	7.9	23	0	1
1979	*Wilson, Steve	35	236	6.8	13	0	2
1980	*Jones, James	54	548	10.1	52	0	
1981	Jones, James	33	188	5.7	17	0	28

INTERCEPTIONS

Year	Player	No.	Yds.	Avg.	Long	TD	NFL/ NFC Rank
1960	Bishop, Don	3	13	4.3	13	0	
	Franckhauser, Tom	3	11	3.7	9	0	
1961	Bishop, Don	8	172	21.5	57	0	
1962	Bishop, Don	6	134	22.3	44	0	
1963	Green, Cornell	7	211	30.1	55	0	
1964	*Renfro, Mel	7	110	15.7	39	1	
1965	Green, Cornell	3	49	16.3	43	0	
	Livingston, Warren	3	5	1.7	5	0	
	*Logan, Obert	3	5	1.7	3	0	
1966	Green, Cornell	4	88	22.0	41	1	
1967	Green, Cornell	7	52	7.4	28	0	
	Renfro, Mel	7	38	5.4	30	0	
1968	Howley, Chuck	6	115	19.2	58	1	
1969	Renfro, Mel	10	118	11.8	41	0	
1970	*Waters, Charlie	5	45	9.0	20	0	1
1971	Adderley, Herb	6	182	30.3	46	0	
1972	Waters, Charlie	6	132	22.0	56	1	
1973	Jordan, Lee Roy	6	78	13.0	31	1	
1974	Harris, Cliff	3	8	2.7	8	0	42
1975	Jordan, Lee Roy	6	80	13.3	38	0	
1976	Washington, Mark	4	49	12.3	22	0	24
1977	Harris, Cliff	5	7	1.4	7	0	1
1978	Barnes, Benny	5	72	14.4	38	0	25
1979	Hughes, Randy	2	91	45.5	68	0	93
	Harris, Cliff	2	35	17.5	20	0	
	Barnes, Benny	2	20	10.0	11	0	
	Lewis, D. D.	2	8	4.0	5	0	
	Kyle, Aaron	2	0	0.0	0	0	
1980	Thurman, Dennis	5	114	22.8	78t	1	24
	Waters, Charlie	5	78	15.6	29	0	24
1981	*Walls, Everson	11	133	12.1	33	0	

*Rookie
**Did Not Qualify (Minimum 14 returns required.)

Cowboys Team Records

1960: 12 games
1961-77: 14 games
1978-81: 16 games

MOST POINTS SCORED
Season
454 1980
445 1966**
Game
59 9/15/68 vs. Detroit
59 10/12/80 vs. San Francisco
FEWEST POINTS SCORED
Season
177 1960
236 1961**
371 1979*
Game
0 11/16/70 vs. St. Louis
OPPONENT/MOST POINTS SCORED
Season
402 1962
Game
54 10/18/70 @ Minnesota
OPPONENT/FEWEST POINTS SCORED
Season
186 1968
208 1978*
Game
0 9 times, last 9/4/78 vs. Baltimore
MOST POINTS, BOTH TEAMS
Game
86 9/19/71 @ Buffalo
(Dallas 49, Buffalo 37)
77 12/12/77 @ San Fran.,
(Dallas 42, San Fran. 35)

FEWEST POINTS, BOTH TEAMS
Game
8 12/12/70 @ Cleveland,
(Dallas 6, Cleveland 2)
MOST DECISIVE WIN
Game
49 10/9/66 vs. Philadelphia,
(Dallas 56, Philadelphia 7)
46 9/15/68 vs. Detroit,
(Dallas 59, Detroit 13)
45 9/18/66 vs. N.Y. Giants,
(Dallas 52, Giants 7)
45 10/12/80 vs. San Fran.,
(Dallas 59, San Fran. 14)
MOST DECISIVE LOSS
Game
41 10/16/60 vs. Cleveland,
(Cleveland 48, Dallas 7)
41 10/18/70 @ Minnesota,
(Minnesota 54, Dallas 13)
MOST TOUCHDOWNS SCORED
Season
60 1980
56 1966**
Game
8 10/9/66 vs. Philadelphia
8 9/15/68 vs. Detroit
8 10/12/80 vs. San Francisco
FEWEST TOUCHDOWNS SCORED
Season
23 1960
29 1961**

OPPONENT/MOST TDS SCORED
Season
52 1962
Game
7 12/9/62 @ St. Louis
OPPONENT/FEWEST TDS SCORED
Season
22 1973
MOST TOUCHDOWNS BY:
RUSHING
Season
26 1980
25 1971**
Game
5 9/19/71 @ Buffalo
PASSING
Season
31 1962
Game
5 5 times, last 12/20/70 vs. Houston

INTERCEPTIONS
Season
3 1966, 67, 68, 75
Game
1 24 times, last 11/23/80 vs. Washington
KO RETURNS
Season
2 1971
PUNT RETURNS
Season
2 1968
FEWEST TOUCHDOWNS BY:
RUSHING
Season
6 1961
6 1962**
PASSING
10 1964
OPPONENT/MOST TOUCHDOWNS BY:
RUSHING
Season
24 1960
Game
5 4 times, last 10/10/65 vs. Philadelphia
PASSING
Season
33 1962
Game
5 10/30/60 vs. Baltimore
5 11/2/69 @ Cleveland
INTERCEPTIONS
Season
6 1961
KO RETURN
3 1966
PUNT RETURNS
Game
1 6 times, last 10/23/77 @ Philadelphia
BLOCKED PUNT

OPPONENT/FEWEST TDS BY:
RUSHING
Season
2 1968
3 1969
13 1978*
PASSING
Season
10 1970
11 1978*
MOST PATS SCORED
Season
59 1980
56 1966**
Game
8 9/15/68 vs. Detroit
8 10/12/80 vs. San Fran.

OPPONENT/MOST PATS SCORED
Season
49 1962
Game
7 12/9/62 @ St. Louis
MOST FGS SCORED
Season
27 1981
22 1975
19 1978*
Game
4 11/24/66 vs. Cleveland
4 11/12/72 vs. St. Louis
4 9/21/75 vs. Los Angeles
4 9/6/81 vs. Washington
4 9/21/81 vs. New England
SCORE BY QUARTERS
1st QUARTER
28 10/19/69 vs. Philadelphia
28 12/4/71 vs. N.Y. Jets
2nd QUARTER
24 9/18/66 vs. N.Y. Giants
24 10/30/66 vs. Pittsburgh
24 9/15/68 vs. Detroit
24 10/24/71 vs. New England
24 10/12/80 vs. San Francisco
3rd QUARTER
21 10/30/66 vs. Pittsburgh
21 9/24/73 vs. New Orleans
21 12/7/74 vs. Cleveland
21 9/28/75 vs. St. Louis
21 10/26/80 vs. San Diego
4th QUARTER
21 12/19/65 @ N.Y. Giants
21 9/15/68 vs. Detroit
21 10/6/75 @ Detroit
21 10/21/73 vs. N.Y. Giants
21 11/27/80 vs. Seattle
SCORE BY HALVES
1st HALF
42 10/19/69 vs. Philadelphia
2nd HALF
31 9/29/68 @ Philadelphia
31 11/17/68 @ Washington
OPPONENT/SCORE BY QUARTERS
1st QUARTER
21 12/3/60 vs. Cleveland
21 10/11/81 @ San Francisco
2nd QUARTER
28 12/16/62 @ N.Y. Giants
3rd QUARTER
21 12/17/61 @ Washington

4th QUARTER
21 12/9/62 @ St. Louis
21 11/28/65 @ Washington
21 11/16/70 vs. St. Louis
21 11/5/72 @ San Diego
OPPONENT/SCORE BY HALVES
1st HALF
35 12/16/62 @ N.Y. Giants
2nd HALF
38 12/9/62 @ St. Louis
SCORE BY QUARTERS, BOTH TEAMS
1st QUARTER
35 10/19/69 vs. Philadelphia
2nd QUARTER
38 11/10/75 vs. Kansas City
3rd QUARTER
35 9/28/75 vs. St. Louis
4th QUARTERS
35 10/21/73 vs. N.Y. Giants
SCORE BY HALVES, BOTH TEAMS
1st HALF
59 12/16/62 @ N.Y. Giants
2nd HALF
52 9/28/75 vs. St. Louis

FIRST DOWNS

MOST FIRST DOWNS
Season
342 1978
297 1968**
Game
32 10/9/66 vs. Philadelphia
32 9/10/78 @ N.Y. Giants
32 11/12/78 @ Green Bay
FEWEST FIRST DOWNS
Season
180 1960
211 1965**
337 1980*
Game
8 10/16/60 vs. Cleveland
8 11/12/61 @ Pittsburgh
8 12/10/61 @ St. Louis
8 11/29/64 vs. Green Bay
8 11/1/70 vs. Philadelphia
OPPONENT/MOST FIRST DOWNS
Season
296 1980
274 1962**
Game
29 10/22/67 @ Pittsburgh
OPPONENT/FEWEST FIRST DOWNS
Season
199 1974
Game
5 11/6/66 @ Philadelphia
5 10/20/74 vs. Philadelphia
MOST FIRST DOWNS, BOTH TEAMS
633 1980
522 1975**
Game
55 10/1/67 vs. Los Angeles
MOST FIRST DOWNS BY:
RUSHING
Season
147 1974
Game
19 12/6/81 vs. Baltimore
17 11/12/78 @ Green Bay
17 11/22/81 vs. Washington
PASSING
Season
195 1979
144 1971**
Game
23 11/10/63 vs. San Francisco
PENALTY
Season
29 1978
24 1966**
Game
5 12/11/60 vs. Detroit
5 12/10/67 vs. Philadelphia
5 11/3/74 vs. St. Louis
5 10/18/81 vs. Los Angeles
FEWEST FIRST DOWNS BY:
RUSHING
Season
57 1960
87 1965**
Game
0 11/16/70 vs. St. Louis
PASSING
Season
95 1970
Game
3 8 times, last 9/23/74 @ Philadelphia
PENALTY
Season
9 1961
9 1962**
9 1971**

*16-game record;
**14-game record

OPPONENT/MOST FIRST DOWNS BY:
RUSHING
Season
122 1961
Game
15 12/3/61 vs. Cleveland
15 9/23/62 vs. Pittsburgh
PASSING
Season
166 1962
Game
21 11/18/62 vs. Chicago
PENALTY
Season
28 1980
27 1967*
Game
5 11/21/65 vs. Cleveland
5 12/7/74 vs. Cleveland
OPPONENT/FEWEST FIRST DOWNS BY:
RUSHING
Season
52 1969
83 1978**
PASSING
Season
94 1977
128 1978*
PENALTY
Season
10 1969
18 1981*

TOTAL YARDS

MOST NET YARDS GAINED
Season
5,968 1979
5,145 1966**
Game
652 10/6/66 vs. Philadelphia
583 9/4/78 vs. Baltimore
578 9/30/73 vs. St. Louis
FEWEST NET YARDS GAINED
3,153 1960
3,704 1964**
5,468 1980*
Game
126 12/10/61 @ St. Louis
OPPONENT/MOST NET YARDS GAINED
Season
5,419 1981
5,325 1963**
Game
529 10/25/81 vs. Miami
527 12/9/62 @ St. Louis
517 12/15/80 @ Los Angeles
OPPONENT/FEWEST NET YDS. GAINED
Season
3,213 1977
4,009 1978*
Game
63 10/24/65 @ Green Bay
80 12/10/67 vs. Philadelphia
MOST NET YARDS, BOTH TEAMS
Season
11,299 1981
10,096 1962**
Game
995 10/25/81 vs. Miami
926 11/10/63 @ San Francisco
874 10/26/80 vs. San Diego

RUSHING

MOST YARDS RUSHING
Season
2,783 1978
2,458 1974**
Game
354 12/6/81 @ Baltimore
FEWEST YARDS RUSHING
Season
1,049 1960
1,608 1965**
Game
41 11/7/65 vs. San Francisco
OPPONENT/MOST YARDS RUSHING
Season
2,242 1960
2,115 1979*
Game
289 10/22/61 vs. Philadelphia

OPPONENT/FEWEST YARDS RUSHING
Season
1,050 1969
1,721 1978*
Game
7 10/30/66 vs. Pittsburgh
MOST YARDS RUSHING, BOTH TEAMS
Season
4,760 1981
4,131 1975**

Game
510 12/6/81 @ Baltimore
466 10/22/61 vs. Philadelphia
450 10/15/61 vs. N.Y. Giants

MOST ATTEMPTS RUSHING
Season
630 1981
571 1975**
Game
59 10/12/80 vs. San Francisco
FEWEST RUSHING ATTEMPTS
Season
311 1960
416 1961**
578 1979*
Game
16 11/7/65 vs. San Francisco
OPPONENT/MOST ATMPTS. RUSHING
Game
54 10/11/70 vs. Atlanta

PASSING

MOST NET YARDS PASSING
Season
3,176 1978
3,026 1968**
Game
440 10/9/66 vs. Philadelphia
FEWEST NET YARDS PASSING
Season
2,013 1964
3,104 1980*
Game
-10 10/24/65 @ Green Bay
OPPONENT/MOST NET YDS. PASSING
Season
3,674 1964
3,370 1981*
Game
437 11/18/62 vs. Chicago
OPPONENT/FEWEST NET YDS. PASS.
Season
1,562 1977
2,288 1980*
Game
-1 10/24/65 @ Green Bay
-1 12/12/75 @ N.Y. Jets
MOST GROSS YARDS PASSING
Season
3,883 1979
3,331 1966**
Game
460 11/10/63 @ San Francisco
FEWEST GROSS YARDS PASSING
Season
2,388 1960
2,445 1970**
3,356 1980*
Game
42 10/24/65 @ Green Bay
OPPONENT/MOST GROSS YDS. PASS.
Season
3,904 1962
3,717 1981*
Game
466 11/18/62 vs. Chicago

OPPONENT/FEWEST GROSS YDS. PASS.
Season
1,991 1977
2,730 1978*
Game
-15 12/21/75 @ N.Y. Jets
MOST PASS ATTEMPTS
Season
503 1979
442 1961**
Game
50 10/26/75 @ Philadelphia
FEWEST PASS ATTEMPTS
Season
297 1970
439 1981*
Game
11 10/21/73 vs. N.Y. Giants
11 10/11/70 vs. Atlanta
OPPONENT/MOST PASS ATTEMPTS
Season
511 1981
482 1967**
Game
49 9/6/81 @ Washington
47 11/18/62 vs. Chicago
OPPONENT/FEWEST PASS ATTEMPTS
Season
293 1960
326 1961**
432 1978*
Game
10 10/3/71 vs. Washington
10 11/22/73 vs. Miami
MOST PASS COMPLETIONS
Season
251 1978
222 1976**
Game
27 10/31/71 @ Chicago
FEWEST PASS COMPLETIONS
Season
149 1970
251 1978*
Game
4 10/11/70 vs. Atlanta

OPPONENT/MOST PASS COMPLETIONS
Season
260 1967
236 1981*
Game
28 11/18/62 vs. Chicago
OPPONENT/FEWEST PASS COMPLNS.
Season
146 1960
154 1977**
202 1978*
Game
2 12/21/75 @ N.Y. Jets
DEFENSE, MOST QB SACKS
Season
60 1966
58 1978*
Game
11 10/6/75 @ Detroit
10 10/27/69 vs. N.Y. Giants

OPPONENT/DFNS., MOST QB SACKS
Season
68 1964
Game
9 10/24/65 @ Green Bay

INTERCEPTIONS

MOST PASSES INTERCEPTED
Season
37 1981
29 1967**
Game
7 9/30/60 vs. Philadelphia
7 9/26/71 @ Philadelphia
FEWEST PASSES INTERCEPTED
Season
13 1974, 79
OPPONENT/MOST PASSES INTER.
Season
33 1960
Game
5 11/5/61 vs. St. Louis
5 11/9/80 @ N.Y. Giants
OPPONENT/FEWEST PASSES INTER.
Season
10 1977
13 1979*

PENALTIES

MOST PENALTIES
Season
107 1980
106 1977**
Game
15 10/18/81 vs. Los Angeles
14 11/6/77 @ N.Y. Giants
14 9/9/79 @ San Francisco
FEWEST PENALTIES
Season
47 1961
96 1978**
Game
0 12/10/61 @ St. Louis
0 11/23/80 vs. Washington
OPPONENT/MOST PENALTIES
Season
106 1980
78 1977**
Game
11 11/1/64 @ Chicago
11 10/9/77 @ St. Louis
11 11/23/78 vs. Washington
11 9/13/81 vs. St. Louis
11 12/6/81 @ Baltimore
OPPONENT/FEWEST PENALTIES
Season
38 1961
70 1979*
Game
0 10/21/62 @ Pittsburgh
0 12/5/65 @ Philadelphia
MOST YARDS PENALIZED
Season
952 1964, 71
Game
161 11/2/70 @ Washington
159 10/13/68 vs. Philadelphia

FEWEST YARDS PENALIZED
Season
427 1961
704 1978*
Game
0 12/5/65 @ Philadelphia
0 10/21/62 @ Pittsburgh
OPPONENT/MOST YARDS PENALIZED
Season
989 1980
1974**
Game
166 10/9/77 @ St. Louis
149 11/6/60 vs. Los Angeles
BOTH TEAMS, FEWEST YDS. PENAL.
Season
789 1961
Game
10 12/10/61 @ St. Louis

PUNTING

MOST PUNTS
Season
83 1977
83 1981*
Game
10 11/15/76 vs. Buffalo
10 10/13/63 vs. Detroit
OPPONENT/MOST PUNTS
Season
108 1978
103 1977**
Game
11 9/30/62 @ Los Angeles
11 9/15/74 @ Atlanta
11 11/15/76 vs. Buffalo
HIGHEST AVERAGE
Season
45.4 1962
Game
53.4 11/3/68 vs. New Orleans (4)
OPPONENT/HIGHEST AVERAGE
Season
45.5 1961
Game
54.3 10/17/65 @ Cleveland (6)

PUNT RETURNS

MOST PUNT RETURNS
63 1978
62 1974**
Game
9 11/15/76 vs. Buffalo
MOST PUNT RETURN YARDS
Season
573 1974
556 1980*
Game
122 12/8/68 vs. Pittsburgh
OPPONENT/MOST PUNT RETURNS
Season
43 1970
40 1978*
Game
7 10/13/63 vs. Detroit
7 12/13/75 vs. Washington
OPPONENT/MOST PUNT RETURN YDS.
Season
343 1974
311 1978*
Game
109 11/16/70 vs. St. Louis

KICKOFF RETURN

MOST KICKOFF RETURNS
Season
68 1979
66 1960***
Game
9 10/18/70 @ Minnesota
MOST KICKOFF RETURN YARDS
Season
1,376 1971
1,322 1979*
Game
260 11/7/65 vs. San Francisco
OPPONENT/MOST KICKOFF RETURNS
Season
78 1966
73 1978, 80*
Game
10 9/15/68 vs. Detroit
OPPONENT/MOST KICKOFF RET. YDS.
Season
1,709 1978
1,699 1966**
Game
261 11/6/66 @ Philadelphia

FUMBLES

MOST FUMBLES
Season
46 1961
45 1981*
Game
7 10/11/71 vs. N.Y. Giants
MOST FUMBLES LOST
Season
21 1961, 71, 79
Game
5 11/13/68 @ New Orleans
5 10/11/71 vs. N.Y. Giants
5 11/10/75 vs. Kansas City
OPPONENT/MOST FUMBLES
Season
44 1973
43 1981*
Game
7 11/28/65 @ Washington
7 11/10/75 vs. Kansas City
OPPONENT/MOST FUMBLES LOST
Season
25 1971
20 1980*
Game
5 10/11/71 vs. N.Y. Giants
5 9/16/73 @ Chicago
5 10/12/80 vs. San Francisco

Cowboys Team Playoff Records

SCORING

MOST POINTS SCORED
52 12/24/67 vs. Cleveland, (Dallas 52, Cleveland 14)
FEWEST POINTS SCORED
3 12/31/72 @ Washington, (Washington 26, Dallas 3)
OPPONENT/MOST POINTS SCORED
38 12/28/69 vs. Cleveland, (Cleveland 38, Dallas 14)
OPPONENT/FEWEST POINTS SCORED
0 12/26/70 vs. Detroit, (Dallas 5, Detroit 0)
0 1/7/79 @ Los Angeles, (Dallas 28, Los Angeles 0)
0 1/2/82 vs. Tampa Bay (Dallas 38, Tampa Bay 0)
MOST DECISIVE WIN
38 1/2/82 vs. Tampa Bay (Dallas 38, Tampa Bay 0)
38 12/24/67 vs. Cleveland, (Dallas 52, Cleveland 14)
MOST DECISIVE LOSS
24 12/28/69 vs. Cleveland, (Cleveland 38, Dallas 14)
MOST POINTS COMBINED
66 12/24/67 vs. Cleveland, (Dallas 52, Cleveland 14)
66 1/21/79 vs. Pittsburgh, (Pittsburgh 35, Dallas 31)

FIRST DOWNS

MOST FIRST DOWNS
29 12/28/80 vs. Los Angeles
FEWEST FIRST DOWNS
8 12/31/72 @ Washington
OPPONENT/MOST FIRST DOWNS
26 1/10/82 @ San Francisco
22 12/28/69 vs. Cleveland
OPPONENT/FEWEST FIRST DOWNS
7 12/26/70 vs. Detroit
MOST FIRST DOWNS BY:
Rushing
19 12/28/80 vs. Los Angeles
Passing
16 1/4/81 @ Atlanta
Penalty
2 8 times, last 1/10/82 @ San Francisco
FEWEST FIRST DOWNS BY:
Rushing
3 4 times, last 12/30/73 vs. Minnesota
Passing
3 12/26/70 vs. Detroit
3 12/31/72 @ Washington
OPPONENT/MOST FIRST DOWNS BY:
Rushing
14 12/30/73 vs. Minnesota
Passing
17 12/28/69 vs. Cleveland
17 1/10/82 @ San Francisco
Penalty
4 1/17/71 vs. Baltimore
OPPONENT/FEWEST FIRST DOWNS BY:
Rushing
1 1/4/76 @ Los Angeles
Passing
1 1/15/78 vs. Denver

TOTAL YARDS

MOST NET YARDS GAINED
528 12/28/80 vs. Los Angeles
FEWEST NET YARDS GAINED
153 12/30/73 vs. Minnesota
OPPONENT/MOST NET YARDS GAINED
393 1/10/82 @ San Francisco
367 1/1/67 vs. Green Bay
OPPONENT/FEWEST NET YARDS GAINED
118 1/4/76 @ Los Angeles

RUSHING

MOST YARDS RUSHING
345 1/2/82 vs. Tampa Bay
338 12/28/80 vs. Los Angeles
FEWEST YARDS RUSHING
85 12/19/76 vs. Los Angeles
OPPONENT/MOST YARDS RUSHING
263 1/11/81 @ Philadelphia
OPPONENT/FEWEST YARDS RUSHING
22 1/4/76 vs. Los Angeles

PASSING

MOST NET YARDS PASSING
310 1/4/81 @ Atlanta
FEWEST NET YARDS PASSING
22 12/26/70 vs. Detroit
OPPONENT/MOST NET YARDS PASSING
291 1/21/79 vs. Pittsburgh
OPPONENT/FEWEST NET YARDS PASSING
35 12/30/78 vs. Atlanta
MOST GROSS YARDS PASSING
322 1/15/78 vs. Denver
FEWEST GROSS YARDS PASSING
38 12/26/70 vs. Detroit
OPPONENT/MOST GROSS YARDS PASSING
320 1/4/81 @ Atlanta
OPPONENT/FEWEST GROSS YARDS PASSING
61 1/15/78 vs. Denver
MOST PASS ATTEMPTS
41 12/23/72 @ San Francisco
FEWEST PASS ATTEMPTS
14 12/25/71 @ Minnesota
14 12/24/77 vs. Chicago
OPPONENT/MOST PASS ATTEMPTS
40 1/3/71 vs. San Francisco
OPPONENT/FEWEST PASS ATTEMPTS
18 12/31/72 @ Washington
MOST PASS COMPLETIONS
25 1/4/81 @ Atlanta
FEWEST PASS COMPLETIONS
4 12/26/70 vs. Detroit
OPPONENT/MOST COMPLETIONS
22 1/10/82 @ San Francisco
20 12/28/69 vs. Cleveland
OPPONENT/FEWEST PASS COMPLETIONS
7 12/26/70 vs. Detroit
7 12/23/73 vs. Los Angeles
DEFENSE, MOST QB SACKS
8 12/31/67 @ Green Bay, (76 yards)
OPPONENT/DFNS., MOST QB SACKS
7 12/23/73 vs. Los Angeles
7 (1/18/76 vs. Pitt.) 52 yds.

INTERCEPTIONS

MOST PASSES INTERCEPTED BY COWBOYS
5 1/7/79 @ Los Angeles
OPPONENT/MOST PASSES INTERCEPTED BY
4 12/21/68 @ Cleveland
4 12/30/73 vs. Minnesota

PENALTIES

MOST PENALTIES
12 1/15/78 vs. Denver
FEWEST PENALTIES
2 7 times, last 1/18/76 vs. Pittsburgh
OPPONENT/MOST PENALTIES
10 1/2/82 vs. Tampa Bay
8 1/19/76 @ Los Angeles
8 1/15/78 vs. Denver
OPPONENT/FEWEST PENALTIES
0 3 times, last 1/18/76 vs. Pittsburgh
MOST YARDS PENALIZED
133 1/17/71 vs. Baltimore
FEWEST YARDS PENALIZED
10 12/24/67 vs. Cleveland
10 12/25/71 @ Minnesota
OPPONENT/MOST YARDS PENALIZED
94 1/19/76 @ Los Angeles

PUNTING

MOST PUNTS
9 1/17/71 vs. Baltimore
FEWEST PUNTS
2 12/24/67 vs. Cleveland
2 12/28/80 vs. Los Angeles
OPPONENT/MOST PUNTS
8 3 times, last 1/1/78 vs. Minnesota
OPPONENT/FEWEST PUNTS
1 12/28/69 vs. Cleveland
HIGHEST COWBOYS AVERAGE
46.7 12/23/73 vs. Los Angeles
HIGHEST OPPONENT AVERAGE
48.8 12/26/70 vs. Detroit

PUNT RETURNS

MOST PUNT RETURNS
5 1/1/78 vs. Minnesota
5 12/28/80 vs. Los Angeles
MOST PUNT RETURN YARDS
155 12/24/67 vs. Cleveland
OPPONENT/MOST PUNT RETURNS
6 12/26/70 vs. Detroit
6 1/11/81 @ Philadelphia
OPPONENT/MOST PUNT RETURN YARDS
69 1/11/81 @ Philadelphia

KICKOFF RETURNS

MOST KICKOFF RETURNS
6 3 times, last 1/4/81 @ Atlanta
MOST KICKOFF RETURN YARDS
153 1/1/67 vs. Green Bay
OPPONENT/MOST KICKOFF RETURNS
8 1/4/76 @ Los Angeles
8 12/26/77 vs. Chicago
OPPONENT/MOST KICKOFF RETURN YARDS
188 12/25/71 @ Minnesota

FUMBLES

MOST FUMBLES
6 12/30/78 vs. Atlanta
6 1/15/78 vs. Denver
MOST FUMBLES LOST
3 12/23/72 @ San Francisco
3 12/28/78 vs. Atlanta
OPPONENT/MOST FUMBLES
5 1/17/71 vs. Baltimore
5 12/23/72 @ San Francisco
5 1/1/78 @ Minnesota
OPPONENT/MOST FUMBLES LOST
4 1/17/71 @ Baltimore
4 1/15/78 vs. Denver
3 1/10/82 @ San Francisco

Cowboys Individual Playoff Records

TOTAL POINTS
18 Craig Baynham (12/24/67 vs. Cleveland), 3 TDs
18 Preston Pearson (1/4/76 @ Los Angeles), 3 TDs
13 Toni Fritsch (1/4/76 @ Los Angeles) (kicker)
13 Efren Herrera (12/26/77 vs. Chicago) (kicker)
TOUCHDOWNS
3 Craig Baynham (12/24/67 vs. Cleveland), 2 runs,
3 1 pass
Preston Pearson (1/4/76 @ Los Angeles), 3 pass
FIELD GOALS MADE
3 Toni Fritsch (12/23/72 @ San Francisco)
3 Toni Fritsch (1/4/76 @ Los Angeles)
3 Efren Herrera (12/26/77 vs. Chicago)
LONGEST FIELD GOAL
48 Rafael Septien 12/30/78 vs. Atlanta)
FIELD GOALS ATTEMPTED
5 Efren Herrera (1/15/78 vs. Denver), 2 FG
EXTRA POINTS ATTEMPTED — MADE
7-7 Danny Villanueva (12/24/67 vs. Cleveland)

RUSHING

RUSHING YARDS
160 Tony Dorsett (12/28/80 vs. Los Angeles), 22 carries
RUSHING ATTEMPTS
30 Duane Thomas (12/26/70 vs. Detroit)
TOUCHDOWNS RUSHING
2 Don Perkins (12/24/67 vs. Cleveland)
2 Craig Baynham (12/24/67 vs. Cleveland)
2 Tony Dorsett (12/26/77 vs. Chicago)
RUSHING AVERAGE (Min. 10 Attempts)
7.2 Tony Dorsett (12/28/80 vs. Los Angeles), 22-160
6.9 Calvin Hill (12/23/72 @ San Francisco), 18-125
6.4 Don Perkins (1/1/67 vs. Green Bay), 17-108
LONGEST RUN
53 Tony Dorsett (1/7/79 @ Los Angeles)

PASSING

PASSING YARDS
322 Danny White (1/4/81 @ Atlanta), 25 of 39
246 Roger Staubach (12/28/75 @ Minnesota), 15 of 24
238 Don Meredith (1/1/67 vs. Green Bay), 15 of 31
PASS ATTEMPTS
39 Danny White (1/4/81 @ Atlanta), 25 completions
37 Roger Staubach (12/19/76 vs. Los Angeles), 15 completions
31 Don Meredith (1/1/67 vs. Green Bay), 15 completions
PASS COMPLETIONS
25 Danny White (1/4/81 @ Atlanta), 39 attempts
17 Roger Staubach (12/28/75 @ Minnesota), 29 attempts
17 Roger Staubach (1/15/78 vs. Denver), 25 attempts
17 Roger Staubach (1/21/79 vs. Pittsburgh), 30 attempts
TOUCHDOWN PASSES
4 Roger Staubach (1/4/76 @ Los Angeles)
PASSES HAD INTERCEPTED
4 Roger Staubach (12/30/73 vs. Minnesota)
COMPLETION PERCENTAGE (Min. 12 completions)
68.0 Roger Staubach (1/15/78 vs. Denver), 17 of 25
64.1 Danny White (1/4/81 @ Atlanta), 25 of 39
LONGEST COMPLETION
86 Don Meredith to Bob Hayes (12/24/67 vs. Cleveland), TD
83 Roger Staubach to Drew Pearson (12/23/73 vs. L.A.), TD
MOST TIMES SACKED
7 Roger Staubach (12/23/73 vs. Los Angeles)
7 Roger Staubach (1/18/76 vs. Pittsburgh)

Miscellaneous Individual Records
PLAYOFFS
Most Games Played

26 — Larry Cole
25 — D. D. Lewis
23 — Jethro Pugh
Charlie Waters

Most Super Bowls Played
5 — Larry Cole, Cliff Harris, D. D. Lewis, Charlie Waters, Rayfield Wright
Most Consecutive Passes Without Interception
99 — Roger Staubach (began vs. Minnesota, Dec. 25, 1971, ended vs. Minnesota, Dec. 30, 1973).
Most Consecutive Games Rush for TD
3 — Duane Thomas (began Dec. 25, 1971 vs. Minnesota, ended January 16, 1972 after Super Bowl victory).
3 — Tony Dorsett (began December 26, 1977 vs. Chicago, ended December 30, 1978 vs. Atlanta).
Most Consecutive Games Catch TD Pass
2 — Golden Richards (vs. Minnesota, January 1, 1978 and vs. Denver, January 15, 1978).
Drew Pearson (vs. Los Angeles, December 28, 1980 and vs. Atlanta, January 4, 1981).
Most Consecutive Games Intercept Pass
3 — Mel Renfro (vs. Detroit, December 26, 1970; vs. San Francisco January 3, 1971; and vs. Baltimore, January 17, 1971).
3 — Randy Hughes (vs. Denver, January 15, 1978; vs. Atlanta, December 30, 1978; and vs. Los Angeles, January 7, 1979).
Most Consecutive Games at Least One Pass Catch
16 — Drew Pearson (began vs. Los Angeles, December 23, 1973; ongoing).
Most Consecutive Games Kick FG
7 — Toni Fritsch (started vs. San Francisco, December 23, 1972, ended after January 18, 1976, vs. Pittsburgh).
Most Consecutive Games Played
22 — Jethro Pugh (started January 1, 1967 vs. Green Bay, ended December 30, 1978 vs. Atlanta).

PASS RECEIVING

RECEPTIONS
7 Billy Parks (12/23/72 @ San Francisco), 136 yards
7 Preston Pearson (1/4/76 @ Los Angeles), 123 yards
RECEIVING YARDS
144 Bob Hayes (12/24/67 vs. Cleveland), 5 receptions
TOUCHDOWNS RECEIVING
3 Preston Pearson (1/4/76 @ Los Angeles)

RUSHING — RECEIVING
188 Tony Dorsett (12/28/80 vs. Los Angeles), 160 rushing, 28 receiving
167 Duane Thomas (1/3/71 vs. San Francisco), 143 rushing, 24 receiving

COMBINED YARDAGE
285 Bob Hayes (12/24/67 vs. Cleveland), 5/144 receiving, 3/141 punt returns

PUNTING

PUNTS
9 Ron Widby (1/17/71 vs. Baltimore), 38.6 average
PUNT AVERAGE
46.7 Marv Bateman (12/23/73 vs. Los Angeles), 7 punts

PUNT RETURNS

PUNT RETURNS
5 James Jones (12/28/80 vs. Los Angeles)
PUNT RETURN YARDAGE
141 Bob Hayes (12/24/67 vs. Cleveland), 3 returns
LONGEST PUNT RETURN
68 Bob Hayes (12/24/67 vs. Cleveland)
PUNT RETURN AVERAGE
47.0 Bob Hayes (12/24/67 vs. Cleveland), 3 for 141 yards
FAIR CATCHES
4 Lance Rentzel (12/21/68 @ Cleveland)
4 Cliff Harris (12/23/72 @ San Francisco)

KICKOFF RETURNS

KICKOFF RETURNS
5 Mel Renfro (1/1/67 vs. Green Bay), 124 yards
KICKOFF RETURN YARDAGE
124 Mel Renfro (1/1/67 vs. Green Bay), 5 returns
LONGEST KICKOFF RETURN
48 Thomas Henderson (1/18/76 vs. Pittsburgh)
KICKOFF RETURN YARDAGE
24.8 Mel Renfro (1/1/67 vs. Green Bay), 5 for 124 yards

INTERCEPTIONS

INTERCEPTIONS
3 Charlie Waters (12/26/77 vs. Chicago)
INTERCEPTION RETURN YARDAGE
68 Thomas Henderson (1/8/79 @ Los Angeles), on 1 int.
LONGEST INTERCEPTION RETURN
68 Thomas Henderson (1/8/79 @ Los Angeles)
PASSES HAD INTERCEPTED
4 Roger Staubach (12/30/73 vs. Minnesota)
COMPLETION PERCENTAGE (Min. 12 completions)
68.0 Roger Staubach (1/15/78 vs. Denver), 17 of 25
66.7 Danny White (1/10/82 @ San Francisco) 16 of 24
64.1 Danny White (1/4/81 @ Atlanta), 25 of 39
LONGEST COMPLETION
86 Don Meredith to Bob Hayes (12/24/67 vs. Cleveland), TD
83 Roger Staubach to Drew Pearson (12/23/73 vs. L.A.), TD
MOST TIMES SACKED
7 Roger Staubach (12/23/73 vs. Los Angeles)
7 Roger Staubach (1/18/76 vs. Pittsburgh)

Cowboys Big Days

RUSHING

(includes all 100-yard days)

206 — Tony Dorsett vs. Philadelphia, Dec. 4, 1977 (23 carries).
183 — Tony Dorsett vs. N.Y. Giants, Nov. 9, 1980 (24 carries).
175 — Tony Dorsett vs. Baltimore, Dec. 6, 1981 (30 carries).
162 — Tony Dorsett vs. New England, Sept. 21, 1981 (19 carries).
*160 — Tony Dorsett vs. Los Angeles, Dec. 28, 1980 (22 carries).
159 — Tony Dorsett vs. Los Angeles, Oct. 18, 1981 (27 carries).
154 — Tony Dorsett vs. St. Louis, Sept. 24, 1978 (21 carries).
153 — Calvin Hill vs. San Francisco, Nov. 10, 1974 (32 carries).
152 — Tony Dorsett vs. New Orleans, Nov. 19, 1978 (25 carries).
150 — Calvin Hill vs. Washington, Nov. 16, 1969 (27 carries).
149 — Tony Dorsett vs. Green Bay, Nov. 12, 1978 (23 carries).
147 — Tony Dorsett vs. Baltimore, Sept. 4, 1978 (15 carries).
145 — Tony Dorsett vs. Minnesota, Oct. 7, 1979 (21 carries).
*143 — Duane Thomas vs. San Francisco, Jan. 3, 1971 (27 carries).
141 — Tony Dorsett vs. St. Louis, Oct. 9, 1977 (14 carries).
140 — Calvin Hill vs. Philadelphia, Oct. 20, 1974 (26 carries).
138 — Calvin Hill vs. New Orleans, Sept. 28, 1969 (23 carries).
137 — Don Perkins vs. St. Louis, Oct. 28, 1962 (24 carries).
137 — Don Perkins vs. N.Y. Giants, Oct. 11, 1964 (17 carries).
*135 — Duane Thomas vs. Detroit, Dec. 26, 1970 (30 carries).
134 — Duane Thomas vs. Kansas City, Oct. 25, 1970 (20 carries).
133 — Don Perkins vs. Green Bay, Oct. 24, 1965 (22 carries).
132 — Tony Dorsett vs. Washington, Sept. 6, 1981 (20 carries).
130 — Calvin Hill vs. Chicago, Sept. 16, 1973 (31 carries).
129 — Tony Dorsett vs. St. Louis, Sept. 13, 1981 (16 carries).
*125 — Calvin Hill vs. San Francisco, Dec. 23, 1972 (18 carries).
124 — Robert Newhouse vs. St. Louis, Dec. 16, 1973 (19 carries).
123 — Don Perkins vs. Cleveland, Dec. 3, 1961 (20 carries).
123 — Duane Thomas vs. Washington, Dec. 6, 1970 (19 carries).
123 — Calvin Hill vs. N.Y. Giants, Oct. 21, 1973 (23 carries).
122 — Tony Dorsett vs. Miami, Oct. 25, 1981 (24 carries).
122 — Scott Laidlaw vs. Washington, Nov. 23, 1978 (16 carries).
122 — Tony Dorsett vs. St. Louis, Nov. 16, 1980 (26 carries).
121 — Walt Garrison vs. Washington, Dec. 9, 1972 (10 carries).
121 — Tony Dorsett vs. N.Y. Jets, Dec. 17, 1978 (29 carries).
120 — Robert Newhouse vs. Seattle, Oct. 3, 1976 (19 carries).
120 — Calvin Hill vs. St. Louis, Dec. 3, 1972 (26 carries).
119 — Tony Dorsett vs. Cincinnati, Sept. 30, 1979 (20 carries).
117 — Tony Dorsett vs. Buffalo, Nov. 9, 1981 (28 carries).
117 — Amos Marsh vs. Cleveland, Dec. 2, 1962 (17 carries).
117 — Calvin Hill vs. Philadelphia, Sept. 20, 1970 (25 carries).
117 — Calvin Hill vs. Atlanta, Oct. 11, 1970 (29 carries).
115 — Tony Dorsett vs. Washington, Nov. 22, 1981 (23 carries).
115 — Duane Thomas vs. Houston, Dec. 20, 1970 (17 carries).
114 — Dan Reeves vs. Cleveland, Sept. 17, 1967 (18 carries).
112 — Duane Thomas vs. N.Y. Jets, Dec. 4, 1971 (14 carries).
111 — Don Perkins vs. Cleveland, Nov. 24, 1966 (23 carries).
111 — Don Perkins vs. Atlanta, Nov. 5, 1967 (21 carries).
111 — Calvin Hill vs. Washington, Dec. 9, 1972 (24 carries).
111 — Tony Dorsett vs. N.Y. Giants, Sept. 10, 1978 (24 carries).
111 — Tony Dorsett vs. St. Louis, Oct. 21, 1979 (20 carries).
110 — Calvin Hill vs. Washington, Dec. 9, 1973 (27 carries).
109 — Amos Marsh vs. Washington, Nov. 4, 1962 (10 carries).
109 — Don Perkins vs. Washington, Sept. 29, 1963 (25 carries).
109 — Calvin Hill vs. New Orleans, No. 9, 1969 (13 carries).
108 — Don Perkins vs. Minnesota, Sept. 24, 1961 (17 carries).
108 — Don Perkins vs. Pittsburgh, Oct. 21, 1962 (20 carries).
108 — Dan Reeves vs. Washington, Dec. 11, 1966 (10 carries).
*108 — Don Perkins vs. Green Bay, Jan. 1, 1967 (17 carries).
108 — Calvin Hill vs. Pittsburgh, Oct. 8, 1972 (23 carries).
108 — Robert Newhouse vs. N.Y. Jets, Dec. 21, 1975 (19 carries).
108 — Robert Newhouse vs. St. Louis, Sept. 2, 1979 (18 carries).
108 — Tony Dorsett vs. Chicago, Sept. 16, 1979 (20 carries).
108 — Tony Dorsett vs. N.Y. Giants, December 2, 1979 (29 carries).
107 — Tony Dorsett vs. Seattle, Nov. 27, 1980 (24 carries).
104 — Duane Thomas vs. Washington, Nov. 22, 1970 (16 carries).
104 — Scott Laidlaw vs. Philadelphia, Sept. 12, 1976 (19 carries).
103 — Don Perkins vs. Washington, Nov. 17, 1968 (13 carries).
103 — Calvin Hill vs. Washington, Oct. 8, 1973 (21 carries).
103 — Tony Dorsett vs. Los Angeles, Oct. 14, 1979 (24 carries).
102 — Walt Garrison vs. N.Y. Giants, Oct. 27, 1969 (16 carries).
101 — Tony Dorsett vs. Philadelphia, Dec. 13, 1981 (28 carries).
*101 — Tony Dorsett vs. Los Angeles, Jan. 8, 1979 (17 carries).
101 — Duane Thomas vs. St. Louis, Nov. 7, 1971 (26 carries).
101 — Preston Pearson vs. Green Bay, Oct. 19, 1975 (15 carries).
101 — Robert Newhouse vs. Green Bay, Nov. 12, 1978 (18 carries).
100 — Calvin Hill vs. Philadelphia, Nov. 19, 1972 (15 carries).
100 — Calvin Hill vs. Philadelphia, Oct. 28, 1973 (25 carries).
100 — Tony Dorsett vs. Tampa Bay, Sept. 21, 1980 (20 carries)

*Playoff Game

PASSING

460 — Don Meredith vs. San Francisco, Nov. 10, 1963 (30 of 48).
406 — Don Meredith vs. Washington, Nov. 13, 1966 (21 of 29).
394 — Don Meredith vs. Philadelphia, Nov. 6, 1966 (14 of 24).
358 — Don Meredith vs. N.Y. Giants, Sept. 18, 1966 (14 of 24).
354 — Danny White vs. Miami, Oct. 25, 1981 (22 of 32).
349 — Craig Morton vs. Houston, Dec. 20, 1970 (13 of 17).
345 — Eddie LeBaron vs. Pittsburgh, Sept. 24, 1960 (15 of 28).
339 — Roger Staubach vs. Baltimore, Sept. 26, 1976 (22 of 28).
336 — Roger Staubach vs. Washington, Dec. 16, 1979 (24 of 42).
326 — Don Meredith vs. St. Louis, Dec. 11, 1965 (16 of 30).
*322 — Danny White vs. Atlanta, Jan. 4, 1981 (25 of 39).
314 — Roger Staubach vs. Philadelphia, Oct. 26, 1975 (27 of 49).
308 — Roger Staubach vs. Philadelphia, November 12, 1979 (17 of 28).
307 — Roger Staubach vs. St. Louis, Sept. 28, 1975 (23 of 34).
306 — Don Meredith vs. Philadelphia, Oct. 13, 1968 (21 of 38).
303 — Roger Staubach vs. Cleveland, Sept. 24, 1979 (21 of 39).
302 — Don Meredith vs. Philadelphia, Nov. 17, 1963 (25 of 33).

RECEIVING

246 — Bob Hayes vs. Washington, Nov. 13, 1966 (9 catches).
241 — Frank Clarke vs. Washington, Sept. 16, 1962 (10 catches).
223 — Lance Rentzel vs. Washington, Nov. 19, 1967 (13 catches).
213 — Tony Hill vs. Philadelphia, November 12, 1979 (7 catches).
195 — Bob Hayes vs. N.Y. Giants, Sept. 18, 1966 (6 catches).
190 — Frank Clarke vs. San Francisco, Nov. 10, 1963 (8 catches).
188 — Drew Pearson vs. Detroit, Oct. 6, 1975 (6 catches).
187 — Bob Hayes vs. Houston, Dec. 20, 1970 (6 catches).
177 — Bob Hayes vs. Philadelphia, Oct. 10, 1965 (8 catches).
170 — Bob Hayes vs. Pittsburgh, Oct. 22, 1967 (7 catches).
168 — Frank Clarke vs. N.Y. Giants, Oct. 20, 1963 (4 catches).
161 — Drew Pearson vs. Philadelphia, Sept. 23, 1974 (10 catches).

Cowboys Longest Plays

LONG RUNS FROM SCRIMMAGE

84 — Tony Dorsett vs. Philadelphia, Dec. 4, 1977 (TD).
77 — Tony Dorsett vs. St. Louis, Oct. 9, 1977 (TD).
75 — Tony Dorsett vs. New England, Sept. 21, 1981 (TD).
73 — Amos Bullocks vs. Chicago, Nov. 18, 1962 (TD).
71 — Amos Marsh vs. New York, Oct. 15, 1961.
70 — Amos Marsh vs. Washington, Nov. 4, 1962.
68 — Les Shy vs. Philadelphia, Oct. 9, 1966.
67 — Dan Reeves vs. Washington, Dec. 11, 1966 (TD).
64 — Jim Stiger vs. Washington, Nov. 22, 1964.
63 — Tony Dorsett vs. New Orleans, Nov. 19, 1978.
59 — James Jones vs. Baltimore, Dec. 6, 1981 (TD).
59 — Don Perkins vs. Pittsburgh, Sept. 27, 1964.
59 — Scott Laidlaw vs. Washington, Nov. 23, 1978.
56 — Frank Clarke vs. New Orleans, Nov. 12, 1967.
56 — Duane Thomas vs. New England, Oct. 24, 1971 (TD).
56 — Tony Dorsett vs. N.Y. Giants, Nov. 9, 1980.
55 — Calvin Hill vs. New Orleans, Nov. 9, 1969.

LONG FORWARD PASSES

95 — Don Meredith to Bob Hayes vs. Washington, Nov. 13, 1966 (TD).
91 — Roger Staubach to Tony Dorsett vs. Baltimore, Sept. 4, 1978 (TD).
89 — Craig Morton to Bob Hayes vs. Kansas City, Oct. 25, 1970 (TD).
*86 — Don Meredith to Bob Hayes vs. Cleveland, Dec. 24, 1967 (TD).
86 — Craig Morton to Lance Rentzel vs. Philadelphia, Nov. 1, 1970 (TD).
85 — Eddie LeBaron to Amos Marsh vs. Los Angeles, Sept. 30, 1962 (TD).
85 — Roger Staubach to Bob Hayes vs. N.Y. Giants, Dec. 12, 1971 (TD).
84 — Don Meredith to Pete Gent vs. Pittsburgh, Oct. 30, 1966 (TD).

LONG PUNTS

84 — Ron Widby vs. New Orleans, Nov. 3, 1968.
75 — Billy Lothridge vs. New York, Oct. 11, 1964.
75 — Sam Baker vs. Los Angeles, Sept. 30, 1962.
73 — Danny White vs. Los Angeles, Oct. 14, 1979.
71 — Billy Lothridge vs. St. Louis, Sept. 12, 1961.
71 — Sam Baker vs. New York, Dec. 16, 1962.

LONG PUNT RETURNS

98 — Dennis Morgan vs. St. Louis, Oct. 13, 1974 (TD).
90 — Bob Hayes vs. Pittsburgh, Dec. 8, 1968 (TD).
69 — Bob Hayes vs. St. Louis, Nov. 23, 1967 (TD).
69 — Mel Renfro vs. Green Bay, Nov. 29, 1964 (TD).
*68 — Bob Hayes vs. Cleveland, Dec. 24, 1967.
63 — Bob Hayes vs. New York, Dec. 15, 1968 (TD).
*63 — Golden Richards vs. Minnesota, Dec. 30, 1973 (TD).
55 — Butch Johnson vs. Philadelphia, Dec. 5, 1976.
52 — James Jones vs. Washington, Nov. 23, 1980.
51 — Mel Renfro vs. Cleveland, Oct. 4, 1964.
50 — Bob Hayes vs. Washington, Nov. 16, 1969.

LONG KICKOFF RETURNS

101 — Amos Marsh vs. Philadelphia, Oct. 14, 1962 (TD).
101 — Ike Thomas vs. New York Jets, Dec. 4, 1971 (TD).
100 — Mark Washington vs. Washington, Nov. 22, 1970 (TD).
100 — Mel Renfro vs. San Francisco, Nov. 7, 1965 (TD).
97 — Thomas Henderson vs. St. Louis, Sept. 28, 1975 (TD).
89 — Ike Thomas vs. Los Angeles, Nov. 25, 1971 (TD).
87 — Mel Renfro vs. Pittsburgh, Oct. 30, 1966 (TD).

LONG INTERCEPTION RETURNS

100 — Mike Gaechter vs. Philadelphia, Oct. 14, 1962 (TD).
96 — Dennis Thurman vs. Washington, Sept. 6, 1981.
90 — Mel Renfro vs. St. Louis, Oct. 4, 1965 (TD).
86 — Mike Gaechter vs. Washington, Nov. 3, 1963.

LONG FUMBLE RETURNS

97 — Chuck Howley vs. Atlanta, Oct. 2, 1966 (TD).
84 — Don Bishop vs. St. Louis, Oct. 28, 1962 (TD).
72 — Benny Barnes vs. San Francisco, Oct. 11, 1981 (TD).
63 — Jim Ridlon vs. Philadelphia, Dec. 6, 1964 (TD).

LONG RETURNS OF FIELD-GOAL ATTEMPTS

94 — Jerry Norton vs. St. Louis, Dec. 9, 1962 (TD).
60 — Mike Gaechter vs. Washington, Nov. 28, 1965 (TD).
60 — Obert Logan vs. New York, Dec. 19, 1965 (TD).
*Playoff Game.

The Last Time . . .

Punt Returned for TD
BY COWBOYS — Charlie Waters (Jay Saldi block), 17 yards, vs. Philadelphia, Oct. 23, 1977. Golden Richards, 43 yards, vs. Philadelphia, Oct. 26, 1975.
BY OPPONENT — Bob Hammond, N.Y. Giants, 68 yards, Sept. 25, 1977.

Kickoff Returned for TD
BY COWBOYS — Thomas Henderson, 97 yards, vs. St. Louis, Sept. 28, 1975.
BY OPPONENT — Roy Green, St. Louis, 106 yards, October 21, 1979. (Playoff Game: Vic Washington, San Francisco, 97 yards, Dec. 23, 1972).

Intercepted Pass Returned for TD
BY COWBOYS — Larry Cole, 43 yards vs. Washington, Nov. 23, 1980.
BY OPPONENT — Ronnie Lott, San Francisco, 41 yards, Oct. 11, 1981.

Shutout Scored
BY COWBOYS — Dallas 38, Baltimore 0, Sept. 4, 1978.
*Dallas 38, Tampa Bay 0, Jan. 2, 1982
BY OPPONENT — St. Louis 38, Dallas 0, Nov. 16, 1970.

Fumble Returned for TD
BY COWBOYS — Benny Barnes, 72 yards vs. San Francisco, Oct. 11, 1981.
BY OPPONENT — Billy Thompson, Denver, 32 yards, Sept. 14, 1980.

PAT Unsuccessful
BY COWBOYS — Rafael Septien vs. Oakland, Dec. 7, 1980.
BY OPPONENT — Joe Danelo, vs. N.Y. Giants, Dec. 19, 1981.

Punt Blocked
BY COWBOYS — Jay Saldi vs. Philadelphia, Oct. 23, 1977.
BY OPPONENT — John Thaxton, St. Louis, Sept. 24, 1978.

*Playoff game.

Miscellaneous Records

INDIVIDUAL

Most Consecutive Passes Completed
12 — Roger Staubach (last 11 vs. Baltimore, Sept. 4, 1978, and first one vs. N.Y. Giants, Sept. 10, 1978).

Most Consecutive Passes Without Interception
166 — Don Meredith (began vs. Philadelphia, Dec. 5, 1965, ended vs. St. Louis, Oct. 16, 1966).

Most Consecutive Games Rush for TD
6 — Tony Dorsett in 1977.

Most Consecutive Games Catch TD Pass
7 — Frank Clarke (final game of 1961 season, first six games in '62). Bob Hayes (final three games of 1965 season, first four games in 1966).

Most Consecutive Games Intercept Pass
5 — Don Bishop in 1961.

Most Consecutive PATs
99 — Mike Clark (last 17 in 1969, all 35 in 1970 and all 47 in 1971).

Most Consecutive Games at Least One Pass Catch
58 — Drew Pearson (final three games of 1974 season, all of 1975, 1976 and 1977, first 13 games of 1978; ended vs. New England, Dec. 3, 1978).

Most Consecutive FG
9 — Rafael Septien (began vs. New England, Sept. 21, 1981, ended vs. Miami, Oct. 25, 1981).

Most Consecutive Games Kick FG
10 — Mike Clark (final nine games of 1969 season, first game in 1970).
Toni Fritsch, twice (final seven games of 1972 season, first three games in 1973; first 10 games in 1975).

Most Consecutive Games Played
196 — Bob Lilly (from 1961 through 1974).

Most Unassisted Tackles in a Game
14 — Lee Roy Jordan vs. Philadelphia, Oct. 28, 1973.

Most Assisted Tackles in a Game
15 — Jerry Tubbs vs. Chicago, Nov. 27, 1960.

Most Tackles Combined in a Game
21 — Lee Roy Jordan vs. Philadelphia, Sept. 26, 1971.

TEAM

Most Consecutive Games Intercept Pass
28 — Every game in 1962 and 1963.

Most Consecutive PATs
162 — 1969, 1970, 1971, 1972, 1973.

Most Consecutive Games Without Losing Fumble
3 — 1973, 1974, 1975, 1976 and 1977.

PAT Record

21 of 23 in 1960	— last 17 straight.	36 of 36 in 1972	— all 36.
29 of 29 in 1961	— all 29.	45 of 46 in 1973	— first 24, last 21.
50 of 51 in 1962	— first 33, last 17.	37 of 38 in 1974	— first 4, last 33.
38 of 40 in 1963	— first 32.	38 of 40 in 1975	— last 34.
28 of 30 in 1964	— last 23.	34 of 34 in 1976	— all 34.
37 of 38 in 1965	— last 24.	39 of 41 in 1977	— first 14, last 16.
56 of 56 in 1966	— all 56.	46 of 48 in 1978	— first 8, last one.
41 of 44 in 1967	— first 8, last 1.	40 of 45 in 1979	— first one, last 26.
54 of 54 in 1968	— all 54.	59 of 60 in 1980	— first 52, last 7.
43 of 44 in 1969	— first 26, last 17.	40 of 40 in 1980	— all 40
35 of 35 in 1970	— all 35.		
50 of 50 in 1971	— all 50.		

Cowboys Individual Records

SCORING

TOTAL POINTS

Career

- 456 Bob Hayes (1965-74), 76 TDs
- 405 Rafael Septien (1978-81), 185 PATs, 73 FGs
- 387 Mike Clark (1968-71, 1973), 180 PATs, 69 FGs
- 317 Toni Fritsch (1971-73, 1975), 119 PATs, 69 FGs
- 306 Frank Clarke (1960-67), 51 TDs

Season

- 122 Rafael Septien (1981), 40 PATs, 27 FGs
- 107 Danny Villanueva (1966), 56 PATs, 17 FGs
- 105 Mike Clark (1968), 54 PATs, 17 FGs
- 104 Toni Fritsch (1975), 38 PATs, 22 FGs
- 103 Mike Clark (1969), 43 PATs, 20 FGs

Game

- 24 Dan Reeves (11/5/67 vs. Atlanta), 4 TDs
- 24 Bob Hayes (12/20/70 vs. Houston), 4 TDs
- 24 Calvin Hill (9/19/71 @ Buffalo), 4 TDs
- 24 Duane Thomas (12/18/71) vs. St. Louis), 4 TDs

Opponent/Game

- 24 Dick James, @ Washington (12/17/61)
- 24 Harold Jackson, @ Los Angeles (10/14/73)

TOUCHDOWNS

Career

- 76 Bob Hayes (1965-74)
- 51 Frank Clarke (1960-67)
- 47 Tony Dorsett (1977-81)
- 45 Don Perkins (1961-68)
- 45 Calvin Hill (1969-74)

Season

- 16 Dan Reeves (1966), 8 run, 8 pass
- 14 Frank Clarke (1962), 14 pass

Game

- 4 Dan Reeves (11/5/67 vs. Atlanta), 2 run 2 pass
- 4 Bob Hayes (12/20/70 vs. Houston), 4 pass
- 4 Calvin Hill (9/19/71 @ Buffalo), 4 run
- 4 Duane Thomas (12/18/71 vs. St. Louis), 3 run, 1 pass

Opponent/Game

- 4 Dick James, @ Washington (12/17/61)
- 4 Harold Jackson, @ Los Angeles (10/14/73)

FIELD GOALS MADE

Career

- 73 Rafael Septien (1978-81) 107 attempts
- 69 Mike Clark (1968-71, 1973) 119 attempts
- 66 Toni Fritsch (1971-73, 1975) 107 attempts
- 46 Rafael Septien (1978-80), 72 attempts

Season

- 27 Rafael Septien (1981), 35 attempts
- 22 Toni Fritsch (1975), 35 attempts
- 21 Toni Fritsch (1972), 36 attempts
- 20 Mike Clark (1969), 36 attempts

Game

- 4 Rafael Septien (9/6/81 @ Washington; 9/21/81 @. New England)
- 4 Danny Villanueva (11/24/66 vs. Cleveland)
- 4 Toni Fritsch (11/12/72 vs. St. Louis)
- 4 Toni Fritsch (9/21/75 vs. Los Angeles)

Longest Field Goal

- 54 Toni Fritsch (9/24/72 @ N.Y. Giants)

Opponent/Game

- 4 Bob Khayat, @ Washington (10/9/60)
- 4 Tommy Davis, San Francisco (11/20/60)
- 4 Sam Baker, @ Philadelphia (12/5/65)
- 4 Fred Cox, @ Minnesota (10/18/70)
- 4 Jim Bakken, St. Louis (12/18/71)

Opponent/Longest Field Goal

- 59 Tony Franklin, Philadelphia (11/12/79)

FIELD GOALS ATTEMPTED

Career

- 119 Mike Clark (1968-71, 1973), 69 FG
- 107 Toni Fritsch (1971-73, 1975), 66 FG
- 107 Rafael Septien (1978-81), 73 FG

Season

- 36 Toni Fritsch (1972), 21 FG
- 36 Mike Clark (1969), 20 FG

Game

- 7 Mike Clark (11/24/68 @ Chicago), 2 FG
- 6 Toni Fritsch (9/21/75 vs. Los Angeles), 4 FG

Opponent/Game

- 7 Sam Baker, @ Philadelphia (12/5/65), 4 FG

EXTRA POINTS MADE

Career

- 185 Rafael Septien (1978-81)
- 180 Mike Clark (1968-71, 1973)
- 134 Danny Villanueva (1965-67)

Season

- 59 Rafael Septien (1980)
- 56 Danny Villanueva (1966)
- 54 Mike Clark (1968)

Game

- 8 Rafael Septien (10/12/80 vs. San Francisco) Att. 8
- 8 Mike Clark (9/15/68 vs. Detroit) Att. 8
- 8 Danny Villanueva (10/9/66 vs. Philadelphia) Att. 8

Opponent/Game

- 7 Gerry Perry, @ St. Louis (12/9/62) Att. 7

RUSHING

TOTAL YARDS

Career

- 6,270 Tony Dorsett (1977-81)
- 6,217 Don Perkins (1961-68)
- 5,009 Calvin Hill (1969-74)
- 4,638 Robert Newhouse (1972-80)

Season

- 1,646 Tony Dorsett (1981), 4.8 per carry
- 1,325 Tony Dorsett (1978), 4.6 per carry
- 1,185 Tony Dorsett (1980), 4.3 per carry
- 1,142 Calvin Hill (1973), 4.2 per carry
- 1,107 Tony Dorsett 1979), 4.4 per carry
- 1,036 Calvin Hill (1972), 4.2 per carry
- 1,007 Tony Dorsett (1977 rookie), 4.8 per carry

Game

- 206 Tony Dorsett (12/4/77 vs. Philadelphia) on 23 carries
- 183 Tony Dorsett (11/9/80 @ N.Y. Giants) on 24 carries
- 175 Tony Dorsett (12/6/81 @ Baltimore) on 30 carries
- 162 Tony Dorsett (9/21/81 @ New England) on 19 carries
- 159 Tony Dorsett (10/18/81 vs. Los Angeles) on 27 carries
- 154 Tony Dorsett (9/24/78 vs. St. Louis) on 21 carries
- 153 Calvin Hill (11/10/74 vs. San Francisco) on 32 carries
- 152 Tony Dorsett (11/19/78 vs. New Orleans) on 25 carries
- 150 Calvin Hill (11/16/69 @ Washington) on 27 carries

Opponent/Game

- 232 Jim Brown, Cleveland (9/22/63)
- 195 Earl Campbell, Houston (11/22/79)
- 194 Wilbert Montgomery, @ Philadelphia (1/11/81 — playoff game)

ATTEMPTS

Career

- 1,500 Don Perkins (1961-68)
- 1,368 Tony Dorsett (1977-81)
- 1,166 Calvin Hill (1969-74)
- 1,151 Robert Newhouse (1972-80)

Season

- 342 Tony Dorsett (1981)
- 290 Tony Dorsett (1978)
- 278 Tony Dorsett (1980)
- 273 Calvin Hill (1973)

Game

- 32 Calvin Hill (11/10/74 vs. San Francisco)
- 31 Calvin Hill (9/16/73 @ Chicago)

Opponent/Game

- 27 Dick James, @ Washington (12/17/61)
- 27 Lydell Mitchell, Baltimore (9/26/76)

TOUCHDOWNS RUSHING

Career

- 42 Don Perkins (1961-68)
- 40 Tony Dorsett (1977-81)
- 39 Calvin Hill (1969-74)
- 30 Robert Newhouse (1972-80)

Season

- 12 Tony Dorsett (1977)
- 11 Tony Dorsett (1980)
- 11 Duane Thomas (1971)

Game

- 4 Calvin Hill (9/19/71 @ Buffalo)

RUSHING AVERAGE

Career

- 4.6 Tony Dorsett (1977-81), 1,368 attempts
- 4.3 Walt Garrison (1966-74), 899 attempts
- 4.3 Calvin Hill (1969-74), 1,166 attempts

Season

- 5.6 Amos Marsh (1962), 144-802
- 5.3 Duane Thomas (1970), 151-803
- 4.8 Tony Dorsett (1981), 342-1,646
- 4.8 Tony Dorsett (1977), 208-1,007

Game (10 attempts)

- 12.1 Walt Garrison (12/9/72 vs. Washington), 10-121
- 10.9 Amos Marsh (11/4/52 @ Washington), 10-109
- 10.8 Dan Reeves (12/11/66 vs. Washington), 10-108

Longest Runs

- 84 Tony Dorsett (12/4/77 vs. Philadelphia) TD
- 77 Tony Dorsett (10/9/77 @ St. Louis) TD
- 75 Tony Dorsett (9/21/81 @ New England) TD
- 73 Amos Bullocks (11/18/62 vs. Chicago) TD
- 71 Amos Marsh (10/15/61 vs. N.Y. Giants)

Opponent/Longest Run

- 76 O. J. Anderson, @ St. Louis (9/2/79)

PASSING

TOTAL YARDS

Career

- 22,700 Roger Staubach (1969-79)
- 17,199 Don Meredith (1960-68)
- 10,279 Craig Morton (1965-74)

Season

- 3,586 Roger Staubach (1979)
- 3,287 Danny White (1980)
- 3,190 Roger Staubach (1978)
- 3,098 Danny White (1981)
- 2,805 Don Meredith (1966)

Game

- 460 Don Meredith (11/10/63 @ San Francisco), 30 of 48
- 406 Don Meredith (11/13/66 @ Washington), 21 of 29
- 394 Don Meredith (11/6/66 @ Philadelphia), 14 of 24
- 358 Don Meredith (9/18/66 vs. N.Y. Giants), 14 of 24

Opponent/Game

- 466 Bill Wade, Chicago (11/18/62), 28 of 46
- 411 Sonny Jurgensen, @ Washington (11/28/65)
- 377 Ed Brown, @ Pittsburgh (10/27/63)
- 371 Don Fouts, San Diego (10/26/80)

PASS ATTEMPTS

Career

- 2,958 Roger Staubach (1969-79)
- 2,808 Don Meredith (1960-68)

Season

- 461 Roger Staubach (1979), 267 completions
- 436 Danny White (1980), 260 completions
- 413 Roger Staubach (1978), 231 completions
- 391 Danny White (1981), 223 completions
- 369 Roger Staubach (1976), 208 completions

Game

- 49 Roger Staubach (10/26/76 @ Philadelphia), 27 completions
- 48 Don Meredith (11/10/63 @ San Francisco), 30 completions

Opponent/Game

- 46 Bill Wade, Chicago (11/18/62)
- 46 Sonny Jurgensen, @ Washington (11/13/66)
- 46 Fran Tarkenton (43), Gary Wood (3), @ N.Y. Giants (12/15/68)
- 46 Jim Hart, St. Louis (11/25/76)

PASS COMPLETIONS

Career

- 1,685 Roger Staubach (1969-79)
- 1,170 Don Meredith (1960-68)

Season

- 267 Roger Staubach (1979), 461 attempts
- 260 Danny White (1980), 436 attempts
- 231 Roger Staubach (1978), 413 attempts
- 223 Danny White (1981), 391 attempts
- 210 Roger Staubach (1977), 361 attempts

Game

- 30 Don Meredith (11/10/63 @ San Francisco), 48 attempts
- 27 Roger Staubach (10/26/75 @ Philadelphia), 49 attempts
- 25 Roger Staubach (12/7/75 @ St. Louis), 41 attempts

Opponent/Game

- 28 Bill Wade, Chicago (11/18/62), 46 attempts
- 28 Kent Nix, @ Pittsburgh (10/22/67), 45 attempts

TOUCHDOWN PASSES

Career

- 153 Roger Staubach (1969-79)
- 135 Don Meredith (1960068)

Season

- 28 Danny White (1980) of 260 completions
- 27 Roger Staubach (1979) of 267 completions
- 25 Roger Staubach (1978) of 231 completions
- 24 Don Meredith (1966) of 177 completions

Game

- 5 Eddie LeBaron (10/21/62 @ Pittsburgh)
- 5 Don Meredith (9/18/66 vs. N.Y. Giants)
- 5 Don Meredith (10/9/66 @ Philadelphia)
- 5 Don Meredith (9/29/68 @ Philadelphia)
- 5 Craig Morton (10/19/69 vs. Philadelphia)
- 5 Craig Morton (12/20/70 vs. Houston)

Opponent/Game

- 6 Y. A. Tittle, @ N.Y. Giants (12/16/62)

PASSES HAD INTERCEPTED

Career

- 111 Don Meredith (1960-68)
- 109 Roger Staubach (1969-79)

Season

- 25 Eddie LeBaron (1960), 225 attempts
- 25 Danny White (1980), 436 attempts
- 21 Craig Morton (1972), 339 attempts
- 18 Don Meredith (1963), 310 attempts

Game

- 5 Eddie LeBaron (9/30/60 vs. Philadelphia), 29 attempts
- 5 Eddie LeBaron (11/5/61 vs. St. Louis), 33 attempts

5 Danny White (11/9/80 @ N.Y. Giants), 23 attempts

Opponent/Game

9 Pete Liske, @ Philadelphia (9/26/71), 29 attempts

LOWEST INTERCEPTION RATE (150 or more attempts)

Season

1.9 Roger Staubach (1971), 4 of 211
2.4 Roger Staubach (1979), 11 of 461
2.5 Roger Staubach (1977), 9 of 361
3.0 Roger Staubach (1976), 11 of 369

COMPLETION PERCENT

Career

58.0 Danny White (1976-81), 539 of 930
57.0 Roger Staubach (1969-79), 1,685 of 2,958
52.4 Craig Morton (1965-74), 685 of 1,308
51.9 Eddie LeBaron (1960-63), 359 of 692
50.7 Don Meredith (1960-68), 1,170 of 2,308

Season

62.6 Roger Staubach (1973), 179 of 286
59.7 Roger Staubach (1971), 126 of 211
59.6 Danny White (1980), 260 of 436

Game (12 or more completions)

84.2 Don Meredith (9/5/68 vs. Detroit) 16 of 19
81.2 Eddie LeBaron (9/16/62 vs. Washington) 13 of 16
80.0 Craig Morton (11/22/70 @ Washington) 12 of 15

LONGEST PASS PLAYS

95 Don Meredith to Bob Hayes (12/13/66 vs. Washington) TD
91 Roger Staubach to Tony Dorsett (9/4/78 vs. Baltimore) TD
89 Craig Morton to Bob Hayes (10/25/70 @ Kansas City) TD

Opponent/Longest Pass Play

94 Norm Snead to Rich Houston, @ N.Y. Giants (9/24/72) TD

PASS RECEIVING

TOTAL RECEPTIONS

Career

416 Drew Pearson (1973-81)
365 Bob Hayes (1965-74)
281 Frank Clarke (1960-67)
248 Billy Joe DuPree (1973-81)

Season

65 Frank Clarke (1964), 973 yards
64 Bob Hayes (1966), 1,232 yards
62 Drew Pearson (1974), 1,087 yards

Game

13 Lance Rentzel (11/19/67 vs. Washington), 223 yards
11 Bill Howton (11/25/62 @ Philadelphia), 102 yards
11 Ron Springs (9/21/81 @ New England), 72 yards

Opponent/Game

12 J. R. Wilburn, @ Pittsburgh (10/22/67), 142 yards

TOTAL RECEIVING YARDS

Career

7,295 Bob Hayes (1965-74)
6,895 Drew Pearson (1973-81)
5,214 Frank Clarke (1960-67)
3,914 Tony Hill (1977-81)
3,521 Lance Rentzel (1967-70)
3,382 Billy Joe DuPree (1973-81)

Season

1,232 Bob Hayes (1966), 64 receptions
1,087 Drew Pearson (1974), 62 receptions
1,062 Tony Hill (1979), 60 receptions
1,055 Tony Hill (1980), 60 receptions
1,043 Frank Clarke (1962), 47 receptions
1,026 Drew Pearson (1979), 55 receptions
1,009 Lance Rentzel (1968), 54 receptions

Game

246 Bob Hayes (11/13/66 @ Washington), 9 receptions
241 Frank Clarke (9/16/62 vs. Washington), 10 receptions
223 Lance Rentzel (11/19/67 vs. Washington), 13 receptions
213 Tony Hill (11/12/79 vs. Philadelphia), 7 receptions

Opponent/Game

238 Harold Jackson, @ Los Angeles (10/14/73), 7 receptions

TOUCHDOWNS RECEIVING

Career

71 Bob Hayes (1965-74)
50 Frank Clarke (1960-67)
40 Drew Pearson (1973-81)
38 Billy Joe DuPree (1973-81)

Season

14 Frank Clarke (1962), 47 receptions
13 Bob Hayes (1966), 64 receptions
12 Lance Rentzel (1969), 43 receptions
12 Bob Hayes (1965), 46 receptions

Game

4 Bob Hayes (12/20/70 vs. Houston)

Opponent/Game

4 Harold Jackson, @ Los Angeles (10/14/73)

RUSHING — RECEIVING

Career

7,884 Tony Dorsett (1977-81), 6,270 rushing, 1,614 receiving
7,527 Don Perkins (1961-68), 6,217 rushing, 1,310 receiving
7,365 Bob Hayes (1965-74), 7,295 receiving, 70 rushing
7,072 Drew Pearson (1973-81), 6,895 receiving, 177 rushing
6,368 Calvin Hill (1969-74), 5,009 rushing, 1,359 receiving

Season

1,971 Tony Dorsett (1981), 1,646 rushing, 325 receiving
1,703 Tony Dorsett (1978), 1,325 rushing, 378 receiving
1,482 Tony Dorsett (1979), 1,107 rushing, 375 receiving
1,448 Tony Dorsett (1980), 1,185 rushing, 263 receiving
1,432 Calvin Hill (1973), 1,142 rushing, 290 receiving

Game

254 Tony Dorsett (9/4/78 vs. Baltimore), 147 rushing, 107 receiving
246 Bob Hayes (11/13/66 @ Washington), 246 receiving
241 Frank Clarke (9/16/62 vs. Washington), 241 receiving
230 Tony Dorsett (12/4/77 vs. Philadelphia), 206 rushing; 24 receiving

COMBINED YARDAGE

Career

8,596 Bob Hayes (1965-74)
7,978 Don Perkins (1961-68)
7,884 Tony Dorsett (1977-81)
7,142 Drew Pearson (1973-81)
6,493 Calvin Hill (1969-74)
6,493 Walt Garrison (1966-74)
6,105 Robert Newhouse (1972-81)

Season

1,998 Amos Marsh (1962), 729 return yards
1,971 Tony Dorsett (1981), no return yards
1,703 Tony Dorsett (1978), no return yards
1,598 Bob Hayes (1965), 603 return yards
1,564 Don Perkins (1961), 451 return yards

Game

285 Bob Hayes (12/24/67 vs. Cleveland — Playoff Game) 5/144 receiving, 3/141 punt returns
285 Calvin Hill (11/16/69 @ Washington) 3/100 kickoff return, 27/150 rushing, 2/35 receiving

PUNTING

TOTAL PUNTS

Career

454 Danny White (1976-81)
247 Ron Widby (1968-71)
192 Danny Villanueva (1965-67)

Season

81 Danny White (1981), 40.8 average
80 Danny White (1977), 39.6 average
76 Danny White (1978), 40.5 average
76 Danny White (1979), 41.7 average

Game

10 Sam Baker (10/13/63 vs. Detroit) 50.3 average
10 Danny White (11/15/76 vs. Buffalo) 39.9 average

AVERAGE YARDS

Career

45.1 Sam Baker (1962-63)

Season

45.4 Sam Baker (1962), 57 punts
44.2 Sam Baker (1963), 71 punts
43.3 Ron Widby (1969), 63 punts

Game (4 or more punts)

53.4 Ron Widby (11/3/68 @ New Orleans)
53.0 Mary Bateman (11/4/73 vs. Cincinnati)

LONGEST PUNT

84 Ron Widby (11/3/68 @ New Orleans)

PUNT RETURNS

TOTAL RETURNS

Career

146 Butch Johnson (1976-80)
109 Mel Renfro (1964-77)
104 Bob Hayes (1965-74)

Season

54 James Jones (1980), 10.1 average
51 Butch Johnson (1978), 7.9 average
50 Butch Johnson (1977), 8.5 average

Game

9 Butch Johnson (11/15/76 vs. Buffalo)

PUNT RETURN YARDAGE

Career

1,313 Butch Johnson (1976-80)
1,158 Bob Hayes (1965-74)

Season

548 James Jones (1980), 10.1 average
489 Butch Johnson (1976), 10.9 average
423 Butch Johnson (1977), 8.5 average

Game

141 Bob Hayes (12/24/67 vs. Cleveland — Playoff Game), 3 returns
122 Bob Hayes (12/8/68 vs Pittsburgh), 3 returns

Longest Punt Return

98 Dennis Morgan (10/13/74 vs. St. Louis)
90 Bob Hayes (12/6/68 vs. Pittsburgh)

AVERAGE YARDS

Career

11.1 Bob Hayes (1965-74), 104 returns
9.0 Butch Johnson (1976-80), 146 returns
8.5 James Jones (1980-81), 87 returns

Season (14 or more returns)

20.8 Bob Hayes (1968), 15 returns
15.1 Dennis Morgan (1974), 19 returns
13.1 Mel Renfro (1964), 32 returns

Game

47.0 Bob Hayes (12/24/67 vs. Cleveland — Playoff Game) 3 for 141 yards

FAIR CATCHES

Career

38 Mel Renfro (1964-77)
38 Butch Johnson (1976-80)
35 Golden Richards (1973-78)

Season

18 Golden Richards (1973)
16 Cliff Harris (1972)
15 Butch Johnson (1977)

Game

4 Golden Richards (11/16/75 @ New England)
4 Golden Richards (11/17/74 @ Washington)
4 Lance Rentzel (12/21/68 vs. Cleveland — playoff game)
4 Cliff Harris (12/23/72 @ San Francisco — playoff game)

KICKOFF RETURNS

TOTAL RETURNS

Career

85 Mel Renfro (1964-77)
79 Butch Johnson (1976-80)

Season

40 Mel Renfro (1964), 25.4 average
38 Ron Springs (1979), 20.5 average
35 Dennis Morgan (1974), 23.5 average

Game

8 Mel Renfro (10/29/64 vs. Green Bay), 156 yards

KICKOFF RETURN YARDAGE

Career

2,246 Mel Renfro (1964-77)
1,832 Butch Johnson (1976-80)

Season

1,017 Mel Renfro (1964), 25.4 average
823 Cliff Harris (1971), 28.4 average
823 Dennis Morgan (1974), 23.5 average

Game

168 Mel Renfro (11/22/64 @ Washington), 4 returns
157 Amos Marsh (10/14/62 vs. Philadelphia), 4 returns

Longest Kickoff Return

101 Amos Marsh (10/14/62 vs. Philadelphia)
101 Ike Thomas (12/4/71 vs. N.Y. Jets)
100 Mark Washington (11/22/70 @ Washington)
100 Mel Renfro (11/7/65 vs. San Francisco)

AVERAGE YARDS

Career

26.4 Mel Renfro (1964-77), 85 returns
25.7 Cliff Harris (1970-79), 63 returns

Season

30.0 Mel Renfro (1965), 21 returns
28.4 Cliff Harris (1971), 29 returns

Game (4 or more)

42.0 Mel Renfro (11/22/64 @ Washington) 4 for 168 yards

INTERCEPTIONS

TOTAL INTERCEPTIONS

Career

52 Mel Renfro (1964-77)
41 Charlie Waters (1970-78, 1981)
34 Cornell Green (1962-74)
32 Lee Roy Jordan (1963-76)

Season

11 Everson Walls (1981), 133 yards
10 Mel Renfro (1969), 118 yards
8 Don Bishop (1961), 172 yards

Game

3 Herb Adderley (9/26/71 @ Philadelphia), 102 yards
3 Lee Roy Jordan (11/4/73 vs. Cincinnati), 49 yards
3 Dennis Thurman (12/13/81 vs. Philadelphia), 37 yards

INTERCEPTION YARDAGE

Career

626 Mel Renfro (1964-77)
584 Charlie Waters (1970-78, 1981)
552 Cornell Green (1962-74)

Season

211 Cornell Green (1963), 7 for 30.1 average
182 Herb Adderley (1971), 6 for 30.3 average

Game

121 Mike Gaechter (11/3/63 vs. Washington) on 2 int.

Longest Interception Return

100 Mike Gaechter (10/14/62 vs. Philadelphia)
96 Dennis Thurman (9/6/81 @ Washington)
90 Mel Renfro (10/4/65 @ St. Louis)

TOUCHDOWN INTERCEPTIONS

Career

3 Mel Renfro (1964-77)
3 Lee Roy Jordan (1963-76)
3 Larry Cole (1968-80)

Cowboys Big Days/Playoffs

100 YARD RUSHING GAMES

160 yards — Tony Dorsett vs. Los Angeles .... December 28, 1980
143 yards — Duane Thomas vs. San Francisco .... January 3, 1971
135 yards — Duane Thomas vs. Detroit .... December 26, 1970
125 yards — Calvin Hill vs. San Francisco .... December 23, 1972
108 yards — Don Perkins vs. Green Bay .... January 1, 1967
101 yards — Tony Dorsett vs. Los Angeles .... January 7, 1979

PASSING

322 yards — Danny White vs. Atlanta .... January 4, 1981
246 yards — Roger Staubach vs. Minnesota .... December 28, 1975
243 yards — Don Meredith vs. Minnesota .... January 5, 1969
238 yards — Don Meredith vs. Green Bay .... January 1, 1967
228 yards — Roger Staubach vs. Pittsburgh .... January 21, 1979
220 yards — Roger Staubach vs. Los Angeles .... January 4, 1976
212 yards — Don Meredith vs. Cleveland .... December 24, 1967
204 yards — Roger Staubach vs. Pittsburgh .... January 18, 1976

RECEIVING

144 yards — Bob Hayes vs. Cleveland .... December 24, 1967
136 yards — Billy Parks vs. San Francisco .... December 23, 1972
123 yards — Preston Pearson vs. Los Angeles .... January 4, 1976
102 yards — Frank Clarke vs. Green Bay .... January 1, 1967
91 yards — Drew Pearson vs. Minnesota .... December 28, 1975
90 yards — Drew Pearson vs. Atlanta .... January 4, 1981

Cowboys Longest Plays/Playoffs

LONG RUNS FROM SCRIMMAGE

53 yards —Tony Dorsett vs. Los Angeles .... January 7, 1979
48 yards —Calvin Hill vs. San Francisco .... December 23, 1972
32 yards —Ron Springs vs. Los Angeles .... December 28, 1980
29 yards —Roger Staubach vs. Washington .... December 31, 1972
29 yards —Tony Dorsett vs. Pittsburgh .... January 21, 1979
27 yards —Billy Joe DuPree vs. Los Angeles .... January 30, 1979
26 yards —Tony Dorsett vs. Los Angeles .... December 30, 1979
26 yards —Tony Dorsett vs. Tampa Bay .... January 2, 1982

LONG FORWARD PASSES

86 yards — Don Meredith to Bob Hayes
vs. Cleveland (TD) .... December 24, 1967
83 yards — Roger Staubach to Drew Pearson
vs. Los Angeles (TD) .... December 23, 1973
68 yards — Don Meredith to Frank Clarke
vs. Green Bay (TD) .... January 1, 1967
51 yards — Don Meredith to Bob Hayes
vs. Minnesota (TD) .... January 5, 1969
50 yards — Roger Staubach to Drew Pearson
vs. Minnesota (TD) .... December 28, 1975
45 yards — Roger Staubach to Butch Johnson
vs. Denver (TD) .... January 15, 1978

LONG PUNT RETURNS

68 yards — Bob Hayes vs. Cleveland .... December 24, 1967
63 yards — Golden Richards vs. Minnesota (TD) .... December 30, 1973
44 yards — Butch Johnson vs. Los Angeles .... December 19, 1976
43 yards — James Jones vs. Los Angeles .... December 28, 1980

LONG KICKOFF RETURNS

48 yards — Thomas Henderson vs. Pittsburgh .... January 18, 1976
34 yards — Cliff Harris vs. Minnesota .... December 30, 1973
33 yards — Cliff Harris vs. San Francisco .... December 23, 1972
33 yards — James Jones vs. Los Angeles .... December 28, 1980

LONG INTERCEPTION RETURNS

68 yards — Thomas Henderson vs. Los Angeles (TD) .... January 7, 1979
60 yards — Cornell Green vs. Cleveland (TD) .... December 24, 1967
41 yards — Chuck Howley vs. Miami .... January 16, 1972
31 yards — Dennis Thurman vs. Tampa Bay .... January 2, 1982
30 yards — Cliff Harris vs. Minnesota .... December 25, 1971
27 yards — Mark Washington vs. Denver .... January 15, 1978
26 yards — Chuck Howley vs. Minnesota .... December 25, 1971

LONG FUMBLE RETURNS

44 yards — Chuck Howley vs. Cleveland (TD) .... December 21, 1968
37 yards — Mike Hegman vs. Pittsburgh (TD) .... January 21, 1979
21 yards — Randy Hughes vs. Denver .... January 15, 1978
20 yards — Charlie Waters vs. Detroit .... December 26, 1970
15 yards — D. D. Lewis vs. Chicago .... December 26, 1977

Cowboys All-Time Results

All-Time Regular Season Record: 196-112-6 Playoff Record: 18-13

*—Designates Home Games

1960 (0-11-1)

Tom Landry, Head Coach

L	*28	Pittsburgh (30,000)	35
L	*25	Philadelphia (18,500)	27
L	14	Washington (21,142)	26
L	* 7	Cleveland (28,500)	48
L	10	St. Louis (20,120)	12
L	* 7	Baltimore (25,500)	45
L	*13	Los Angeles (16,000)	38
L	7	Green Bay (32,294)	41
L	*14	San Francisco (10,000)	26
L	7	Chicago (39,951)	17
T	31	New York (55,033)	31
L	14	Detroit (43,272)	23
	177		369

1961 (4-9-1)

Tom Landry, Head Coach

W	*27	Pittsburgh (23,500)	24
W	*21	Minnesota (20,500)	7
L	7	Cleveland (43,638)	25
W	28	Minnesota (33,070)	0
L	*10	New York (41,500)	31
L	* 7	Philadelphia (25,000)	43
W	17	New York (60,254)	16
L	*17	St. Louis (20,500)	31
L	7	Pittsburgh (17,519)	37
T	*28	Washington (17,500)	28
L	13	Philadelphia (60,127)	35
L	*17	Cleveland (23,500)	38
L	13	St. Louis (15,384)	31
L	24	Washington (21,451)	34
	236		380

1962 (5-8-1)

Tom Landry, Head Coach

T	*35	Washington (15,730)	35
L	*28	Pittsburgh (19,478)	30
W	27	Los Angeles (26,907)	17
L	10	Cleveland (44,040)	19
W	*41	Philadelphia (18,645)	19
W	42	Pittsburgh (23,106)	27
L	*24	St. Louis (16,027)	28
W	38	Washington (49,888)	10
L	*10	New York (45,668)	41
L	*33	Chicago (12,692)	34
L	14	Philadelphia (58,070)	28
W	*45	Cleveland (24,226)	21
L	20	St. Louis (14,102)	52
L	31	New York (62,694)	41
	398		402

1963 (4-10)

Tom Landry, Head Coach

L	* 7	St. Louis (36,432)	34
L	*24	Cleveland (28,710)	41
L	17	Washington (40,101)	21
L	21	Philadelphia (60,671)	24
W	*17	Detroit (27,264)	14
L	21	New York (62,889)	37
L	21	Pittsburgh (19,047)	27
W	*35	Washington (18,838)	20
L	24	San Francisco (29,563)	31
W	*27	Philadelphia (23,694)	20
L	17	Cleveland (55,096)	27
L	*27	New York (29,653)	34
L	*19	Pittsburgh (24,136)	24
W	28	St. Louis (12,695)	24
	305		378

1964 (5-8-1)

Tom Landry, Head Coach

L	* 6	St. Louis (36,605)	16
W	*24	Washington (25,158)	18
L	17	Pittsburgh (35,594)	23
L	6	Cleveland (72,062)	27
T	*13	New York (33,324)	13
L	*16	Cleveland (37,456)	20
W	31	St. Louis (28,253)	13
W	24	Chicago (47,527)	10
W	31	New York (63,031)	21
L	*14	Philadelphia (55,972)	17
L	16	Washington (49,219)	28
L	*21	Green Bay (44,975)	45
L	14	Philadelphia (60,671)	24
W	*17	Pittsburgh (35,271)	14
	250		289

1965 (7-7)

Tom Landry, Head Coach

W	*31	New York (59,366)	2
W	*27	Washington (61,577)	7
L	13	St. Louis (32,034)	20
L	*24	Philadelphia (56,249)	35
L	17	Cleveland (80,451)	23
L	3	Green Bay (48,311)	13
L	13	Pittsburgh (37,804)	22
W	*39	San Francisco (39,677)	31
W	*24	Pittsburgh (57,293)	17
L	*17	Cleveland (76,251)	24
L	31	Washington (50,205)	34
W	21	Philadelphia (54,714)	19
W	*27	St. Louis (38,499)	13
W	38	New York (62,871)	20
	325		280

PLAYOFF BOWL GAME (Miami)

L	3	Baltimore (65,569)	35

1966 (10-3-1)

Tom Landry, Head Coach

W	*52	New York (60,010)	7
W	*28	Minnesota (64,116)	17
W	47	Atlanta (56,990)	14
W	*56	Philadelphia (69,372)	7
T	10	St. Louis (50,673)	10
L	21	Cleveland (84,721)	30
W	*52	Pittsburgh (58,453)	21
L	23	Philadelphia (60,658)	24
W	31	Washington (50, 927)	30
W	20	Pittsburgh (42,185)	7
W	*26	Cleveland (80,259)	14
W	*31	St. Louis (76,965)	17
L	*31	Washington (64,198)	34
W	17	New York (62,735)	7
	445		239

1966 CHAMPIONSHIP GAME (Dls.)

L	27	Green Bay (75,504)	34

1967 (9-5)

Tom Landry, Head Coach

W	21	Cleveland (81,039)	14
W	*38	New York (66,209)	24
L	*13	Los Angeles (75,229)	35
W	17	Washington (50,566)	14
W	*14	New Orleans (64,128)	10
W	24	Pittsburgh (39,641)	21
L	14	Philadelphia (60,740)	21
W	*37	Atlanta (54,751)	7
W	27	New Orleans (83,437)	10
L	*20	Washington (75,538)	27
W	*46	St. Louis (68,787)	21
L	17	Baltimore (60,238)	23
W	*38	Philadelphia (55,834)	17
L	16	San Francisco (27,182)	24
	342		268

1967 EASTERN CHAMPIONSHIP GAME (Dallas)

W	52	Cleveland (70,786)	14

1967 CHAMPIONSHIP GAME (Green Bay)

L	17	Green Bay (50,861)	21

1968 (12-2)

Tom Landry, Head Coach

W	*59	Detroit (61,382)	13
W	*28	Cleveland (68,733)	7
W	45	Philadelphia (60,858)	13
W	27	St. Louis (48, 296)	10
W	*34	Philadelphia (72,083)	14
W	20	Minnesota (47, 644)	7
L	*17	Green Bay (74,604)	28
W	17	New Orleans (84,728)	3
L	*21	New York (72,163)	27
W	44	Washington (50,816)	24
W	34	Chicago (46,667)	3
W	*29	Washington (66,076)	20
W	*28	Pittsburgh (55,069)	7
W	28	New York (62,617)	10
	431		186

1968 EASTERN CHAMPIONSHIP GAME (Cleveland)

L	20	Cleveland (81,497)	31

PLAYOFF BOWL GAME (Miami)

W	17	Minnesota (22,961)	13

1969 (11-2-1)

Tom Landry, Head Coach

W	*24	St. Louis (62,134)	3
W	21	New Orleans (79,567)	17
W	38	Philadelphia (60,658)	7
W	24	Atlanta (54,833)	17
W	*49	Philadelphia (71,509)	14
W	*25	New York (58,964)	3
L	10	Cleveland (84,850)	42
W	*33	New Orleans (68,282)	17
W	41	Washington (50, 474)	28
L	23	Los Angeles (79,105)	24
T	*24	San Francisco (62,348)	24
W	10	Pittsburgh (24,990)	7
W	*27	Baltimore (63,191)	10
W	*20	Washington (56,924)	10
	369		223

1969 EASTERN CHAMPIONSHIP GAME (Dallas)

L	14	Cleveland (69,321)	38

PLAYOFF BOWL GAME (Miami)

L	0	Los Angeles (31,151)	31

1970 (10-4)

Tom Landry, Head Coach

W	17	Philadelphia (59,728)	7
W	*28	N.Y. Giants (57,239)	10
L	7	St. Louis (50,780)	20
W	*13	Atlanta (53,611)	0
L	13	Minnesota (47,900)	54
W	27	Kansas City (51,158)	16
W	*21	Philadelphia (55,736)	17
L	20	N.Y. Giants (62,928)	23
L	* 0	St. Louis (69,323)	38
W	45	Washington (50,415)	21
W	*16	Green Bay (67,182)	3
W	*34	Washington (57,936)	0
W	6	Cleveland (75,458)	2
W	*52	Houston (50,504)	10
	299		221

1970 DIVISIONAL PLAYOFF (Dallas)

W	5	Detroit (73,167)	0

1970 NFC CHAMPIONSHIP GAME (San Francisco)

W	17	San Francisco (59,625)	10

SUPER BOWL V (Miami)

L	13	Baltimore (80,055)	16

1971 (11-3)

Tom Landry, Head Coach

W	49	Buffalo (46,206)	37
W	42	Philadelphia (65,358)	7
L	*16	Washington (72,000)	20
W	*20	N. Y. Giants (68,378)	13
L	14	New Orleans (83,088)	24
W	*44	New England (65,708)	21
L	19	Chicago (55,049)	23
W	16	St. Louis (50,486)	13
W	*20	Philadelphia (60,178)	7
W	13	Washington (53,041)	0
W	*28	Los Angeles (66,595)	21
W	*52	N. Y. Jets (66,689)	10
W	42	N. Y. Giants (62,815)	14
W	*31	St. Louis (66,672)	12
	406		222

1971 DIVISIONAL PLAYOFF (Minnesota)

W	20	Minnesota (49,100)	12

1971 NFC CHAMPIONSHIP GAME (Dallas)

W	14	San Francisco (66,311)	3

SUPER BOWL VI (New Orleans)

W	24	Miami (81,035)	3

1972 (10-4)

Tom Landry, Head Coach

W	*28	Philadelphia (55,850)	6
W	23	N. Y. Giants (62,725)	14
L	13	Green Bay (47,103)	16
W	*17	Pittsburgh (65,682)	13
W	21	Baltimore (58,992)	0
L	20	Washington (53,039)	24
W	*28	Detroit (65,378)	24
W	34	San Diego (54,476)	28
W	*33	St. Louis (65,218)	24
W	28	Philadelphia (65,720)	7
L	*10	San Francisco (65,124)	31
W	27	St. Louis (49,797)	6
W	*34	Washington (65,136)	24
L	* 3	N. Y. Giants (64,602)	23
	319		240

1972 DIVISIONAL PLAYOFF (San Francisco)

W	30	San Francisco (61,214)	28

1972 NFC CHAMPIONSHIP GAME (Washington)

L	3	Washington (53,129)	26

1973 (10-4)

Tom Landry, Head Coach

W	20	Chicago (55,701)	17
W	*40	New Orleans (53,972)	3
W	*45	St. Louis (64,815)	10
L	7	Washington (54,314)	14
L	31	Los Angeles (81,428)	37
W	*45	N. Y. Giants (64,898)	28
L	16	Philadelphia (65,954)	30
W	*38	Cincinnati (58,802)	10
W	23	N. Y. Giants (70,128)	10
W	*31	Philadelphia (61,985)	10
L	* 7	Miami (64,100)	14
W	22	Denver (51,706)	10
W	*27	Washington (64,458-†)	7
W	30	St. Louis (43,946)	3
	382		203

1973 DIVISIONAL PLAYOFF (Dallas)

W	27	Los Angeles (64,291)	16

1973 NFC CHAMPIONSHIP GAME (Dallas)

L	10	Minnesota (64,524)	27

1974 (8-6)

Tom Landry, Head Coach

W	24	Atlanta (52,322)	0
L	10	Philadelphia (64,088)	13
L	* 6	N. Y. Giants (45,841)	14
L	*21	Minnesota (57,847)	23
L	28	St. Louis (49,885)	31
W	*31	Philadelphia (43,586)	24
W	21	N. Y. Giants (61,918)	7
W	*17	St. Louis (64,146)	14
W	*20	San Francisco (50,018)	14
L	21	Washington (54,395)	28
W	10	Houston (49,775)	0
W	*24	Washington (63,243)	23
W	*41	Cleveland (48,754)	17
L	23	Oakland (45,850)	27
	297		235

1975 (10-4)

Tom Landry, Head Coach

W	*18	Los Angeles (49,091)	7
W	*37	St. Louis (52,417) (OT)	31
W	36	Detroit (79,784)	10
W	13	N. Y. Giants (56,511)	7
L	*17	Green Bay (64,934)	19
W	20	Philadelphia (64,889)	17
L	24	Washington (55,004) (OT)	30
L	*31	Kansas City (63,539)	34
W	34	New England (60,905)	31
W	*27	Philadelphia (57,893)	17
W	*14	N. Y. Giants (53,329)	3
L	17	St. Louis (49,701)	31
W	*31	Washington (61,091)	10
W	31	N. Y. Jets (37,279)	21
	350		268

1975 DIVISIONAL PLAYOFF (Minnesota)

W	17	Minnesota (48,341)	14

1975 NFC CHAMPIONSHIP GAME (Los Angeles)

W	37	Los Angeles (84,483)	7

SUPER BOWL X (Miami)

L	17	Pittsburgh (80,187)	21

1976 (11-3)

Tom Landry, Head Coach

W	*27	Philadelphia (54,052)	7
W	24	New Orleans (61,413)	6
W	*30	Baltimore (64,237)	27
W	28	Seattle (62,027)	13
W	24	N. Y. Giants (76,042)	14
L	17	St. Louis (50,317)	21
W	*31	Chicago (61,346)	21
W	20	Washington (55,004)	7
W	* 9	N. Y. Giants (58,870)	3
W	*17	Buffalo (51,779)	10
L	10	Atlanta (54,992)	17
W	*19	St. Louis (62,498)	14
W	26	Philadelphia (55,072)	7
L	*14	Washington (59,916)	27
	296		194

1976 DIVISIONAL PLAYOFF (Dallas)

L	12	Los Angeles (62,436)	14

1977 (12-2)

Tom Landry, Head Coach

W	16	Minnesota (47,678) (OT)	10
W	*41	N.Y. Giants (64,215)	21
W	*23	Tampa Bay (55,316)	7
W	30	St. Louis (50,129)	24
W	*34	Washington (62,115)	16
W	16	Philadelphia (65,507)	10
W	*37	Detroit (63,160)	0
W	24	N.Y. Giants (74,532)	10
L	*17	St. Louis (64,038)	24
L	13	Pittsburgh (49,761)	28
W	14	Washington (55,031)	7
W	*24	Philadelphia (60,289)	14
W	42	San Francisco (55,848)	35
W	*14	Denver (63,752)	6
	345		212

1977 DIVISIONAL PLAYOFF (Dallas)

W	37	Chicago (62,920)	7

1977 NFC CHAMPIONSHIP GAME (Dallas)

W	23	Minnesota (61,968)	6

SUPER BOWL XII (New Orleans)

W	27	Denver (76,400)	10

1978 (12-4)

Tom Landry, Head Coach

W	*38	Baltimore (64,224)	0
W	34	N.Y. Giants (73,265)	24
L	14	Los Angeles (65,749)	27
W	*21	St. Louis (62,760)	12
L	5	Washington (55,031)	9
W	*24	N.Y. Giants (63,420)	3
W	24	St. Louis (48,991) (OT)	21
W	*14	Philadelphia (60,525)	7
L	*10	Minnesota (61,848)	21
L	16	Miami (69,414)	23
W	42	Green Bay (55,256)	14
W	*27	New Orleans (57,920)	7
W	*37	Washington (64,905)	10
W	*17	New England (63,263)	10
W	31	Philadelphia (64,667)	13
W	30	N.Y. Jets (52,532)	7
	384		208

1978 DIVISIONAL PLAYOFF (Dallas)

W	27	Atlanta (60,338)	20

1978 NFC CHAMPIONSHIP GAME (Los Angeles)

W	28	Los Angeles (67,470)	0

SUPER BOWL XIII (Miami)

L	31	Pittsburgh (78,656)	35

1979 (11-5)

Tom Landry, Head Coach

W	22	St. Louis (50,855)	21
W	21	San Francisco (56,728)	13
W	*24	Chicago (64,056)	20
L	7	Cleveland (80,123)	26
W	*38	Cincinnati (63,179)	13
W	36	Minnesota (47,572)	20
W	*30	Los Angeles (64,462)	6
W	*22	St. Louis (64,300)	13
L	3	Pittsburgh (50,199)	14
W	16	New York (76,490)	14
L	*21	Philadelphia (62,417)	31
L	20	Washington (55,031)	34
L	*24	Houston (63,897)	30
W	*28	New York (63,787)	7
W	24	Philadelphia (71,434)	17
W	*35	Washington (62,867)	34
	371		313

1979 DIVISIONAL PLAYOFF (Dallas)

L	*19	Los Angeles (64,792)	21

1980 (12-4)

Tom Landry, Head Coach

W	17	Washington (55,045)	3
L	20	Denver (74,919)	41
W	*28	Tampa Bay (62,750)	17
W	28	Green Bay (54,776)	7
W	*24	N.Y. Giants (59,126)	3
W	*59	San Francisco (63,399)	14
L	10	Philadelphia (70,696)	17
W	*42	San Diego (60,639)	31
W	27	St. Louis (50,701)	24
L	35	N.Y. Giants (68,343)	38
W	*31	St. Louis (52,567)	21
W	*14	Washington (58,809)	10
W	*51	Seattle (57,540)	7
W	19	Oakland (53,194)	13
L	14	Los Angeles (65,154)	38
W	*35	Philadelphia (62,548)	27

1980 NFC WILD CARD PLAYOFF (Dallas)

W	*34	Los Angeles (64,533)	13

1980 DIVISIONAL PLAYOFF (Atlanta)

W	30	Atlanta (60,022)	27

1980 NFC CHAMPIONSHIP GAME (Philadelphia)

L	7	Philadelphia (70,696)	20

1981 (12-4)

Tom Landry, Head Coach

W	17	Washington (55,045)	3
W	*30	St. Louis (63,602)	17
W	35	New England (60,311)	21
W	*18	N.Y. Giants (63,449)	10
L	17	St. Louis (49,777)	20
L	14	San Francisco (57,574)	45
W	*29	Los Angeles (64,649)	17
W	*28	Miami (64,221)	27
W	17	Philadelphia (72,111)	14
W	*27	Buffalo (62,583)	14
L	24	Detroit (79,694)	27
W	*24	Washington (64,583)	10
W	*10	Chicago (63,499)	9
W	37	Baltimore (54,871)	13
W	*21	Philadelphia (64,955)	10
L	10	N.Y. Giants (73,009) (OT)	13

1981 DIVISIONAL PLAYOFF (Dallas)

W	38	Tampa Bay (64,848)	0

1981 NFC CHAMPIONSHIP GAME (San Francisco)

L	27	San Francisco (60,525)	28

Cowboys All-Time Pre-Season Results

1960 (1-5)

DAL.			OPP.
10	San Francisco (22,000)	@ Seattle	16
13	St. Louis (14,000)	@ San Antonio	20
10	Baltimore (40,000)	@ Dallas	14
14	New York (10,663)	@ Louisville	3
14	Los Angeles (13,500)	@ Pendleton	49
23	Green Bay (20,121)	@ Minn.	28

1961 (2-3)

DAL.			OPP.
38	Minnesota (4,954)	@ Sioux Falls	13
7	Green Bay (30,000)	@ Dallas	30
10	N.Y. (21,500)	@ Albuquerque	28
35	Baltimore (19,000)	@ Norman	24
10	S.F. (22,130)	@ Sacramento	24

1962 (0-5)

DAL.			OPP.
7	Green Bay (54,500)	@ Dallas	31
24	Detroit (77,683)	@ Cleveland	35
10	Baltimore (14,000)	@ Roanoke	24
7	S.F. (20,000)	@ Sacramento	26
26	Minnesota (12,500)	@ Atlanta	45

1963 (3-2)

DAL.			OPP.
17	Los Angeles (70,675)	@ L.A.	14
10	Green Bay (53,121)	@ Dallas	31
17	Los Angeles (29,349)	@ Portland	20
37	S.F. (9,927)	@ Bakersfield	24
27	Detroit (51,218)	@ New Orleans	17

1964 (1-4)

DAL.			OPP.
6	Los Angeles (57,450)	@ L.A.	17
34	S.F. (24,679)	@ Portland	23
16	Los Angeles (30,565)	@ Portland	25
3	Green Bay (60,057)	@ Dallas	35
6	Chicago (35,000)	@ New Orleans	21

1965 (2-3)

DAL.			OPP.
0	Los Angeles (31,579)	@ L.A.	9
7	S.F. (24,837)	@ Portland	27
21	Green Bay (67,954)	@ Dallas	12
17	Minn. (41,500)	@ Birmingham	57
34	Chicago (33,525)	@ Tulsa	21

1966 (5-0)

DAL.			OPP.
24	San Francisco (28,899)	@ S.F.	13
20	Los Angeles (44,217)	@ L.A.	10
21	Green Bay (75,504)	@ Dallas	3
20	Detroit (31,250)	@ Tulsa	10
28	Minnesota (58,316)	@ Dallas	24

1967 (2-3)

DAL.			OPP.
6	Los Angeles (57,595)	@ L.A.	20
30	San Francisco (31,212)	@ S.F.	24
3	Green Bay (78,087)	@ Dallas	20
30	Houston (53,125)	@ Houston	17
7	Baltimore (58,492)	@ Dallas	33

1968 (3-3)

DAL.			OPP.
24	Chicago (14,578)	@ Canton	30
16	San Francisco (27,530)	@ S.F.	14
42	Los Angeles (64,978)	@ L.A.	10
27	Green Bay (72,014)	@ Dallas	31
33	Houston (52,289)	@ Houston	19
10	Baltimore (69,520)	@ Dallas	16

1969 (4-2)

DAL.			OPP.
17	Los Angeles (87,381)	@ L.A.	24
20	San Francisco (33,894)	@ S.F.	17
31	Green Bay (73,764)	@ Dallas	13
14	Houston (55,310)	@ Houston	11
25	N.Y. Jets (74,771)	@ Dallas	9
7	Baltimore (58,975)	@ Dallas	23

1970 (1-5)

DAL.			OPP.
20	San Diego (39,392)	@ San Diego	10
10	Los Angeles (64,646)	@ L.A.	17
34	Green Bay (72,389)	@ Dallas	35
21	Houston (46,548)	@ Houston	37
0	Kansas City (69,055)	@ Dallas	13
21	New York Jets (55,297)	@ Dallas	29

1971 (6-0)

DAL.			OPP.
45	Los Angeles (87,187)	@ L.A.	21
36	New Orleans (73,560)	@ Dallas	21
16	Cleveland (69,099)	@ Dallas	15
28	Houston (49,078)	@ Houston	20
27	Baltimore (22,291)	@ Baltimore	14
24	Kansas City (74,035)	@ Dallas	17

1972 (6-1)

DAL.			OPP.
20	College All-Stars (54,162)	@ Chi.	7
26	Houston (65,405)	@ Dallas	24
27	Los Angeles (66,051)	@ L.A.	13
30	New Orleans (81,070)	@ N.O.	7
34	N.Y. Jets (65,386)	@ Dallas	27
10	Kansas City (79,592)	@ K.C.	20
16	Oakland (62,607)	@ Dallas	10

1973 (4-2)

DAL.			OPP.
24	Los Angeles (75,461)	@ L.A.	7
26	Oakland (53,723)	@ Oakland	27
24	New Orleans (61,022)	@ Dallas	14
24	Houston (46,942)	@ Houston	27
27	Kansas City (57,468)	@ Dallas	16
26	Miami (61,378)	@ Dallas	23

1974 (3-3)

DAL.			OPP.
7	Oakland (41,049)	@ Oakland	27
13	Los Angeles (46,468)	@ L.A.	6
19	Houston (53,148)	@ Dallas (OT)	13
7	N. Orleans (56,563)	@ N. Orleans	16
25	Kansas City (43,492)	@ Dallas	16
15	Pittsburgh (43,900)	@ Dallas	41

1975 (2-4)

DAL.			OPP.
7	Los Angeles (62,843)	@ L.A.	35
20	Kansas City (35,630)	@ K.C.	26
13	Minnesota (45,395)	@ Dallas	16
17	Houston (46,951)	@ Houston	14
20	Oakland (39,562)	@ Dallas	31
17	Pittsburgh (43,186)	@ Dallas	16

1970 (3-3)

DAL.			OPP.
14	Oakland (52,391)	@ Oakland	17
14	Los Angeles (60,158)	@ L.A.	26
9	Denver (54,567)	@ Dallas	13
36	Detroit (30,340)	@ Memphis	16
20	Pittsburgh (64,264)	@ Dallas	10
26	Houston (58,844)	@ Dallas (OT)	20

1977 (3-3)

DAL.			OPP.
34	San Diego (59,504)	@ Dallas	14
17	Seattle (58,789)	@ Seattle (OT)	23
14	Miami (56,820)	@ Dallas	20
23	Baltimore (54,835)	@ Dallas	21
14	Houston (49,777)	@ Houston	23
30	Pittsburgh (49,824)	@ Dallas	0

1978 (3-1)

DAL.			OPP.
41	San Francisco (63,736)	@ Dallas	24
21	Denver (74,619)	@ Denver	14
13	Houston (62,242)	@ Dallas	27
16	Pittsburgh (59,747)	@ Dallas	13

1979 (3-2)

DAL.			OPP.
13	Oakland (20,648)	@ Canton, Ohio	20
7	Denver (61,192)	@ Dallas	6
17	Seattle (59,803)	@ Seattle	27
16	Houston (62,803)	@ Dallas	13
16	Pittsburgh (64,543)	@ Dallas	14

1980 (3-1)

DAL.			OPP.
17	Green Bay (54,876)	@ Dallas	14
19	Los Angeles (63,283)	@ Anaheim	16
20	Houston (63,658)	@ Dallas	13
10	Pittsburgh (62,795)	@ Dallas	31

1981 (2-2)

DAL.			OPP.
17	Green Bay (55,087)	@ Dallas	21
21	Los Angeles (61,459)	@ Anaheim	33
24	Pittsburgh (63,504)	@ Dallas	14
28	Houston (63,799)	@ Dallas	20

1981 NFL Final Standings

AMERICAN FOOTBALL CONFERENCE

Eastern Division

	W	L	T	Pct.	Pts.	OP
*Miami	11	4	1	.719	345	275
#N.Y. Jets	10	5	1	.656	355	287
#Buffalo	10	6	0	.625	311	276
Baltimore	2	14	0	.125	259	533
New England	2	14	0	.125	322	370

Central Division

	W	L	T	Pct.	Pts.	OP
*Cincinnati	12	4	0	.750	421	304
Pittsburgh	8	8	0	.500	356	297
Houston	7	9	0	.438	281	355
Cleveland	5	11	0	.313	276	375

Western Division

	W	L	T	Pct.	Pts.	OP
*San Diego	10	6	0	.625	478	390
Denver	10	6	0	.625	321	289
Kansas City	9	7	0	.563	343	290
Oakland	7	9	0	.438	273	343
Seattle	6	10	0	.375	322	388

NATIONAL FOOTBALL CONFERENCE

Eastern Division

	W	L	T	Pct.	Pts.	OP
*Dallas	12	4	0	.750	367	277
#Philadelphia	10	6	0	.625	368	221
#N.Y. Giants	9	7	0	.563	295	257
Washington	8	8	0	.500	347	349
St. Louis	7	9	0	.438	315	408

Central Division

	W	L	T	Pct.	Pts.	OP
*Tampa Bay	9	7	0	.563	315	268
Detroit	8	8	0	.500	397	322
Green Bay	8	8	0	.500	324	361
Minnesota	7	9	0	.438	325	369
Chicago	6	10	0	.375	253	324

Western Division

	W	L	T	Pct.	Pts.	OP
*San Francisco	13	3	0	.813	357	250
Atlanta	7	9	0	.438	426	355
Los Angeles	6	10	0	.375	303	351
New Orleans	4	12	0	.250	207	378

*Division Champion; #Wild Card for Playoffs

NOTE: San Diego won AFC Western title over Denver on the basis of a better division record (6-2 to 5-3).

WILD CARD GAMES

Buffalo 31, @ N.Y. Jets 27

N.Y. Giants 27, @ Philadelphia 21

DIVISIONAL PLAYOFFS

San Diego 41, @ Miami 38 (OT)

@ Cincinnati 28, Buffalo 21

@ DALLAS 38, Tampa Bay 0

@ San Francisco 38, N.Y. Giants 24

CONFERENCE CHAMPIONSHIPS

@ Cincinnati 27, San Diego 7

@ San Francisco 28, Dallas 27

SUPER BOWL XVI

San Francisco 26, Cincinnati 21

AFC-NFC PRO BOWL

AFC 16, NFC 13

PART VI

DALLAS
COWBOYS

Kim Rockel enjoys dancing and being on the go as a Cheerleader.

Dallas Cowboys Cheerleaders: Ladies with Heart

"Missing the cheerleaders in Dallas would be nearly as bad as missing a touchdown . . ."

— CBS-TV producer Chuck Milton in the Wall Street Journal

It all began in the blink of an eye back in January of 1976 when a Dallas Cowboys Cheerleader, standing on the sidelines in Miami's Orange Bowl, winked at the attending network television cameras. That innocent gesture, made during the heat of Super Bowl X, quickened the heartbeats of millions.

The Cowboys lost, 21-17, to the Pittsburgh Steelers that day, but that wink started something that would grow beyond logical expectation. It was, in the truest sense of the word, the beginning of a phenomenon. While the Steelers were being hailed as the new dynasty team of the National Football League (a title they would carry only briefly), the Dallas Cowboys Cheerleaders were being applauded as the new darlings of the sports world.

Teams throughout the NFL rushed cheerleader groups of their own onto the fields, proving the aged axiom that imitation is the highest form of flattery. Yet the Dallas group, pioneers in the concept of sideline show biz, continued to get the lion's share of public attention. In time their annual tryouts would draw as many as 2,000 applicants from throughout the nation; they would grace the covers of national magazines, appear on a variety of network TV shows, be featured in two highly successful made-for-TV movies, have a long list of nationally sold merchandise, and travel millions of miles on six foreign tours sponsored by the USO and Department of Defense.

Requests for appearances arrive in the office of Cheerleaders Vice-President and Director Suzanne Mitchell in a steady flow. The girls are wanted for state and county fairs, TV commercials, grand openings, charity telethons, guest appearances on variety shows and college halftimes. Ms. Mitchell, careful to protect the image of the 36 girls who make up the Cheerleaders' roster, turns down far more requests than she accepts.

(Top Left) Teri Richardson is the senior veteran Cheerleader. This is her fifth year as an enthusiastic member of the squad. *(Top Right)* Melissa White, in her second year as a Cheerleader, says that being a member of the squad is a "wonderful experience." *(Below)* The Cheerleaders add pizzazz to pre-game doldrums as they enter the field.

And when she does agree to have her girls appear, the rules she sets forth are unbending. She demanded and received full script approval for the ABC-TV movies, "Dallas Cowboys Cheerleaders," (which earned a 48 percent audience share when aired in January of 1979, making it the second highest rated made-for-TV movie in the industry's history) and "Dallas Cowboys Cheerleaders II" as well as the two "Love Boat" segments in which the girls appeared.

No similar group, it goes without saying, has so captured the fancy of Hollywood producers. In 1977 they made two network appearances, the "NBC Rock 'n Roll Sports Classic" and ABC's "Osmond Brothers Special." The next year they did a TV commercial for Faberge shampoo, and kicked off the season for Monday Night Football with their own one-hour special for ABC titled, appropriately, "The 36 Most Beautiful Girls in Texas." To date, the Cheerleaders have made 19 non-football network appearances and the demand shows no sign of slowing.

Clearly the Dallas Cowboys Cheerleaders, Inc., have made a strong impression on the consciousness of the nation. That it has happened, however, was never a part of any master plan.

The Cowboys have had cheerleaders as long as they've been in the pro football business. When the franchise started in 1960, a group of local male and female high school students were organized, outfitted in traditional cheerleader uniforms, and were called the Belles and Beaux. They were virtually unnoticed as they tried to persuade disinterested Cotton Bowl crowds to do the traditional "two bits, four bits" sort of cheers.

When the Cowboys left the Cotton Bowl for the modernized atmosphere of Irving's Texas Stadium in 1975, however, Team President and General Manager Tex Schramm, ever the innovator, decided it was time to bring more show biz to his sidelines. A designer was commissioned to come up with new uniforms and local dance instructor Texie Waterman was asked to conduct tryouts, select a squad, and then work out disco-like routines to be performed.

(Top) For every five-minute routine the Cheerleaders perform, it takes approximately 30 hours of rehearsals. *(Bottom)* Texie Waterman has been the Dallas Cowboys Cheerleaders' Choreographer for the past 10 years.

The debut of the "new" Dallas Cowboys Cheerleaders drew applause. For every person who objected there were thousands who cheered their arrival on the sports scene. Network TV cameramen, on hand for Cowboys home games, found focusing on the squad members a good way to pass the idle moments created by time-outs. The love affair had begun.

"One of the things that has made all this work," says Ms. Mitchell, "is that Mr. Schramm believed in it from the beginning. He made that clear to me, then stepped away from it; he gave me complete control."

Aided by choreographer Texie Waterman and a pair of former Cheerleaders, Shannon Baker Werthmann and Kim Kilway Nippler, Ms. Mitchell oversees the tryouts, workouts, performances, and sets the rules members of the squad must live by.

"There is a great deal of hard work and sacrifice involved in being a Cheerleader," Suzanne says, "but by being a part of the squad a girl gains experiences she otherwise would never have known. They're given a gift and an opportunity to give back to other people. How many people in this world are given the chance to make millions of people happy?"

To realize that opportunity, to be a part of the celebrated group, is far from easy.

Applicants must advance through preliminaries, semi-finals and finals which are conducted over a two-month time span. When the original group of nearly 2,000 is reduced to approximately 150 for the semi-final round of competition, Mrs. Waterman and Mrs. Werthmann teach applicants a dance routine, and their ability to perform it well and learn quickly is part of the criteria on which they are judged. Applicants who are called back for the finals have one week to prepare for an exam on football, write an autobiography and develop a talent presentation. Personal interviews are conducted with all finalists. Veteran members of the squad automatically advance to the finals but must compete for the spots against all newcomers.

Each candidate must meet these basic requirements: She must be at least 18 years old at the time of her audition, must be a high school graduate, must maintain a full-time job or be attending school, and, if selected to the squad, must make the Dallas-Fort Worth area her home.

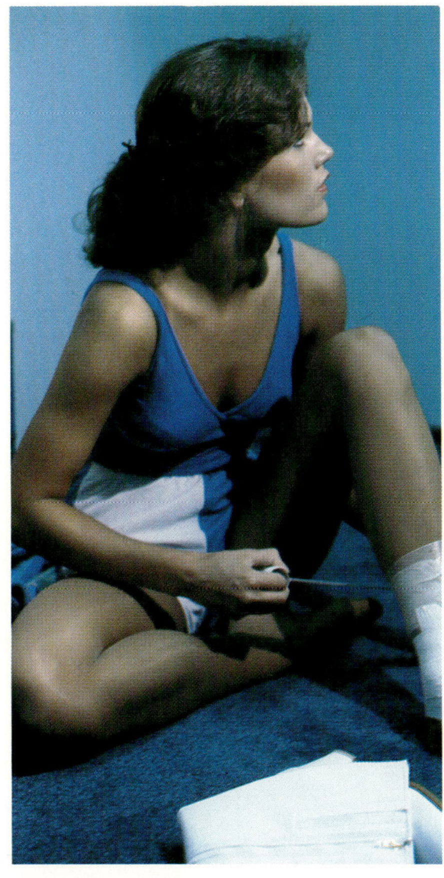

(Top Left) Just like football players, Cheerleaders also tape to prepare for practice. *(Top Middle and Right)* Veteran Dana Presley and rookie Annie Adkins give it their best during the talent presentations of the final round of Cheerleaders' auditions. *(Bottom)* Conditioning is extremely important to the Cheerleaders' preparation, so bar and floor-stretching exercises precede every rehearsal. *(Below)* The first former Cheerleader to join administrative ranks was Shannon Baker Werthmann, at right, in 1981 as Assistant Choreographer. She is joined this year by Kim Kilway Nippler as Associate Choreographer.

Young women willing to relocate have come from throughout the United States and Canada. On this year's roster, which features 12 returnees and 24 rookies, are girls from Vancouver, Canada; Waterloo, Iowa; Deland, Florida; Winston-Salem, North Carolina; and Bartlesville, Oklahoma.

Rules governing the Cheerleaders, who earn $15 per game, are strict. "I'm old-fashioned," admits Ms. Mitchell, "and I run the Cheerleaders by the same guidelines I was raised on." If a girl misses one of the two studio rehearsals or three stadium rehearsals during a week preceding a home game, she is not allowed to participate on Sunday. No girls are allowed to appear in uniform where liquor is served and they are not allowed to appear at any promotional event or social function alone or without organizational approval. Dating members of the Dallas Cowboys team is prohibited.

Soon after the squad is selected the girls begin learning the numerous routines they will be performing over the course of the season. The schedule is demanding as over 50 routines are learned, rehearsed and smoothed for eventual game-day performance.

Ms. Mitchell estimates that every five-minute dance the Cheerleaders perform represents 30 hours of rehearsal. And members of the squad's show group who perform at fairs and on tour are required to do even more rehearsing. There are, however, few members of the show group who will suggest it is not time well spent.

Almost without exception, those who have made overseas tours point to that experience as one of the most memorable of their lives. The Cheerleaders first went abroad in 1978 for a 10-day tour of Japan, performing in theaters and parades, on national television shows and at the Mirage Bowl game. While there they also did several television commercials for Mitsubishi Motor Corporation.

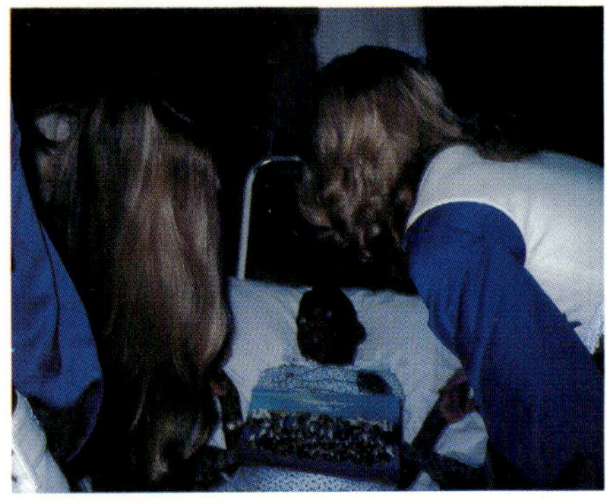

(Top) The Cheerleaders bring warmth to a Variety Club Handicapped Children's telethon in St. Louis, Missouri. *(Bottom)* The Cheerleaders spread good cheer during a visit to a children's hospital in Umatilla.

A year later the U.S. Department of Defense requested the Cheerleaders' presence on a USO Christmas tour of Korea where they performed for thousands of American troops. So successful was that tour that the Cheerleaders were sent to West Germany in March of 1980, returned to Korea during Christmas of that year, and in the spring of '81 made a two-week tour of military bases in Greece and Crete. In December and January of 1981-82 they made a two-week tour of Korea, the Philippines and the Indian Ocean, and in the spring of '82 made another two-week tour of Turkey.

Melinda May, who begins her second season with the Cheerleaders this year, says she had difficulty sleeping for days after her return from last fall's 15-day, 35,000-mile trip which stretched from the Demilitarized Zone in Korea to the Philippines and Diego Garcia and, finally, the Indian Ocean. "One night, shortly after we got back," she recalls, "I was up at two in the morning because I couldn't sleep, watching television. The station I was watching was signing off and the National Anthem came on. Without thinking, I stood up, sang along, and cried."

Such is the effect the tour had. Tears were very much a part of the experience, shed not only by the 12 visiting performers but by many of the 23,000 who welcomed the sight of someone from home.

"It is absolutely impossible to describe the emotion involved in something like that," Ms. Mitchell says. "To look out in an audience of young men and women and see them applauding while tears stream down their faces is something you'll never forget. There's no way you can go through some of the experiences we've gone through and not come away proud to be an American—and proud of the job our military is doing. I just wish people could see what is going on over there from the same vantage point we've had.

(Top Left) The Cheerleaders' Show Group delights sailors aboard ship in the middle of the Indian Ocean. *(Bottom)* One of the many non-football appearances the Cheerleaders have made includes this appearance for the March of Dimes in Spokane, Washington. *(Top Right)* The Cheerleaders get a warm welcome from a flight crew in Ankara, Turkey, during their spring '82 military tour.

"Everywhere we went there was always a look of disbelief on the faces of the men. They knew, of course, that we were coming, but I don't think many of them believed it until we actually arrived.

"Last Christmas Eve, we visited eight bases on the DMZ. We went to camps and guard posts where there were 15 to 20 men. To walk into one of those guard posts where a guy has nothing but a gun and a telescope and maybe a little Christmas tree he's decorated makes you realize how important it is for you to be there."

Teri Richardson, the veteran member of the Cheerleaders squad who will enter her fifth season this fall, has made every tour with the group. "I'm always moved by the trips," she says. "Each time I come home hoping this time I'll really be able to describe what went on to my friends, but it is impossibie. I know this: when you see what those guys are doing and what they're having to deal with and then compare it to the comfort you have at home, you have to stop and think."

Among the many souvenirs Teri has brought home is a letter hastily written to her by a soldier who had seen the Cheerleaders' performance aboard the USS Flint. "Thirty minutes after the show he came rushing up with it and gave it to me. He just thanked us for taking time to come and perform."

The girls always return to Dallas with cards and letters and phone numbers of families and friends. "We ask the guys if we can get in touch with their wives or girlfriends or parents when we get back," Ms. Mitchell explains. For days after their return, the girls forward mail, write letters and make trips to the Cowboys office to make long distance phone calls.

"As I said," Ms. Richardson notes, "the whole experience is just impossible to describe. It's all in your heart."

It is this feeling, an opportunity to give, that elevates the definition of cheerleading to a higher meaning.

Annie Adkins

Graduate of Drake University this former cheerleader captain is a native of Waterloo, Iowa, and has been active in athletics most of her 22 years. A Libra, she participated in swimming, gymnastics and track in high school before majoring in physical education in college. For three years she spent her summers singing and dancing at Adventureland Amusement Park and was a finalist in the Miss Iowa pageant. Athletic and fun-loving, Annie has also taught gymnastics to elementary students and has worked as a lifeguard. "College cheerleading was a great experience," she says, "and now I'm looking forward to the challenge of being a member of the Cowboys Cheerleaders."

Kim Bateman

A cheerleader for six years in junior high and high school in Azle, Tex., the eighteen-year-old Aquarius plans to major in communications in college. The active, blue-eyed blonde served as Student Council President, was selected Homecoming Queen in her senior year and was voted her school's Best Actress after her performance in the lead role in "Annie Get Your Gun." She was also listed in "Who's Who Among American High School Students." In addition to her hobbies of horseback riding and skiing, she takes ballet, jazz and voice lessons. "Being a member of the Cowboys Cheerleaders," she says, "will be beneficial to me, I'm sure. I feel the educational experience will help me greatly in attaining future goals I have for myself."

Annette Birdwell

Born on St. Patrick's Day in 1961, she is now in her third season as a member of the Cowboys Cheerleaders. A newlywed as of June 5, 1982, Annette is a legal secretary and native Texan. She graduated from Irving's Nimitz High School, and was active in student government, drill team and YMCA. Twice the energetic Pisces was chosen Homecoming Princess. Following graduation she attended North Lake Junior College. A gymnastics and tumbling instructor for youngsters, she also enjoys dancing and skiing and has recently taken up tennis. Last year's USO Tour ranks as the most memorable experience of her career with the Cheerleaders. "I'll never forget that New Year's Eve aboard the USS Constellation, hearing the sound of a 21-gun salute and 5,000 very proud sailors singing 'God Bless America.' It put us all in tears. That night brought a whole new meaning to our trip."

Kaye Boone

The eighteen-year-old Bartlesville, Oklahoma native became interested in the Cowboys Cheerleaders as a little girl watching Cowboys games on television and dreamed of one day performing with them. In high school, she was a cheerleader and second runner-up in the Oklahoma Junior Miss pageant. Upon graduation she was awarded a dance scholarship to Kilgore Junior College and listed in the "Who's Who of American Drill Teams." She plans to attend North Texas State University with a major in dance. The Active Aries spent last summer as an instructor at the Dallas-based Superstar Drill Team Camps.

Leslie Bowling

Four years as a cheerleader for Plano High School provides the nineteen-year-old blonde with a strong background as she enters her first season as a Cowboys Cheerleader. The native Texan will, in fact, be familiar with the Texas Stadium sidelines since she's been there before, cheering her high school team on in the schoolboy state championship playoffs. "Just being in that stadium was exhilarating," she says. She attended Abilene Christian University after graduation and now works as a receptionist for an employment agency. Describing herself as gregarious, she enjoys the outdoors, horseback riding, hunting, fishing and water-skiing.

Kim Chapman

Already well-traveled, the twenty-five-year-old English teacher has toured 14 foreign countries as a friendship ambassador for the U.S. State Department. A native Texan from Longview, the busy Capricorn was a twirler and drum major in high school and was also an accomplished pianist and dancer. While attending Kilgore Junior College she was a member of the famed Rangerettes drill team and was voted a Ranger Beauty. At Stephen F. Austin State University she double majored in physical education and English, then took a job teaching at Carlisle High School in Price, Tex. There she also served as cheerleading sponsor, choreographing all routines. She also teaches twirling. Her hobbies include calligraphy, drawing sketches, tennis, water and snow skiing and sewing. She has been dancing since she was six years old.

Lorie Clark

A freshman at North Texas State University, majoring in dance and physical therapy, the eighteen-year-old Pisces is a native Texan who graduated from Berkner High School in Richardson. There she was a member of the drill team and was the lead dancer in two musical productions. In addition to occasional modeling, she enjoys swimming, tennis, horseback riding, dancing and "working with people." A longtime fan of the Cowboys, she decided to audition because "being a Dallas Cowboys Cheerleader would provide me a way to stay active and also to support my favorite football team." She began dancing at age five.

Michelle Cole

Competitive athletics have long been a way of life for the nineteen-year-old Texas Woman's University student. While attending high school in her hometown of Denton, the blue-eyed Scorpio excelled at softball, basketball and track, earning a scholarship to Baylor University in the latter. She also served as an officer of the Denton High drill team, was a cheerleader, and was selected Homecoming Queen in her senior year. She was first runner-up in the national finals of America's Homecoming Queen pageant held in Memphis, Tenn., and was also named to the All-America Drill Team. A self-described farm girl, she transferred to TWU following her freshman year to pursue a major in occupational therapy and a minor in dance. She also models and has taken five years of ballet and tap dancing lessons.

A native of San Bernardino, Calif., the former Cal State University at Fullerton cheerleader and Homecoming Queen is in her second season as a member of the Cowboys Cheerleaders squad. Now a twenty-year-old executive secretary for a Dallas bank, she hopes eventually to attend law school. While in high school she was a cheerleader for four years and was named Homecoming Queen. As a collegian majoring in English, she was regularly named to the Dean's List. She was also selected Miss Fullerton in a city-wide contest. She has traveled throughout the United States as a professional cheerleading instructor. "Last year was very exciting and memorable for me," she says. "Being a member of the Cowboys Cheerleaders has been a dream come true. Moving away from my family and friends in California was difficult, but now I feel I've found a second home in Dallas."

In the trophy case of the twenty-one-year-old Aries from Kilgore, Tex., are awards for 35 first and second place finishes in competitive diving competitions as well as mementoes from beauty contests she began entering at age nine. Among the titles she has won are Miss Kilgore and East Texas Junior Miss. After serving as a cheerleader for four years she attended Kilgore Junior College where she was a member of the famed Rangerettes, was active in campus politics and taught a youth Sunday School class. Now a computer operator and an assistant office manager, she still finds time for occasional diving, jogging, gymnastics, dancing and piano practice. She also models and would like eventually to model professionally and hopes to own her own dance studio. "The Lord has given me energy to share with others," she says. "Being a Cowboys Cheerleader gives me the opportunity to do that."

A native of Lubbock, the twenty-year-old broadcast journalism major at Southern Methodist is entering her second year as a Cheerleader. Daughter of an SMU mathematics professor, she was named to "Who's Who" and to the Society of Distinguished American High School Students. "The Dallas Cowboys Cheerleaders stand for everything I believe in," she says, "and to be a part of the organization is an honor I will forever cherish."

A native Texan who attended Thomas Jefferson High School in San Antonio, then earned a journalism degree from the University of Texas, the twenty-eight-year-old married Aquarius was listed among the "Who's Who of American Businesswomen" for 1980-81. As an oncology sales representative for Bristol Laboratories, she is a member of the Medical Service Representatives Society of Dallas and has taken jazz and tap dancing and ballet for several years from Cowboys Cheerleaders choreographer Texie Waterman and the Buster Cooper School of Dance. In addition to her dancing, she enjoys hunting, fishing, racquetball and snow skiing. "Being selected to the squad," she says, "is something I've dreamed of. My professional career is very exciting and rewarding, but the excitement of being a Cowboys Cheerleader is something special."

Dianna Hart

This nineteen-year-old graduate of Irving High School makes her debut this season. In the summer of 1980 she was a regular performer at Six Flags over Texas and in 1981 made numerous appearances on the Grapevine Opry Show. After attending North Lake Junior College she took a job as a secretary. The auburn-haired Leo says, "Being a Cheerleader is not only an honor, but will be a wonderful learning experience." Her busy schedule will hopefully keep her from missing her family which recently moved to Alaska to do missionary work. "I'm very proud of them for what they're doing."

Sandy Matthews

A brother living in the Dallas area was the one who persuaded the eighteen-year-old Sagittarius to travel from her home in Deland, Fla., to try out for a spot on the Dallas Cowboys Cheerleaders squad. A majorette in junior high and high school, she began taking twirling lessons at age five. Her hobbies include horseback riding, water skiing, dirt biking, and tennis. A student at Daytona Beach Community College before moving to Dallas, she plans to continue her education, working toward a major in law, communications and advertising.

Sherri Mallard

From being named Our Little Miss Louisiana at age 11 to becoming a member of the Cowboys Cheerleaders squad at 20 is a big step for the energetic North Texas State graduate. A Scorpio, she has been taking dancing lessons for 13 years and was a member of the Twin City Civic Ballet Company in her hometown of Monroe, La., for six years. She was a member of the drill team in high school before entering Kilgore Junior College where she was a member of the famed Rangerettes. At North Texas she earned an Associate of Arts degree and plans to begin teaching. While working for the Superstar Drill Team Company she has traveled throughout the country as an instructor and has been active in Little Theater musical productions. Among her many hobbies are motorcycle riding, painting, sewing and playing golf and tennis. "I love to see people happy and enjoying themselves," she says, "and as a performer and dancer I feel I'm capable of making people feel good."

Melinda May

An All-District guard for her high school basketball team in Crosby, Tex., she collected more than 500 trophies for her abilities as a twirler. A cum laude business management graduate of Texas A&M University, the twenty-three-year-old Capricorn is a certified twirling coach and judge and placed high in A&M's Junior Olympic Fencing Finals. Valedictorian of her high school she was also FFA Sweetheart and president of the National Honor Society. In her second year as a Cheerleader, she remembers the USO tours with special fondness. "The tours were magnificent," she says. "In meeting so many servicemen I was deeply touched by their patriotism and love of God."

The twenty-year-old married Texas native served as captain of her high school drill team at North Mesquite, winning several medals for her high kick and jazz routines. For three years now, the brown-eyed Taurus has been taking dancing lessons and will put them to use this fall as a rookie member of the Cowboys Cheerleaders squad. A payroll processor for a Dallas electronics data system firm, she enjoys outdoor activities such as skiing and boating and is also a movie buff. Her biggest supporter is her father, Bennie Milano. And during Cowboys games he's not far away. In fact he's just down the Texas Stadium sidelines, cueing the officials when network broadcasters take a break in the action for commercial announcements.

A student at North Texas State University, the Dallas native was captain of the drill team at J.J. Pearce High School and was runner-up in the Miss Texas Drill Team competition in 1980. Majoring in English with a minor in Spanish, the energetic nineteen-year-old Leo also co-captained the NTSU drill team. In addition to staying busy with dancing and gymnastics, she was a member of the National Honor Society in high school and currently teaches a jazzercise class. This is her first season as a Cowboys Cheerleader after making two audition trips.

Now in her fourth season with the Cowboys Cheerleaders (the only four-year veteran), she also serves as a gymnastics coach and an executive secretary for a Dallas tool firm. As a student at Irving High School she won numerous honors in gymnastics competition. She also attended North Lake Community College. The twenty-two-year-old Libra enjoys ice skating, the outdoors, traveling, riding horses and football. One of her most cherished memories as a Cheerleader is the time spent at Camp Kunsan in Korea during last year's USO tour. "After we did our show in a big airplane hangar there was this lady waiting to thank us. When I reached to shake her hand, she saluted me as a tear rolled down her face. Never before have I felt such a feeling of accomplishment. I wish I could find words to describe that moment."

Now in her second year as a member of the Cheerleaders squad, she is a graduate of Burleson High School where she was a cheerleader for three years, active in thespian productions and named Miss Burleson High. In 1979 she was named Miss Lake Whitney. The twenty-one-year-old Virgo has performed in Fort Worth's Casa Manana musicals, sung with a rock-and-roll band and competed on television's Hollywood Squares and Gambit game shows. A former North Texas State University student, she hopes to return to college to major in radio/television. "After being a member of the squad for a year and having more fun than I've ever had in my life," she says, "I can't think of a better way to spend another year."

Teri Richardson

Beginning her fifth year as a Cowboys Cheerleader, she is the senior veteran member of the 1982 squad. The twenty-three-year-old jazzercise/aerobics dance instructor grew up in Sugar Land, Tex., and was a communications major at North Texas State University. A Leo, she recently completed studies at a commercial real estate college. "During my years as a Cheerleader there have been moments when I wanted to laugh and cry," she says. "The most special moments are the times we spent on USO tours. It really gives me a good feeling to know I've helped some lonely soldier's day pass just a little more quickly." She enjoys skating, photography, swimming and dance.

Robin Roberts

Though only 21, she brings an outstanding dance background to her first year as a Cowboys Cheerleader. She was invited by Auther Mitchell to attend his summer workshop at The Dance Theater of Harlem in New York and is a dance instructor at a Dallas studio. As a high school senior at Richardson's J.J. Pearce, she was named the outstanding performer on the Pacesetters drill team. She has been dancing for 11 years. A Sagittarius, she attended Richland Junior College and will enroll at Southern Methodist University to work toward a degree in dance. "The only thing I can imagine being more exciting than being a Cowboys Cheerleader," she says, "would be to dance in a Broadway show."

Kim Rockel

The daughter of an Air Force officer, she has been on the go for most of her 21 years. A Taurus, she was born in Oxnard, Calif., completed high school in Satellite Beach, Fla., and was a cheerleader for Brevard College in Melbourne, Fla., Weber State College in Ogden, Utah, and at the University of California at Santa Barbara. Enrolled in North Texas State University, she's working toward a degree in public relations. She also traveled throughout Europe with the Consortium of International Education. "The travel I've enjoyed has been fun," she says, "but being a Dallas Cowboys Cheerleader last year was the most fantastic experience I've ever had."

Cindy Rodriguez

Dancing since age four, the San Antonio native has performed in theater groups and in USO shows staged at Kelly and Lackland Air Force Bases. As a student at Thomas Jefferson High she was a cheerleader, a member of the drill team, Student Council officer, honor student and won speech and drama awards. She has been a scholarship student at the Natalia Krassauska Ballet. Majoring in business at North Texas State University, she is also a sales and marketing representative for an Arlington office interiors firm and teaches piano and ballet. A Pisces, she also enjoys playing tennis.

Lori Sandridge

Born on Christmas Day in 1960, the Houston native spent four years as a member of the Northbrook High drill team, was named to the National Superstar Drill Team, and received a scholarship for her efforts to Blinn Junior College. There she was choreographer for the drill team. After transferring to the University of Houston where she majored in dance, she was a member of the Cougar Dolls and a Homecoming Queen candidate. She also did volunteer work at the M.D. Anderson Cancer and Tumor Institute, working with children. Recently married, she works as a secretary.

Stacy Stanaland

Dancing since she was three years old, the Southern Methodist University business major will be making her debut as a member of the Cowboys Cheerleaders. The twenty-year-old Capricorn was a member of the Richardson High School drill team and was twice voted an outstanding member of the squad. She has been taking ballet and tap dance lessons for 13 years. She also enjoys snow skiing, music, horseback riding and travel.

Tisha Sulak

An honor student at the University of Texas at Arlington, the twenty-year-old Libra is a native Texan. At Fort Worth's Nolan High School she was a cheerleader, a member of the track team, voted Most Attractive and Basketball Sweetheart and was on the honor roll for four years. She was also a semifinalist in the Miss Teenage Fort Worth competition. A systems analyst major, she has been taking ballet and jazz for 12 years. She also enjoys tennis, skiing and travel and last year coached a sixth grade cheerleading squad which placed third in city-wide competition.

Nasha Thomas

A native of New York and a graduate of the High School of Performing Arts, the nineteen-year-old Southern Methodist University dance major has been performing since she was 14. As a member of the Bernice Johnson Theater of Dance company, she has appeared in Carnegie Hall, Lincoln Center, the Felt Forum and the Brooklyn Academy of Music. She also appeared in the off-Broadway production of "Paper Bird." She has studied at the American Ballet Theater, the Alvin Ailey American Dance Center and the Joffrey Ballet School. In 1980 she was a Presidential Scholar of the Arts winner and was flown to Washington, D.C. along with other winners to perform for an audience which included then President Jimmy Carter. A Virgo, she has taught a jazz exercise class on the SMU campus and enjoys reading, backgammon, movies and animals.

Judy Trammell

Now in her third season with the Cowboys Cheerleaders and fourth year of marriage, she is a receptionist for three physicians in Garland. The twenty-four-year-old Taurus is a native of Houston and at R.L. Turner High was voted Most Beautiful and captained the Lionettes Drill team. She has won over 100 medals and trophies in twirling competitions. She has also taught twirling, tap dance, ballet and gymnastics. She enjoys skiing, working on the trampoline, twirling and tossing the frisbee around with her husband, Dick. "As a Cheerleader," she says, "I've been very fortunate to travel around the world and touch peoples' lives and make new friends. The experience has been very worthwhile for me."

Toni Washington

This is her third season as a member of the Cheerleaders. Born in Los Angeles, she moved to Dallas 10 years ago and was an honor graduate of Grady Spruce High School. The twenty-one-year-old Aries is studying computer programming at El Centro College and is a supervisor for a temporary help service. In her spare time she enjoys drawing and sewing. "I feel that being a Dallas Cowboys Cheerleader gives one the opportunity to put a little sunshine in other peoples' lives. It has been a very inspirational experience for me," she says.

Melissa White

A native of Houston now studying advertising art at North Texas State University, she is in her second year as a member of the Cowboys Cheerleaders squad. At Friendswood High she was an honor student and was twice chosen Most Beautiful and Football Sweetheart. She also competed in track and volleyball and was listed in "Who's Who." She was voted Miss High Kick and Outstanding Three-Year Member of her high school drill team. Her hobbies include snow and water skiing, gourmet cooking and country and western dancing. A Libra, the twenty-year-old says, "Being a Cheerleader last year was a wonderful experience for me. I learned a great deal about working with other people, about developing my own character, and about life in general."

Susan Widmer

Having lived in Dallas for five years, she is an honor graduate of Bauder Fashion College in Arlington and was selected Miss Bauder Fashion College in 1980. A native of Bartlesville, Oklahoma, the twenty-three-year-old Aquarius was voted Miss Personality at her Sooner High School and was also a member of the National Honor Society and was listed in "Who's Who." She has 18 years of dance experience and currently is a secretary. In her spare time she enjoys roller skating, fishing and antique collecting. This will be her first season with the Cheerleaders.

A magna cum laude dance graduate of Utah State University, the twenty-four-year-old Aries is in her second season as a member of the Cowboys Cheerleaders. A native of Ogden, Utah, she is now a physical education and dance teacher in the Garland Independent School District. As a collegian she was president of the dance-drill team and a member of Mortar Board, College of Education Council and Phi Kappa Phi Honorary Society. She also has an associate's degree in business and is interested in real estate and hopes to one day own her own dance studio. Daughter of a club golf professional, she competed in junior tournaments and won numerous awards in gymnastics. In addition to reading, tennis and swimming, she enjoys jogging and hopes to one day compete in a marathon. "Being a Cowboys Cheerleader," she says, "has helped me to grow and learn a great deal about myself."

The 1982-83 Dallas Cowboys Cheerleaders

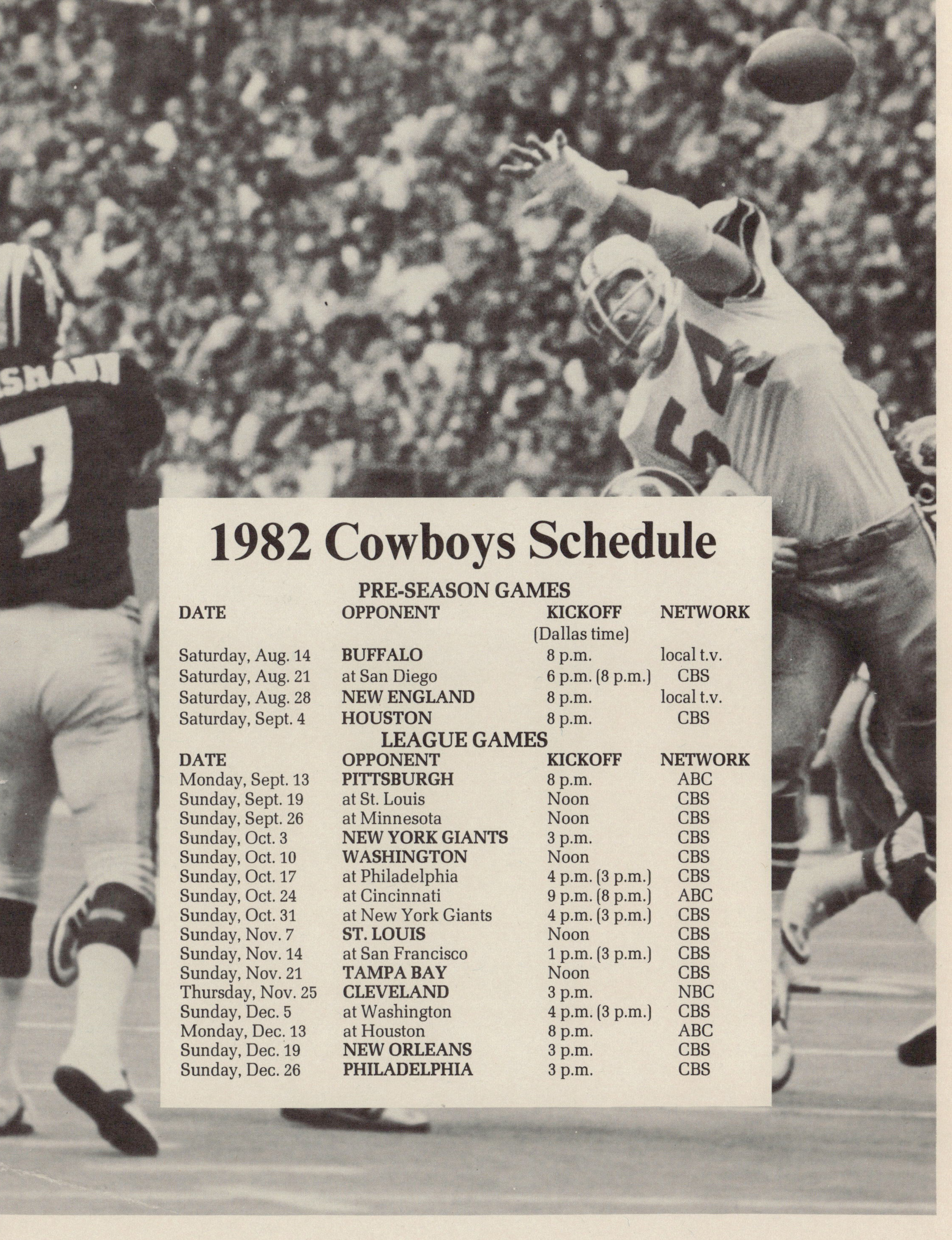

1982 Cowboys Schedule

PRE-SEASON GAMES

DATE	OPPONENT	KICKOFF (Dallas time)	NETWORK
Saturday, Aug. 14	**BUFFALO**	8 p.m.	local t.v.
Saturday, Aug. 21	at San Diego	6 p.m. (8 p.m.)	CBS
Saturday, Aug. 28	**NEW ENGLAND**	8 p.m.	local t.v.
Saturday, Sept. 4	**HOUSTON**	8 p.m.	CBS

LEAGUE GAMES

DATE	OPPONENT	KICKOFF	NETWORK
Monday, Sept. 13	**PITTSBURGH**	8 p.m.	ABC
Sunday, Sept. 19	at St. Louis	Noon	CBS
Sunday, Sept. 26	at Minnesota	Noon	CBS
Sunday, Oct. 3	**NEW YORK GIANTS**	3 p.m.	CBS
Sunday, Oct. 10	**WASHINGTON**	Noon	CBS
Sunday, Oct. 17	at Philadelphia	4 p.m. (3 p.m.)	CBS
Sunday, Oct. 24	at Cincinnati	9 p.m. (8 p.m.)	ABC
Sunday, Oct. 31	at New York Giants	4 p.m. (3 p.m.)	CBS
Sunday, Nov. 7	**ST. LOUIS**	Noon	CBS
Sunday, Nov. 14	at San Francisco	1 p.m. (3 p.m.)	CBS
Sunday, Nov. 21	**TAMPA BAY**	Noon	CBS
Thursday, Nov. 25	**CLEVELAND**	3 p.m.	NBC
Sunday, Dec. 5	at Washington	4 p.m. (3 p.m.)	CBS
Monday, Dec. 13	at Houston	8 p.m.	ABC
Sunday, Dec. 19	**NEW ORLEANS**	3 p.m.	CBS
Sunday, Dec. 26	**PHILADELPHIA**	3 p.m.	CBS

1982 NFL SCHEDULE

CBS/NBC-TV Doubleheader Games To Be Determined (All Times Local)

SUNDAY, SEPTEMBER 12 (First Weekend)

Atlanta at New York Giants	1:00	
Chicago at Detroit	1:00	
Cleveland at Seattle	1:00	
Houston at Cincinnati	1:00	
Kansas City at Buffalo	1:00	NBC-TV
Los Angeles vs. Green Bay at Milw.	12:00	Doubleheader
Miami at New York Jets	4:00	Week
New England at Baltimore	2:00	
Oakland at San Francisco	1:00	
St. Louis at New Orleans	12:00	
San Diego at Denver	2:00	
Tampa Bay at Minnesota	12:00	
Washington at Philadelphia	1:00	

MONDAY, SEPTEMBER 13

Pittsburgh at Dallas **8:00**

THURSDAY, SEPTEMBER 16 (Second Weekend)

Minnesota at Buffalo 8:30

SUNDAY, SEPTEMBER 19

Baltimore at Miami	4:00	
Cincinnati at Pittsburgh	1:00	
Dallas at St. Louis	**12:00**	
Detroit at Los Angeles	1:00	
New Orleans at Chicago	12:00	CBS-TV
New York Jets at New England	1:00	Doubleheader
Oakland at Atlanta	1:00	Week
Philadelphia at Cleveland	1:00	
San Diego at Kansas City	12:00	
San Francisco at Denver	2:00	
Seattle at Houston	3:00	
Washington at Tampa Bay	4:00	

MONDAY, SEPTEMBER 20

Green Bay at New York Giants 9:00

THURSDAY, SEPTEMBER 23 (Third Weekend)

Atlanta at Kansas City 7:30

SUNDAY, SEPTEMBER 26

Buffalo at Houston	12:00	
Chicago at San Francisco	1:00	
Dallas at Minnesota	**12:00**	
Denver at New Orleans	12:00	NBC-TV
Los Angeles at Philadelphia	1:00	Doubleheader
Miami at Green Bay	12:00	Week
New York Giants at Pittsburgh	1:00	
New York Jets at Baltimore	4:00	
Oakland at San Diego	1:00	
St. Louis at Washington	1:00	
Seattle at New England	1:00	
Tampa Bay at Detroit	1:00	

MONDAY, SEPTEMBER 27

Cincinnati at Cleveland 9:00

SUNDAY, OCTOBER 3 (Fourth Weekend)

Baltimore at Detroit	1:00	
Cleveland at Washington	1:00	
Houston at New York Jets	1:00	
Kansas City at Seattle	1:00	
Los Angeles at St. Louis	12:00	CBS-TV
Miami at Cincinnati	1:00	Doubleheader
Minnesota at Chicago	12:00	Week
New England at Buffalo	1:00	
New Orleans at Oakland	1:00	
New York Giants at Dallas	**3:00**	
Philadelphia vs. Green Bay at Milw.	12:00	
Pittsburgh at Denver	2:00	
San Diego at Atlanta	1:00	

MONDAY, OCTOBER 4

San Francisco at Tampa Bay 9:00

SUNDAY, OCTOBER 10 Fifth Weekend

Atlanta at Los Angeles	1:00	
Buffalo at Baltimore	2:00	
Cincinnati at New England	1:00	
Cleveland at Oakland	1:00	
Denver at New York Jets	4:00	NBC-TV
Detroit at Miami	4:00	Doubleheader
Green Bay at Chicago	12:00	Week
Houston at Kansas City	12:00	
Minnesota at Tampa Bay	1:00	
St. Louis at New York Giants	1:00	
San Francisco at New Orleans	12:00	
Seattle at San Diego	1:00	
Washington at Dallas	**12:00**	

MONDAY, OCTOBER 11

Philadelphia at Pittsburgh 9:00

SUNDAY, OCTOBER 17 (Sixth Weekend)

Atlanta at Detroit	1:00	
Baltimore at Cleveland	1:00	
Chicago at St. Louis	12:00	
Cincinnati at New York Giants	1:00	
Dallas at Philadelphia	**4:00**	CBS-TV
Denver at Houston	12:00	Doubleheader
Kansas City at San Diego	1:00	Week
Los Angeles at San Francisco	1:00	
New England at Miami	1:00	
New Orleans at Minnesota	12:00	
Oakland at Seattle	1:00	
Pittsburgh at Washington	1:00	
Tampa Bay at Green Bay	12:00	